Teaching English as a Second Language: Techniques and Procedures

CHRISTINA BRATT PAULSTON

MARY NEWTON BRUDER

English Language Institute
Department of General Linguistics
University of Pittsburgh

Little, Brown and Company
Boston   Toronto

Teaching English as a Second Language: Techniques and Procedures

Library of Congress Cataloging in Publication Data

PAULSTON, CHRISTINA BRATT,
  Teaching English as a second language:
  techniques and procedures.

  Includes bibliographical references.
  1. English language—Study and teaching—Foreign
  students. I. BRUDER, MARY NEWTON,
  joint author. II. Title.
  PE1128.A2P34   428′.2′4   75–38835
  ISBN 0–316–695106

Library of Congress Catalog Card No. 75–38835

ISBN 0-316-69510-6

14   13   12   11   10

HAL
Published simultaneously in Canada
by Little, Brown & Company (Canada) Limited

Printed in the United States of America

Contents

INTRODUCTION   ix

1

GRAMMAR   1

Teaching Grammar   1
   Introduction 1

A Classification of Structural Pattern Drills   3
   Introduction 3
   Mechanical Drills 4
   Meaningful Drills 6
   Communicative Drills 8

A Typology of Structural Pattern Drills 10
  Introduction 10
  I. Repetition Drills 12
  II. Discrimination Drills 15
  III. Alternation Drills 18
  IV. Reply 27
  Concluding Remarks 33

Design of a Grammar Lesson 33

Classroom Procedures 34
  Step 1. Presentation of Pattern in Context 34
  Step 2. Comprehension Questions 35
  Step 3. Identification of the Pattern 36
  Step 4. Formal Explanation 37
  Step 5. Mechanical Drills 39
  Step 6. Functional Explication 40
  Step 7. Meaningful Drills 40
  Step 8. Communicative Drills 42
  Conducting and Correcting Drills 43
  Conclusions 46

Appendix 47

2

SPEAKING   55

Communicative Competence 55
  Communicative Competence: Goals 58

Communicative Interaction Activities 60
  1. Social Formulas and Dialogues 60
  2. Community-oriented Tasks 63
  3. Problem-solving Activities 67
  4. Role Play 70

3

PRONUNCIATION   81

Introduction 81

Goals and Objectives 81

Discussion of Phonology 83
  Phonemes and Allophones—Segmental 83
  Consonants 84
  Vowels 88
  *Language Differences in Segmentals Which
  Interfere with Pronunciation 90*
  Suprasegmentals 91

General Elements of a Pronunciation Lesson 94
  Teaching the Segmental Phonemes 95
  Teaching the Suprasegmental Phonemes 106
  Intonation 107
  Stress and Rhythm 109
  Correcting Pronunciation Mistakes 115

4

LISTENING COMPREHENSION   127

Introduction 127

General Principles in Teaching Listening Comprehension 129

Practice in Listening Comprehension 130
  Format and Presentation of the Exercise 131

Techniques for Specific Teaching Points 132
  *Decoding Sounds, Stress and Intonation,
  and Sound-Symbol Correspondence 133*
  Decoding Structures 134
  Listening for the Message 137
  Teaching Variations of Style 143

Total Meaning of a Passage: Listening to
Lectures and Taking Notes 145

Sources and Uses of Natural Materials for Listening 153

Conclusion 155

5

READING   157

Reading and Vocabulary Study 157
Introduction 157
Some Primary Considerations 159

Intensive Reading 163
Checking Comprehension Questions 165
Introduction of the Next Reading Assignment: 168
Intensive Study of Grammar Patterns for
Recognition 175
List of Grammatical Patterns to be Taught
for Recognition in Reading 178
Activities 182
Extensive Reading 199

6

WRITING 203

Writing 203
Motives and Objectives 203
Techniques and Procedures 205

Composition: Correct Language Forms 205
Controlled Composition 206
Typology of Exercises 208
Procedures 228
Free Composition 230
Mechanics of Punctuation 234
Organization of Content 236

INDEX   251

Introduction

Teaching English as a Second Language: Techniques and Procedures is directed primarily to classroom teachers and the trainers of such teachers. It is intended to be a modest and useful book by which we mean that it is not theoretical in its orientation. There may seem to be no need for one more book on the teaching of English as a second language; there are already many (some of them good)[1] but *this* book is different.

In language teaching we distinguish among approach, method, and technique. Approach is the "set of correlative assumptions dealing with the nature of language and the nature of language and learning."[2] Approach is the theoretical foundation upon which any systematic method is based. Many of the assumptions held are

---

[1] See C. B. Paulston, "A Biased Bibliography: Comments on Selecting Texts for a Methods Course in TESOL," *Language Learning* 23 (1973) :1.

[2] Edward M. Anthony, "Approach Method and Technique," in H. Allen and R. Campbell, eds., *Teaching English as a Second Language* (New York: McGraw-Hill, 1972), p. 5.

axiomatic in that they cannot be proved either true or false. As such, the merit of any approach is unarguable in terms of theory, and one must look at the effectiveness of the method which it has generated. Methods refer to the procedures of language teaching, to an "overall plan for the orderly presentation of language material, no part of which contradicts, and all of which is based upon, the selected approach."[3] The lesson plan, the curriculum, the scheduling of classes, and the selection of textbooks, in fact most of the decisions made about language teaching outside the classroom, form part of the method and should of course be in harmony with the basic tenets of the approach. The method is implemented by techniques, by actual classroom behavior of the specific strategies which the teacher selects to achieve his objectives. The selection and sequencing of these strategies as well as the strategies themselves are based on the method and hence are in accord with the theoretical issues of the approach.

Most standard texts on language teaching discuss the approach and method of language teaching; there exist virtually no books on the technique level, on what the teacher is supposed to say and do in his classroom once he has shut the door behind him. Chastain for instance makes very clear that his book is not intended as a "cookbook."[4] This book, on the other hand, is intended to be just such a cookbook, outlining procedures and techniques that the teacher can utilize in his teaching. Most books on language teaching usually ignore two important aspects: the hard work that language teaching constitutes, and the importance of the personal relationship between the teacher and student in effective teaching. The building of personal relationships belongs to the "art" of teaching and cannot be learned from books. This book tries to alleviate somewhat the hard work of teaching by gathering together a number of useful techniques for easy reference, for new ideas, and for facilitating that sense of play and experimentation which is the sustaining foundation of all good teaching.

We don't want to give the impression that we discredit the importance of a solid theoretical foundation in language teaching.

---

[3] Ibid, p. 6.

[4] Kenneth Chastain, *The Development of Modern Language Skills: Theory to Practice* (Philadelphia: The Center for Curriculum Development, 1971), p. 1.

We hold it of the utmost importance, and in a teacher training program this book needs to be complemented by a text which deals with theoretical concerns. Our own approach to language teaching is eclectic, that is, the assumptions we hold about language learning are not based solely on one theoretical school of thought. The pure audiolinguist will find as much to disagree with as the strict cognitive codist. But we know that assumptions about language teaching ultimately have to be evaluated by the effectiveness of their techniques, and are convinced that these techniques do work, whatever we may think about language teaching on a theoretical level.

Our own thinking about language teaching is permeated by the practical concerns and contextual constraints in running the English Language Institute at the University of Pittsburgh, an institute that prepares foreign students for academic work at American universities. We know that we must so structure a learning program that in a meager six month's time it allows monolingual students from a multitude of language backgrounds to gain enough proficiency in English to follow successfully an academic program in that language. We simply cannot afford procedures and techniques which are not efficient in language teaching, and we feel somewhat about language teaching as the Irish feel about their horses: Handsome is as handsome does. We use two main criteria in evaluating this efficacy: the first, quite mundanely, is that our students must score well on the standardized proficiency test (like the TOEFL—Test of English as a Foreign Language, Educational Testing Service, Princeton, N.J.) which they are required to take for university admission evaluation, and the second is that they must be able to handle academic work — to follow lectures, read textbooks, write term papers, and give reports. But since the TOEFL is also designed to evaluate these skills, our criteria of evaluation are not really disparate in nature, and it is readily apparent that these skills are merely substitutes for listening, speaking, reading, and writing--the classic breakdown of skills in language teaching. So that even if our techniques for teaching English as a second language have been designed and tested for a specific situation, we are reasonably certain that they will remain effective even in other situations.

Our book, then, is a discussion of what we have found to be efficient techniques and procedures in language learning and teaching from a very beginning level through intermediate to advanced levels, based on our work in the Institute. Frequently techniques which are useful at one level do not work at another, and we have taken care to identify such techniques. We have long needed such a book for our own teacher training, and the impetus for the book lies exactly in the problems and needs of classroom teachers. We owe a great debt to our own staff who through the years have implemented and experimented with different ways of teaching. This book is the result of our combined attempts to deal with our mutual problems.

Pittsburgh   C.B.P.
                                                                            M.N.B.

Teaching English as a Second Language: Techniques and Procedures

1
Grammar

TEACHING GRAMMAR

Introduction

In this chapter we will discuss procedures and techniques for teaching grammar. There are as many definitions of grammar as there are linguistic schools of thought, but here we simply mean: the possible forms and arrangements of words in phrases and sentences. We begin with a classification of drills, followed by a typology, and close with a discussion of actual classroom procedures and techniques of teaching grammar.

Grammar permeates all language skills, and the objective of teaching grammar, as we discuss it here, is the oral use of the target language for communicative purposes. Separate references to grammar will also be found in the discussions of listening comprehension, pronunciation, reading and writing, which skills involve distinct aspects of grammar.

The chapter discusses how to teach grammar, not *what* to

teach—i.e., a linguistic analysis of English from a pedagogical view point, which is outside the scope of this book. Normally teachers are supplied with textbooks which determine what they teach. Occasionally, teachers who employ the grammar-translation approach to language teaching only work with reading selections. For their benefit we have included as an appendix a list of grammar patterns in English, sequenced primarily according to (1) a range from simple to complex, (2) saliency for communicative purposes, and (3) the interrelationship of grammatical points, e.g., *already* and *yet* are taught in the same lesson as the present perfect tense.

We believe, however, that the sequencing of patterns is not as important as the use and practice the students put these patterns to, and the list should only be regarded as a guideline and a checklist.

We would like at this point to make a brief detour. Throughout the book, there are references to beginning, intermediate, and advanced students. There is a wide discrepancy in the general definitions of these levels, and the reader should be familiar with the criteria we use in assigning students to particular levels. We use standardized test scores as follows:

Level	TOEFL examination	Michigan examination
Beginning	250-350	0-60
Intermediate	350-450	60-75
Advanced	450-	75-

Very beginning students are just that, monolingual in the mother tongue; beginning students in general correspond roughly with the end of a first year college language class in ability. Intermediate students are perfectly capable of getting around in the target language culture, they can do brief speeches, and they can do extensive reading. They still make many, many mistakes, they have a limited vocabulary, and their pronunciation often leaves much to be desired. Test scores for advanced students are much less indicative than they are for beginning and intermediate students. Students with a TOEFL score of 500 and above may come from a country where English is taught through reading; they will need practice in listening comprehension and speaking skills of the same type as the intermediate students although the homework and assignments may use more sophisticated English. Similarly, they may come from a nonreading culture, and be poor readers although fairly fluent in English. We often use the same basic procedures for intermediate and advanced students and we have no course exclusively in grammar at that level; what grammar they need depends on the skill they need improvement in and is incorporated in the lessons on speaking, reading, and writing.

A CLASSIFICATION OF STRUCTURAL PATTERN DRILLS

Introduction

The following classification, previously outlined in two articles by Paulston[1], is based on the following assumptions: (1) there are (at least) two levels of language—mechanical skill and thought; (2) these levels correlate with Katona's[2] two methods of learning—a "direct practice" and a "method of understanding," or as Rivers paraphrases "a mechanical level and a level which involves understanding of how one is learning and the essential elements of what is being learned;"[3] and (3) language learning as the formation of language habits is not mutually exclusive with the establishment of rule-governed behavior but rather the two methods are complementary. And finally, what is more an observation than an assumption, in courses whose objective is the oral use of language for communicative purposes, the methods of learning must reflect that objective; students should spend maximum time in the actual production of the target language where the ultimate purpose of every activity ultimately is communication.[4]

---

[1] Christina Bratt Paulston, "Structural Pattern Drills: A Classification," *Foreign Language Annals* IV, no. 2 (December 1970): 187-193; and "The Sequencing of Structural Pattern Drills," *TESOL Quarterly* 5, no. 3 (September 1971): 197-208.

[2] G. Katona, *Organzing and Memorizing* (New York: 1940).

[3] Wilga Rivers, *The Psychologist and The Foreign Language Learner* (Chicago: University of Chicago Press, 1964), p. 50.

[4] The relative merits of these assumptions may be defended either by theoretical speculation (which is outside the scope of this book) or by empirical investigation. The reader is referred to the dissertations of Sandra Savignon, "Study of the Effect of Training in Communicative Skills as Part of a Beginning College French Course on Student Attitude and Achievement in Linguistic and Communicative Competence" (Ph.D. dissertation, University of Illinois at Urbana, Campaign, 1971), Robert A. Morrey, "The Effects of Sequential Oral Drilling with Second Conjugation French Verbs upon Student Performance" (Ph.D. dissertation, Stanford University, 1970); Elizabeth G. Joiner, "Communicative Versus Noncommunicative Language Practice in the Teaching of Beginning College French: A Comparison of Two Treatments (Ph.D. dissertation, Ohio State University, 1974). All three are experimental investigations and support the view expressed here.

The implications for the classroom are simple: a grammar lesson should consist of grammatical rules which explain the particularities of the structural pattern to be learned plus a series of drills from a mechanical level to a communicative in order to give the students optimum practice in language production.

Paulston argues that there are three classes of drills: mechanical, meaningful, and communicative, and that these can be distinguished from each other if they are analyzed in terms of (1) expected terminal behavior, (2) degree of response control, (3) type of learning process involved and (4) criteria for the selection of utterance response.

Mechanical Drills

A mechanical drill is defined as a drill where there is complete control of the response, where there is only one correct way of responding. Because of the *complete* control, students need not even understand the drill although they respond correctly, as in the first Spanish drill below. Repetition drills are the most extreme example of this class of drill. Substitution drills also lend themselves particularly well to this.

There are two kinds of mechanical drills, mechanical memorizing drills and mechanical testing drills.

The concord of person and noun in Spanish serves as a good example of a memorizing drill:

```
Model:   andar (tú)      R:     andas
         cantar (tú)            cantas
Continue the drill:
Cue:     trabajar (tú)   R:
         pasar (tú)
         hablar (tú)
```

The purpose of this drill is primarily to help students memorize the pattern with virtually no possibility for mistakes, and even the reader who does not know Spanish can complete the drill above correctly.

But as soon as we change the cues to include all persons, that is, to change the cues so as to require an answer of more than minimal items, we require that students know all the verb endings for the *ar* verbs, present tense, and by their responses we know whether they do or not. The response depends on the conscious choices of the students:

```
Model:   andar (tú)       R: andas
         cantar (Vd.)     R: canta
Continue the drill:
Cue:     trabajar (él)    R:
```

Only those students who have previously memorized these patterns can complete the drill successfully.

Mechanical testing drills not only provide feedback for the teacher, but they also help students organize the information they have learned into wholes or contrasts. Students who have only drilled "I am" separate from "He is" may never realize they belong to the same structure. Similarly, without a testing drill, students might never realize that "I'm walking" and "I'm going to walk" are different structures.

The difference between a mechanical memorizing drill and a mechanical testing drill lies in the ability of the students to respond, again depending on how well they have memorized certain patterns; but understanding what they are saying is not a necessary requisite. It is perfectly possible to supply a verb with a correct ending, for example, in Spanish, without necessarily knowing what the verb means. Given the cue: *gratar* (*nosotros*), any docile student will respond with *gratamos*; yet the student, no more than we, will know the meaning of that nonsense word. The ability to practice mechanical drills without necessarily understanding them is an important criterion in distinguishing them from meaningful drills.

Transformation drills may be mechanical:

```
John kicked the door.
The door was kicked by John.
```

All students need memorize is the structural change, and they can complete such a drill without understanding exactly what they are saying. Response drills, which so frequently masquerade as communication, can be some of the easiest mechanical drills for students:

```
Which would you prefer, tea or coffee?
                       wine or beer?
                       nectar or ambrosia?
```

The student will answer *ambrosia* without the foggiest notion of what it is.

The expected terminal behavior of such drills is the automatic use of manipulative patterns and is commensurate with the assumption that language learning is habit formation. It involves the classical Skinnerian method of learning through instrumental conditioning by immediate reinforcement of the right response. Learning takes place through analogy and allows transfer of identical patterns. This is clearly the mechanical level of learning, and this class of drills provides practice in mechanical associations such as adjective-noun agreement, verb endings, question forms, and the like. This is a very necessary step in language learning; and as long as the student is learning, he won't mind the mechanical nature of the drill. The teacher needs to remember that students can drill without understanding and *to make sure that in fact they do understand*. Because of the response control, it is eminently suited for choral drills.

The student knows how to select the utterance response on the basis of the teacher's cue, be it oral or pictorial; but the teacher is the sole criterion for supplying the correct response. This becomes an important distinction between meaningful and communicative drills.

Meaningful Drills

If the teacher is unsure of whether a drill is mechanical or meaningful (the borders are not completely clear), it can be tested with a nonsense word.

Example:

		I walk to school every day.
Cue: run	Response:	I run to school every day.
Teacher: skip	Student:	I skip to school every day.
Teacher: somersault	Student:	I somersault to school every day.
Teacher: boing	Student:	I boing to school every day.

Complexity of pattern is not an issue.

Example: John kicked the door.
The door was kicked by John.

Cue	Response
The dog bit the woman.	The woman was bitten by the dog.
The boing boinged the boing.	The boing was boinged by the boing.

That is a mechanical drill. For the language teacher who is fluent in the target language, it is difficult to appreciate the enormous difference in difficulty between mechanical and meaningful drills.

Much of the criticism of the audio-lingual method is based on the mechanical drill or rather the overuse to which it has been put. While not denying the need for mechanical drills, we may note that on the mechanical level alone students certainly cannot yet express their own ideas fluently. He next needs to work through a set of meaningful drills:[5]

1. Teacher: She's outside. 2. Teacher: She's eating.
   Student 1: Where is she? Student 1: What's she doing?
   Student 2: She's outside. Student 2: She's eating.

3. She's at home. 4. She's going home.

(Note that Student 2's response is not meaningful; it is repetition.)

In a meaningful drill there is still control of the response although it may be correctly expressed in more than one way and as such is less suitable for choral drilling. There is a right answer and the student is supplied with the information necessary for responding, either by the teacher, the classroom situation, or the assigned reading; but in all cases the teacher always knows what the student ought to answer. Everyone is always aware that these drills are only language exercises and that any answer will do as well as another as long as it is grammatically correct and conforms to the information supplied. The student cannot complete these drills without fully understanding structurally and semantically what is being said. One might attempt to exclude lexical meaning from structural in the definition of meaningful drills, but it is doubtful that it is either possible or desirable. The result is that some pattern drills come very close to being vocabulary drills. Compare the above "Which would you rather have, tea or coffee?" with "Which would you rather be, rich and healthy or sick and poor?" In other words, some meaningful drills may have the check for feedback which shows that the student really understands the pattern built into the lexical components.

---

[5]William E. Rutherford, *Modern English: A Textbook for Foreign Students* (New York: Harcourt Brace & World, 1968), p. 11.

Comprehension type questions and answers based on assigned readings fall in this class of drills:

Teacher: What color is Little Red Ridinghood's hood?
Student: Little Red Ridinghood's hood is red;

as well as much "situational" teaching, as in this drill on postnominal modification using prepositional phrases, where the students were instructed to describe each other:

Teacher: Which boy is in your class?
Student: The thin boy with long sideburns.
The handsome boy with black hair.

It will be noticed that in the question-answer drill above, the long answers were given. The expected terminal behavior is the same as for mechanical drills. We still want an automatic use of language manipulation; we are still working on habit formation. But the method is different. Mechanical drills by their nature can be drilled without grammatical analysis with the students left to "analogize" the pattern on their own. This is not possible with meaningful drills. Unless the students understand what they are doing, i.e., recognize the characteristic features involved in the language manipulation, they cannot complete the drill. Politzer reports an interesting experiment in "The Role and Place of the Explanation in the Pattern Drill" and points out that an early introduction of the explanation seems to be a more effective treatment than its postponement or omission, and that it is preferable to show the application and relevance of the new material in some sort of context before explaining it.[6] Explanations of grammatical rules will be discussed later in the chapter, and it suffices here to state that meaningful drills must be preceded by some kind of grammatical analysis. The learning process varies depending on the structural pattern drilled, and while there may still be instrumental conditioning involved, there is most often a trial-and-error process involved in finding the correct response.

Communicative Drills

At this point, however, there is still no real communication taking place. Students have a tendency to learn what they are taught rather

---

[6] Robert L. Politzer, "The Role and Place of the Explanation in the Pattern Drill," IRAL VI, no. 4 (November 1968): 315-331.

than what we think we are teaching. If we want fluency in expressing their own opinions, then we have to teach that. The expected terminal behavior in communicative drills is normal speech for communication or, if one prefers, the free transfer of learned language patterns to appropriate situations.

The degree of control in a communicative drill is a moot point. Paulston originally stated that there is no control of the response, that students have free choice to say whatever they want. However, this turns out not to be true. All classroom teachers, using this system of sequencing drills, have reported that there is indeed control, not of lexical items as we had at first thought but of structural patterns. The difficulty lies in retaining this control so that the students indeed practice what they have learned; they themselves lose track of the fact that they are drilling and become engrossed in exchanging information. But it is a drill rather than free communication because we are still within the realm of the cue-response pattern.

To recapitulate, the differences between a meaningful drill and a communicative drill lie in the expected terminal behavior (automatic use of language manipulation versus free transfer of learned language patterns to appropriate situations), and in response control. But the main difference between a meaningful drill and a communicative drill is that in the latter the speaker adds *new* information about the real world. In mechanical and meaningful drills the teacher and the class always know what answer to expect; although the grammatical patterns used to encode the information may vary, the content is already known and there is a right or wrong answer. No one ever forgets that these drills are only language exercises; in the real world it would seem foolish to ask questions the answers to which you already know. The answer to "What color is your shirt?" is merely meaningful; the situation supplies that information, and the teacher knows the answer as well as the student. But the answer to "Do you have a date for Saturday night?" is communicative; here the class gets a piece of information it did not have before.

Communicative drills are the most time consuming and the most difficult to arrange, but if we want fluency in expressing personal opinions, we must teach that. Role playing within a set situation—ordering a meal, carrying on a telephone conversation, buying groceries—is one way of working with communicative drills. Soliciting opinions rather than factual answers from reading passages is another. The simplest way of working with communicative drills is just to instruct students to answer truthfully.

Guided Reply[7]

1. Do you read the *Daily News* editorials?

    No. { The *Times* is the paper whose editorials I read.

    { The paper whose editorials I read is the *Times*.

2. Are you familiar with Burma's problems?

    No. { Thailand is the country whose problems I am familiar with.

    { The country whose problems I am familiar with is Thailand.

3. Did you fly over here on a United Airlines plane?
4. Are you taking Professor Wiley's course?

Communicative drills provide John Carroll's " 'problem-solving' situation in which the student must find . . . appropriate verbal responses for solving the problem, 'learning' by a trial-and-error process, to communicate rather than merely to utter the speech patterns in the lesson."[8] We are clearly working within a level of language that involves thought and opinion, and teaching it in a way which necessitates an understanding of the essential elements of what is being learned. It is a very different experience from mechanical drilling. It is practice in performance by practice in generating new utterances in order to internalize the rules of the grammar.

It should be emphasized that these drills do not involve free communication, and that if that is the ultimate goal of the class, then these drills should be followed by interaction activities, situations so structured that the students learn through free communication with their peers. Interaction activities are discussed in Chapter 2.

A TYPOLOGY OF STRUCTURAL PATTERN DRILLS[9]

Introduction

Few texts will incorporate a complete sequence of mechanical, meaningful, and communicative drills. Audio-lingually oriented texts primarily contain mechanical drills; cognitive code-oriented texts

---

[7] Rutherford, p. 219.

[8] John B. Carroll, *The Study of Language* (Cambridge, Massachusetts: Harvard University Press, 1953), p. 188.

[9] This part of the chapter is based on the article "A Typology of Structural Pattern Drill," by Bruder and Paulston, forthcoming in *Studia Anglica Posnaniensia*, an International Review of English Studies.

typically lack any mechanical drills, and the teacher has to supplement his text with those drills which are missing. A typology of drills is a useful guide to constructing drills, and it is to that purpose that we include the following discussion of types of drills.

Types of drills refer to the type of restructuring of a model, what Francis Johnson has named the "restructuring range."[10] The restructuring range indicates the type of rearrangement and the complexity of this rearrangement which the learner goes through in order to arrive at a response.

What follows is a discussion of our typology of structural pattern drills. The basic criterion for assigning drills to the various types is in terms of the types of restructuring.

Here is an overview of the total typology:

    I. Repetition Drills
        A. Verbatim repetition
        B. Open-ended repetition
        C. Dialogue repetition
   II. Discrimination Drills
        A. Pattern recognition
        B. Context recognition
        C. Function coding
  III. Alternation Drills
        A. Morpho-lexical Drills
            1. Single slot substitution
            2. Double slot substitution
            3. Multiple slot substitution
            4. Moving slot substitution
            5. Correlative substitution
               a. simple
               b. complex
        B. Syntactic Drills
            1. Expansion
            2. Completion
            3. Reduction
            4. Transformation
            5. Integration
  IV. Reply
        A. Two Stage Drills
            1. Short answer

---

[10] Personal Communication from Dr. Francis C. Johnson, then Professor of English, University of Papua and New Guinea, July 31, 1970.

2. Comprehension questions
3. Rejoinder
4. Comment
5. Free response
   B. Three Stage Drills

We have included several examples of the various types in order to demonstrate their use at different levels in the curriculum. The designation T-1, T-2, T-3 refers to approximate TOEFL level of students' proficiency: T-1 250; T-2 350; T-3 450, i.e., very beginning, beginning, and intermediate. Advanced students should not be doing these types of drills.

I. Repetition Drills

Repetition drills are just what they sound like, plain repetition of the cue. By varying the nature of the cue, one can achieve different subtypes of repetition drills.

One might well question the justification for including mindless parroting in a language class. In the first place, the teacher must make very sure that it is not mindless parroting. Students can do some of these drills without understanding them and the teacher therefore has to make extra sure that they do understand. As for justification, these drills serve two purposes. At the beginning stages of language learning, repetition drills are very useful in building up "kinetic memory," i.e., for the training of the perceptual motor skills. We have forgotten the rules for the word order of the French oblique personal pronouns but we can still use them correctly, the tongue trips along its memorized path, as it were. We suspect that the function of kinetic memory in language learning is more important than what it presently is given credit for being, and repetition drills are excellent for its development.

As Francis Johnson has pointed out, part of language learning is also the ability to control increasing amounts of language in mechanical manipulation.[11] Beginning students can remember and repeat only relatively short sentences. Repetition drills of steadily increasing lengths are very useful for developing auditory memory, for increased competence in recognition and recall of long utterances of language.

---

[11] Ibid.

A. *Verbatim Repetition*

The students repeat the cue exactly as given. The drills are useful in teaching subject-verb agreement, adjective-noun order and word order in general.

T-1		NP + BE + adjective	(Mechanical)
	Repeat:	The campus is confusing.	
		The boy is handsome.	
		The house is white.	
		The car is small.[12]	

T-2		*There* + BE + NP	(Mechanical)
	Repeat:	There's a good restaurant down the street.	
		There's a drug store in the next block.	
		There are some new students in the class.	

Verbatim repetition tends to be very boring for more advanced students; but by increasing the length of the utterances as the students increase in proficiency, the students' memory is challenged and the drills seem to be regarded as games.

T-3	Perfect modals – negative		(Mechanical)
	Listen:	I didn't see Judy at the party.	
	Repeat:	She may not have been there—she had to finish a paper.	
	Listen:	John wasn't in class when it began.	
	Repeat:	He might not have been on time—he overslept this morning.	
	Listen:	I got up late, so I didn't go to the store for a *New York Times.*	
	Repeat:	They might not have had any during the truckers' strike.	

B. *Open-ended Repetition (Chain Drills)*

These drills are done individually and each student repeats all the responses prior to his own and adds his own piece of information. Since the students tend to regard them as games, they work well for extra practice on complicated patterns when verbatim repetition might be rejected. The drills also require the students to listen to each other, and attention is diverted from the fact that they are drilling and toward actual use of the language.

---

[12] All further drills in this chapter, unless footnoted, come from Mary Newton Bruder, *MMC → Developing Communicative Competence in English as a Second Language* (Pittsburgh: University of Pittsburgh,) University Center for International Studies, 1974).

T-1 *going to* future (Meaningful)

Teacher presents Situation: You have $50.00. The stores are having "end-of-season" sales. What are you going to buy?

S1: I'm going to buy (a coat).[13]
S2: I'm going to buy a coat and (a hat).
S3: I'm going to buy a coat and a hat and (a scarf).

In the previous example, the concord between subject and verb can be practiced by expanding the drill to include the other students' full statements. (She's going to buy a coat, he's going to buy a hat, and I'm going to buy a scarf.)

The following example is a variation of a chain drill in that each student repeats only part of the previous student's answer as he adds to the information concerning the proposed situation.

T-2 Conditional (Meaningful)

T: Imagine a situation where it is possible for you to go to New York. Make a series of statements, each of which is based on the preceding one.

S1: If we receive some money, we will go to New York.
S2: If we go to New York, we will go by plane.
S3: If we go by plane, we will arrive at Kennedy Airport.
S4: If we arrive at Kennedy Airport. . . .[14]

Chain drills can be varied by altering the pattern of student responses. At first the students should answer in order around the class so as to reduce the number of elements they must remember (pattern, item, order); later the teacher can call on students at random and finally, the student himself can choose the next to answer. We make it a rule in our classes that no one is allowed to write down the items because the challenge of remembering seems to be important to the success of the drills.

C. Dialogue Repetition Drills

In these drills a sequence of specified patterns is repeated with minor variations. They are excellent for practice in the changing of tenses, formation of questions and changing word order, as well as

---

[13] The parentheses indicate elements of free choice to the student.

[14] Robert Krohn, *English Sentence Structure* (Ann Arbor: University of Michigan Press, 1971), p. 259.

for practice in conversational exchanges. The students concentrate on the exchange and forget they are drilling.

T-2   Irregular past   (Meaningful)

    T: He teaches the class every day.
    S1:   Then he taught the class yesterday.
    S2:   No, he didn't teach it yesterday.
    S1:   Why not?
    S2:   (He was sick.)
    S1:   When *did* he teach it?
    S2:   He taught it (the day before yesterday).

    T: She makes a cake every week.
    S1:   Then she made a cake last week.
    S2:   No, she didn't make one last week.
    S1:   Why not?
    S2:   (She was busy.)
    S1:   When *did* she make one?
    S2:   She made one (the week before last).

    T: Bill catches up on his sleep every Saturday.
          Nancy has a date every weekend.
          Chen makes a long distance phone call every Sunday.

If the drills are to be used for conversational exchanges, care must be taken to make the language as "natural" as possible. In the example above, use of the pronouns *it* and *one* make the dialogue much more realistic even though they increase the complexity of the drill considerably.

It is important to recognize drills of this type for what they are, i.e., simply repetitions. However, well done they look impressive and can easily delude an observer into thinking that actual communication is taking place.

II. Discrimination Drills

Discrimination drills are by nature testing drills, i.e., drills where the correct answer (there is only one) depends on conscious choice by the student. Discrimination drills are useful when introducing new patterns which vary only slightly from previous patterns (e.g., singular/plural; third person; present perfect/present continuous), and the students must recognize subtle differences for accurate encoding. Very little time should be spent on this type of drill since the students are talking about language rather than using it. However, these drills do reduce the necessity for grammatical explanations;

they assure students' grasp of the function of the pattern; and they give valuable practice in listening comprehension in that they serve to focus the students' attention on syntactic cues.

A. Pattern Recognition

The "same-different" responses are most often found in pronunciation exercises but can be helpful in determining discrimination of grammatical patterns as well. More common in grammar drills are those in which the student is required to identify the patterns on the basis of some specified feature.

```
T-1   BE — singular/plural                    (Mechanical-testing)
      T:   If you hear a sentence in the singular, raise one finger;
           if plural, raise two fingers.
           The girl is tall.     S:    (1)
           The girls are tall.         (2)
           The boys are lost.          (2)
```

In order to avoid the linguistic terminology, examples of the patterns are sometimes written on the board and labeled A and B. The students then respond by saying the appropriate letter.

```
T-1   Adjective/noun                           (Mechanical-testing)
        A                                          B
He's an American.                          He's American.
You're Brazilians.                         You're Brazilian.
She's a Thai.                              She's Thai.
We're Arabs.                               We're Arab.[15]
```

B. Context Recognition

Similar surface structures may have different underlying deep structures, i.e., similar sounding words and phrases may have different meanings, for example, *Whose/who's*. These drills ascertain whether the students have grasped the various functions of such words and phrases, a determination not always possible in drills requiring encoding.

```
T-1   Who's/whose                             (Mechanical-testing)
      T:   Whose book is this?       S:    Possession
           Who's going downtown?           Person
           Whose is this?                  Possession
           Who's a doctor?                 Person
           Whose is the VW?                Possession
```

---

[15] Rutherford, p. 4.

T-2 *Could*   (Mechanical-testing)

    T: Could you tell me the time?   S: Request
          Could you speak English
          before you came?   Ability
          Could you go tomorrow?   Possibility
          Could he come later?   Possibility
          Could she cook before she
          was married?   Ability
          Could you lend me a dime?   Request

T-3 Uses of *if* clauses   (Mechanical-testing)

    T: If you have time, I'd like some
          suggestions.   S: Request
    T: If he has a test, he studies for
          three days.   S: Habit
    T: If you've learned the acronyms,
          you've learned the language. S: Generalization
    T: If my friend is late, I try to
          cover up for her.   S: Habit
    T: If you've read one English book,
          you've read them all.   S: Generalization

C. Function Coding

T-2 Modal verbs   (Mechanical-testing)

    T: go to our friends' party   S: We might go to our
          (possibility)   friends' party.
    T: write to my parents   S: I should write to my
          (good idea)   parents.
    T: pay his bills by Monday   S: He has to pay his
          (obligation)   bills by Monday.

These drills might be said to be the reverse of the context recognition drills. Rather than decoding a specific function, the student here has to encode it. Our students find them useful for sorting out the meanings of the various modals.

T-3 Modal *have to*/ causative *have*   (Meaningful)

    T: cut the grass (necessity)   S: (I) have to cut the grass.
    T: cut the grass (cause)   S: (I'm going to) have the
                                        grass cut.

    T: type the term paper (cause)
          wash the windows (necessity)
          fix the car (cause)
          type the letters (necessity)

III. Alternation Drills

These are the drills familiar to all who have used the audio-lingual texts; substitution, transformation, expansion drills, and so on. They are all encoding drills which provide the students with practice with the *rules* of the grammar where the purpose is to internalize the structure by practicing the pattern.

A. MORPHO-LEXICAL DRILLS

The teaching point of these drills focuses on morphological structure or lexical items like frequency adverbs, prepositions, etc. Some drills combine practice of more than one grammatical feature, and such drills are much more difficult. All of these drills involve manipulation of a single sentence utterance where the constituents (i.e., slot and filler in the tagmemic sense) remain in the same order and of the same number as in the model utterance.

1. Single slot substitution

T-1/2	Negative modal		(Mechanical)
	Repeat:	I might not go to class today.	
	Substitute:	go shopping	S: I might not go shopping today.
		do the laundry	
		finish the lesson	
		see John	
		have time to do the assignment	

Only one constituent is changed throughout the drill. The drills are useful for practicing the word order of difficult patterns or for function words like the frequency adverbs. They also lend themselves to teaching vocabulary. At the beginning stages of language learning, the substituted constituent is likely to be a single word, but the drills should steadily be made more difficult by increasing the length of the constituent.

T-2/3	*If* clauses—condition		(Mechanical)
	Repeat:	John would help the students if he knew the answers to their questions.	
	Substitute:	if he could	S: John would help the students if he could.
	Substitute:	if he had time	S: John would help the students if he had time.

Substitute:	if he didn't have so much to do	S:	John would help the students if he didn't have so much to do.
Substitute:	if he wanted to if someone asked him to if he could understand their English[16]		

2. Double slot substitution

T-1	Count nouns		(Mechanical)
	Repeat:	We don't smoke many cigarettes.	
	Substitute:	eat/vegetables	S: We don't eat many vegetables.
		use/eggs read/books[17]	

In these drills the student changes two constituents from the model. The drills are useful for practicing comparison, and for highlighting many structural contrasts.

T-2	Comparison (*the same* NP *as*)		(Mechanical)
	Repeat:	My coat is the same size as yours.	
	Substitute:	city/size	S: My city is the same size as
		book/price	yours.
		hat/shape	
		car/color	

T-2	BE-past + *going to* + verb	(Mechanical)
	T:	fly to Paris/fly to London
	S:	I was going to fly to Paris; I'm going to fly to London instead.
	T:	study English/study French
	S:	I was going to study English; I'm going to study French instead.
	T:	read a novel/read a biography buy a VW/buy a Chevrolet work all day/sleep all day

3. Multiple slot substitution   Three or more constituents are replaced in the model with each student response. These drills are excellent for practicing comparisons and can be used as problem-solving activities even for quite advanced students, especially if the order of the cues is different from that expected in the response.

---

[16] Substitution drills must be carefully checked to guard against a cue fitting in more than one slot. If the cue is "Boys like sports.—girls," the response is more likely to be "Boys like girls" than the expected "Girls like sports."

[17] Note that this kind of drill can cover many more items than a single slot substitution which would be restricted to smokable or edible lexical items.

T-2 Comparison (*the same* NP *as*)   (Mechanical-testing)

T:	VW/Volvo (size)	S:	My VW is the same size as her Volvo.
	hat/coat (color)		My hat is the same color as her coat.
	novel/short story (length)		
	Ford/Oldsmobile (width)		

4. *Moving slot substitution* With each student response one constituent is changed but it is a different constituent in each response. The drills are very useful for extended practice on verb tenses or virtually any pattern on which the students need extra practice, since the drills are usually regarded as games.

T-1 *Going to* future   (Mechanical-testing)

Repeat:	He's going to buy a new car.		
Substitute:	radio	S:	He's going to buy a new radio.
	get		He's going to get a new radio.
	I		I'm going to get a new radio.
	house		

T-2 Past continuous   (Mechanical)

Repeat:	I was watching TV at 10:00 last night.		
Substitute:	we	S:	We were watching TV at 10:00 last night.
	sleeping		
	11:00		
	yesterday		
	the children		

T-3 Past perfect continuous   (Mechanical)

Repeat:	I'd been travelling for three months when I met him.		
Substitute:	working	S:	I'd been working for three months when I met him.
Substitute:	two months	S:	I'd been working for two months when I met him.
Substitute:	saw	S:	I'd been working for two months when I saw him.
Substitute:	her	S:	I'd been working for two months when I saw her.
Substitute:	we	S:	We'd been working for two months when we saw her.
Substitute:	studying		
	two days		
	them		

5. *Correlative substitution* The cue triggers a morphological or syntactic correlative change in the pattern. The drills are excellent for testing the students' ability to encode grammatical relationships such as subject-verb agreement, indefinite article choice, count-mass nouns, pronoun forms—in short, any structure which contrasts minimally in its various patterns. All correlative drills are by nature testing drills.

   a. Simple   These drills are single slot substitutions which require the students to make some adjustment in another part of the pattern in order to respond correctly.

T-1   Indefinite article   (Mechanical)
      Repeat: The girl is a student.
      Substitute: teacher   S: The girl is a teacher.
                    artist   The girl is an artist.
                    actress
                    spy

T-2   Reflexive pronouns   (Mechanical-testing)
      Repeat: I'd rather do it by myself.
      Substitute: she   S: She'd rather do it by herself.
                    he
                    we
                    you and Joe

T-2/3   Conjunction *but*   (Mechanical-testing)
      Repeat: We don't understand the game, but Jack does.
      Substitute: We didn't see the   S: We didn't see the game,
                    game.   but Jack did.
      Substitute: We saw the game.   S: We saw the game, but
                                              Jack didn't.
      Substitute: We aren't having a picnic.
                    We can understand the rules.
                    We won't have time.

   b. Complex   If the student must replace two or more constituents, correlative changes add greatly to the complexity of producing the expected response. In the following example, note that a lexical change is also required:

T-2/3   Relative clauses   (Mechanical-testing)
      Repeat: The boy who is coming is my brother.
      Substitute: boys   S: The boys who are coming are my
                                  brothers.
                    girl   The girl who is coming is my
                                  sister.
                    girls   The girls who are coming are my
                                  sisters.
                    woman
                    man

In the following example the students must know the semantic relationship between the items in order to do the drill successfully.

T-2   Comparison (*like/the same as*)   (Mechanical-testing)

    T: Pepsi/Coke   S: Pepsi is like Coke.
          autumn/fall   Autumn is the same as fall.
          frozen water/ice   Frozen water is the same as ice.
          VW/Volvo   A VW is like a Volvo.

In the next example, Student 1 must infer from the double cue the expected response in order to postulate the correct question form.

T-2   Question words and time expressions   (Mechanical-testing)

T:	Paris/three weeks	S1:	*How long* were you in Paris?
		S2:	I was in Paris *for* three weeks.
	Paris/1965	S1:	*When* were you in Paris?
		S2:	I was in Paris *in* 1965.
	Paris/April 5	S1:	*When* were you in Paris?
		S2:	I was in Paris *on* April 5.
	London/July 14		
	Caracas/a month		

T-3   Modal verbs—present/past   (Mechanical-testing)

Repeat:	I could have looked up the words yesterday.		
Substitute:	today	S:	I could look up the words today.
	my friends	S:	I could look up my friends today.
	yesterday	S:	I could have looked up my friends yesterday.

B. SYNTACTIC DRILLS

In syntactic drills the student manipulates either the number or the order of the constituents in the cue. The teaching point of these drills tends to involve syntactical relationships of features such as question formation, formation of negative statements, word order, changes from phrase to clause and from clause to phrase.

1. Expansion

T-1   Frequency adverbs   (Mechanical-testing)

T:	The baby cries. (often)	S:	The baby often cries.
	He's hungry. (always)		He's always hungry.
	There's a nurse in the hall. (usually)		There's usually a nurse in the hall.
	The girls fight. (never)		The girls never fight.[18]

---

[18] Francine Stieglitz, *Progressive Audio-Lingual Drills in English* (New York: Regents, 1970), p. 32.

T-1   Adjective phrase   (Mechanical-testing)

T:	The napkins are on the table.	S:	The napkins are on the table.
T:	two	S:	The two napkins are on the table.
T:	paper	S:	The two paper napkins are on the table.
T:	pretty yellow[19]		

The student's response contains more constituents than does the model but their relative word order remains the same. These drills are useful for practice on word order in adjective phrases and of frequency adverbs, and for tag questions.

Expansion drills can combine with various kinds of substitution drills, as in the following example, in which the student is required to expand the basic Noun Phrase + BE + Noun Phrase pattern by adding an adjective of his choice to each NP.

T-1   Adjective + noun   (Meaningful)

| T: | man/lawyer women/students | S: | The (big) man is a (bad) lawyer. The (thin) women are (good) students. |
| | women/actresses men/hairdressers children/actors | | |

T-2   *There*—subject   (Mechanical-testing)

T:	some letters on the desk		There are some letters on the desk.
	a good restaurant near here		There's a good restaurant near here.
	a phone call for John some bills for you		

2. *Completion*   As with the expansion drills, the student's response will contain more constituents than the cue, but in these drills the cue is always just part of an utterance which the student must complete.

T-2   *Since/ago* + time expression   (Meaningful)

| T: | They had an election _____. | S: | They had an election (a year ago). |

[19] Fe R. Dacanay, *Techniques and Procedures in Second Language Teaching* (Dobbs Ferry, New York: Oceana Publications, 1963), p. 120.

	T:	They haven't had an election _____.	S:	They haven't had an election (since 19____).
	T:	She hasn't smoked a cigarette _____.		
		We saw the new movie _____.		
		Nancy has read three books _____.		

T-2 Conjunctions (Meaningful)

	T:	He smiled but _____.	S:	He smiled but (refused).
	T:	They were laughing and _____	S:	They were laughing and (telling jokes).
	T:	He usually eats here or _____.	S:	He usually eats here or (in a restaurant).
	T:	I'll take sugar but _____.		
		She went to the door and _____.		
		We'll see you on Thursday or _____.[20]		

These drills are useful for moving the student away from the extremely structured nature of most of the preceding types of drills to a point where he can begin to express his own thoughts. Completion drills can be used with virtually any pattern, but they are particularly useful for contrasting such structural patterns as conjunctions and time expressions which occur with specific tenses. In the preceding examples, note that the teaching point of the first drill is the structural relationship, in the second the semantic relationship of the features in the pattern.

Here are two more examples of completion drills, one from a beginning lesson and one quite advanced:

T-1 Count/noncount nouns (Meaningful)

	T:	Carlos uses a few _____.	S:	Carlos uses a few (eggs).
		Jim doesn't smoke many _____.		Jim doesn't smoke many (cigars).
		Jane wants a little _____.		
		Bill doesn't use much _____.		
		Paul spends a little _____.		

T-3 Transitive verb + complement (Meaningful)

	T:	I feel it is my duty to _____.	S:	I feel it my duty to (tell you that you're wasting your time).
	T:	We call it failure when _____.	S:	We call it failure when (you don't accomplish your objective).

---

[20] Rutherford, p. 78.

T: I find it impossible to   S:

_____ .

They regard it as an insult that _____ .
Do you consider it correct to _____ ?[21]

3. Reduction   These drills are the converse of expansion drills. that is, the order of the constituents remains the same, but the number is fewer in the response than in the cue. They are most common in the practice of pronoun forms and are frequently accompanied by correlative changes as in the second of the following examples.

T-1   Subject pronouns   (Mechanical-testing)
      T: The car is small.   S: It's small.
            The girl is beautiful   She's beautiful.
            The man is tall.   He's tall.
            The house is big.   It's big.
T-2   Indefinite pronouns   (Mechanical-testing)
      T: All of the people are coming.   S: Everyone is coming.
            All of the people like Coke.   Everyone likes Coke.
            All of the people want clean air.   Everyone wants clean
                                                 air.

4. Transformation   In transformation drills the order of constituents in the cue is changed in the response. The number of constituents in the cue may also vary from that in the response. The drills can be used to practice tense, question, and negative formations as well as many noun modifications.

T-1   BE—question formation   (Mechanical-testing)
      T: You're lost.   S: Are you lost?
            He's a good student.   Is he a good student?
            She's lost.   Is she lost?
            They're good instructors.   Are they good instructors?
T-2   Noun modification   (Mechanical)
      T: the club for the faculty   S: the faculty club
            a room in the dormitory   a dormitory room
            delivery of the mail
            the people in the office
            a frame for the picture[22]

---

[21] Ibid, p. 362.
[22] Ibid, p. 46.

T-2	Irregular past	(Meaningful)
T:	They're beginning the program promptly at six today.	S: (Yesterday) they began it at five.
T:	She's singing with an orchestra this time.	S: (Last time) she sang with (only a piano).
T:	The bells usually ring every Sunday at eleven.	

T: This semester he's sitting in the front of the room.

T: They're throwing a big party at their place this weekend.[23]

T-3	Relative clause formation	(Mechanical-testing)
T:	Do you know any superstitious people?	S: Do you know any people who are superstitious?
T:	Do you like exciting stories?	S: Do you like stories which are exciting?
T:	Does the store have any cheap paperbacks?	S: Does the store have any paperbacks which are cheap?

Of all the types of structural pattern drills, transformation drills vary the widest in degree of difficulty, from very easy ones as in the examples above to the very difficult (from the students' point of view) question formation types found in most audio-lingual texts on any language.

T: John wrote *the letter.*
S: What did John write?

It seems fairly obvious that the degree of difficulty is directly proportional to the number of changes performed on the cue in order to arrive at the response. Consider the following examples from drills on WH question formation:

a. One change required (Movement of the WH word)
   T: Did John drive somewhere?
   S: Where did John drive?
b. Two changes required (Formation of past question; movement of WH word)
   T: John drove somewhere.
   S: Where did John drive?
c. Three changes required (Formation of past question; supply and movement of the WH word.)
   T: John drove home.
   S: Where did John drive?

[23] Ibid. p. 38.

In all three examples the student response is the same, but the last is the most difficult because it involves the most operations. In our experience, when a transformation drill has gone astray, it has been because the number of transformations is beyond the ability or training of the students.

5. *Integration* All of the previous types of drills have involved a single sentence utterance; integration drills require the students to combine two utterances into one, a manipulation which frequently requires some transformation or correlative change in the pattern. Integration drills are useful in practicing conjunction and subordination, relative clause formation, and other rather complex structures.

T-2 BE + adjective/adverb + present participle (Mechanical-testing)

T: Is he busy? Is he doing his assignment?
S: Is he busy doing his assignment?

T: Are they in the kitchen? Are they eating?
S: Are they in the kitchen eating?

T: Is she outside? Is she waiting?
S: Is she outside waiting?

T: Is he sitting? Is he reading? Are they at the bank? Are they cashing a check? Is she back home? Is she watching TV?[24]

T-2 Adjective phrase (Mechanical-testing)

T: This apartment is cheap. She can rent it.
S: This apartment is cheap enough for her to rent.

T: This car is big. ( ) can't drive it.
S: This car is too big for ( ) to drive.

T: These chairs are heavy. We can't lift them.
S: These chairs are too heavy for us to lift.

T-3 Relative clause formation (Mechanical-testing)

T: The man broke his leg. He's in my class.
S: The man who broke his leg is in my class.

T: The women are studying computer science. They're waiting to see the professor.
S: The women who are studying computer science are waiting to see the professor.

T: The man came to dinner. He stayed for three weeks.
S: The man who came to dinner stayed for three weeks.

IV. Reply

We consider all types of drills which consist of a conversation-like exchange to belong to this category. With these drills it is especially important to keep the class of the drill in mind for it is easy to

---

[24]Ibid, p. 11.

mistake mechanical manipulation for communicative activity. (This type of drill does, however, lend itself well to communicative drills.) The drills are important in training the students to interact with others in the foreign language.

A. TWO STAGE DRILLS

In two stage drills, the exchange is completed by the teacher cue and the student response. The cue may consist of a question or a statement which requires an appropriate controlled or free reply by the student. The reply types of drills are grouped according to the nature of the expected response and the degree of control by the teacher.

1. Short Answer Much natural language exchange consists of partial utterances or short answers in responses to inquiries. The students must be trained in this usage if they are to sound natural in real conversation and not as if they are still doing language classroom drills.

T-1 Tag question responses   (Mechanical-testing)

T: Big cars increase pollution,   S: Yes, they do.
      don't they?
      He has a VW, doesn't he?   Yes, he does.
      You come from Libya, don't you?   Yes, I do.
      The weather gets hot, doesn't it?   Yes, it does.

T-2/3 Conjunctions   (Meaningful-Communicative)

T: Do you have to
      make a lot of   Yes, I do.   { But (I can't).
      money?   { And (I will).
                         S:
                                   No, I don't. { But (I hope to).
                                                 { And (I won't).

T: Do you overeat?
                                   Yes, I do.   { But (I shouldn't).
                                                 { And (I like to).
                         S:
                                                 { But (they're always
                                   No, I don't. { encouraging me to).
                                                 { And (I don't ever
                                                 { expect to).

T: Do you ever eat in American homes?
      Did you enjoy yourself?
      Did they go out of their way to give you a good time?[25]

---

[25] Ibid, p. 157.

2. Rejoinder These drills are useful for training the students in the use of phatic language—the conversational formulas which serve as introductions, leave takings, change of topics, etc.

T-2/3   "By the way"   (Meaningful)

    T: With an F visa you   S: By the way, (will they order
        have a Temporary   us to do military service?)
        Entry Permit.

    T: Jim Barlett wrote   S: By the way, (I saw his wife's
        me a nice letter.   name in the paper).

    T: (Christmas) will soon be here.
        I have to see my advisor tomorrow.[26]

3. Guided Comment or Reply The student replies to a comment or a question by the teacher using a specified structure.

T-2   Prenominal Modification   (Mechanical-testing)

    T: What's a service for   S: It's a check-
        cashing checks?   cashing service.

    T: What's an operation   S: It's a time con-
        that consumes time?   suming operation.

    T: What's an operating   S: It's a high
        cost that's high?   operating cost.

    T: What's an expert in reading minds?
        What's a display that catches the eye?[27]

T-2   Comparison   (Meaningful)

    T: She's 35, but he's   S: He's older than
        45.   she is.

    T: The Hudson is an   S: The Mississippi is
        important river,   more important
        but the Mississippi   than the Hudson.
        is very important.

    T: He made some progress, but she made a lot of progress.
        It's easy to go by train, but it's very easy to go by bus.[28]

T-2/3   Modals (perfect)—*must*   (Meaningful-Communicative)

    T: John slept in until   S: (He must have stayed
        10:00 this morning.   out late last night.)
                        (He must have been
                        tired.)

---

[26] Ibid, p. 130.
[27] Ibid, p. 273.
[28] Ibid, p. 44.

T: Bill and Jim had to break a window to get into their apartment.	S: (They must have lost their key.)

T: When the professor returned the exams, Jane looked sad. Nancy's mother was angry with her.

4. Comprehension Questions Questions which test the student's understanding of material read or heard are usually more common in reading exercises, but they can be used in the grammar class to check on the comprehension of a dialogue or narrative used to introduce the grammar patterns.

Grammar drills which contain alternative questions are really tests of the student's comprehension.

T-2   *In order to/for*   (Meaningful Communicative)

I   T   What do you go to   S: You go to the post
the post office for,   office for stamps.
stamps or envelopes?

T: What do you go to   S: You go to the bank
the bank for, to   to take out money.
take out money or
to buy tickets?

T: Why do you go to   S: You go to school
school, to study or   to study.
to have a good time?

Neither. You go to
school to (get an
education).

T: What do you go to school for, an education or a good time?
What do you study English for, to get a better job or to be
able to communicate?[29]

5. Free Response Free response drills are just that—the student is free to respond as he wants. They lend themselves particularly well to being communicative; although such drills are designed to practice a specific pattern, there is no guarantee that the student will actually use the target pattern in his response. As often as not he does, as Rivers points out, because he is uncertain in his knowledge of the language.[30]

T-1   BE—present   (Communicative)
T: Describe the capital   S: (It's a beautiful
of your country.   city.)

---

[29] Ibid, p. 160.

[30] Wilga M. Rivers, "Talking Off the Tops of Their Heads," *TESOL Quarterly* VI no. 1 (March 1972): 75.

T: Describe the people   (They're friendly
     of your country.   people.)
     Describe a big university in your country.
     Describe the leader of your country.
     Describe the houses in your country.

T:2 Reflexives   (Communicative)
     T: What kinds of things   S: (I like to study
          do you like to do   alone, but I don't
          by yourself?   like to eat by myself.)
     T: Do you always type your own papers?
          Did you come here by yourself?
          Do you live alone or do you have a roommate?

T-3 *Have*—Causative   (Communicative)
     T: Do you wash and   S: (Yes, I do.)
          iron your clothes   (No, I don't. I have
          yourself?   them done at the
                                     laundry down the
                                     street.)
     T: Where do you have your clothes cleaned?
          Does your roommate cut your hair?
          Do you polish your shoes yourself?
          If you tear your shirt, do you fix it yourself?

B. THREE STAGE DRILLS

The cue, either a question or a statement by the teacher, sets up a conversational exchange among the students. The most common of these are the directed dialogues, the "Ask him . . ." type of exercise. These tend to be in the meaningful and communicative classes of drills, but it is possible by using pictures or objects to construct mechanical-testing drills of this type.

T-1 Tenses/time expressions   (Mechanical-testing)
always   Student A: Is he always thirsty?
             Student B: No, he isn't always thirsty.
now   Student A: Are they busy now?
             Student B: No, they aren't busy now.
last night   Student A: Was he hungry last night?
             Student B: No, he wasn't hungry last night.

tomorrow
always
now
last night [31]

---

[31] Robert Lado and C. C. Fries, *English Pattern Practices* (Ann Arbor: The University of Michigan Press, 1958), p. 59

The relative difficulty of these drills depends on the nature of the manipulation from the cue to the first response. The example above is an expansion, but note the increased complexity caused by the required transformations in the next example.

T-3 Subordinators (Meaningful)
T: Was (Cecelia) stand-   S1: (José,), (do you recall)
ing near the door   whether (Cecelia) was
when you came in?   standing near the door
                         when we came in?
                  S2: I (didn't notice)
                         whether she was or not.
T: Did today's weather report say anything about rain?
Were you sitting in the right laboratory booth yesterday?
Do New York City and Long Island have different area codes?[32]

Communicative drills result when the structures for the exchange are not specified in the model. Students get the information by use of any patterns at their command.

T-2 Simple past (Communicative)
T: Find out when (Ali) S1: (When did you
called long distance and   call long distance?)
what kind of call   S2: (Last weekend
it was?   I called Iran.)
                  S1: (Did you call
                         person-to-person?)
                  S2: (No, station-to-
                         station.)
T: Find out when ( ) called long distance and who dialed the number, ( ) or the operator.
Find out if ( ) ever called a wrong number long distance and what happened.

T-3 Modal *have to*/ causative *have* (Communicative)
T: Find out if ( ) has S1: (What do you have
to do something   to do today?) (Do
today.   you have to do
                            something today?)
                  S2: (Nothing. I'm free
                         all day.) (I have
                         to finish my research
                         paper.)

[32] Rutherford, p. 278.

T:	Find out if ( ) has something done every week.	S1:	(Do you have your laundry done every week?)
		S2:	(No, I do it myself at the laundromat.)

T: Find out if ( ) and ( ) had to do something last week.
Find out if ( ) and ( ) will have something done this afternoon.
Find out if ( ) had to go somewhere last weekend.

Concluding Remarks

We presume that drills can be found which do not fit exactly into any of the categories discussed, but if so, we are reasonably certain that such drills will be combinations of the basic types in this typology.[33]

Typologies are boring, but so is writing supplementary drills for a bad text. In this section it has been our intention to alert teachers to potential troublespots in different types of drills so that such drills can be avoided or changed, and to provide models for facilitating the writing of supplementary drills.

DESIGN OF A GRAMMAR LESSON

A grammar lesson may take many formats, and we are perfectly ready to concede that there are other ways of teaching grammar than ours. The design of a grammar lesson which we discuss here is based on the theoretical framework which we outlined in the beginning of the chapter, and we are satisfied after years of experimentation by trial and error in the English Language Institute that these procedures achieve a maximum efficiency in language learning while maintaining a reasonable degree of student satisfaction.

The procedures are designed for a fifty minute class devoted exclusively to grammar. In a class which is designed to teach all four skills, the procedures will have to be modified by shortening the lesson but the order of activities should remain essentially the same. The teacher may well want to begin a new day's lesson with the

---

[33]The drill on p. 22 on Time Expressions is a good example. It really belongs with the Reply drills, but it is also a double slot substitution.

addition of a few rapid mechanical drills as review, a procedure which would not have been necessary had the lesson not been interrupted with a unit on reading or writing.

The format of the lesson looks like this:

Step 1.	Presentation of Pattern in Context
Step 2.	Comprehension questions
Step 3.	Identification of the Pattern
Step 4.	Mechanical Drills–Formal Explanations
Step 5.	Mechanical Drills
Step 6.	Functional Explication
Step 7.	Meaningful Drills
Step 8.	Communicative Drills
Step 9.	(Communicative Activity)

CLASSROOM PROCEDURES

Step 1. Presentation of Pattern in Context

The structural pattern that the students are to learn should first be introduced to them in context, in a passage of natural language. The context may take a variety of forms, from dialogues and reading selections to letters, diaries, news stories, etc. One has to be careful in the selection of contextual passages; cartoons, for example, often carry so much cultural meaning that the time spent in explanation makes them not worth the effort.

In a course where the objectives are oral use of language, we prefer dialogues for two reasons. First, a written dialogue demonstrates how the pattern is used in actual oral language, our objective of the course. Second, some students find it helpful to memorize dialogues while it would never occur to anyone to memorize letters or diaries. We do not require students to memorize dialogues; for many (ourselves included) it is a waste of time and tedious to boot, but for those who find it useful, opportunity for dialogue memorization should be available.

The teacher first presents any new vocabulary which is crucial to an understanding of the passage. In a dialogue about a student who is in the hospital because of food poisoning, the whole passage would be incomprehensible if the students did not understand the expression *food poisoning.* Such words can also be assigned as homework prior to the introduction of the passage. The simplest way to explain words in class, if it is possible in the teaching situation, is by giving the direct equivalent in the mother tongue, i.e., by old-fashioned translation. The chapter on Reading and Word Study contains a discussion of procedures for explaining new words. It is helpful if the teacher writes the important new words on the blackboard or refers to which line of the passage they appear in, so that the students can find them easily. In many texts, passages contain a multitude of new words. We do not mean that all new words should be discussed prior to the reading of the dialogue but only those words which are crucial to the drift of the passage. This is also the place in the lesson where the lexical meaning of new structural patterns is explained.

Next, the teacher reads the dialogue while the students follow along in their own books. They keep their books open because the purpose of this activity is to introduce structural patterns in context. Listening with books closed amounts to a listening comprehension exercise, and there are better ways of developing listening comprehension. Nor do the students read the dialogue aloud; that is a pronunciation exercise and there are better ways of teaching pronunciation. No harm of course is done by having students read the dialogue or having them listen with their books closed (the teacher will have to read the selection several times if the students are to get anything out of the activity), but is very time consuming and an inefficient use of class time, considering what students learn from such activities. The purpose of the dialogue or reading selection is to introduce the structural patterns, and time is better spent on students' practice of those patterns.

Step 2. Comprehension Questions

After the teacher has read the introductory passage, he asks some (the number depends on the length of the passage) comprehension questions to make sure that the students have understood. If the questions are skillfully constructed, the students can be made to answer using the examples of the target structural pattern where they occur in the passage, thus making the model patterns familiar. To do this the students must be allowed to keep their books open or they will get the new patterns wrong. In any case, we are checking comprehension, not memory of details, and it is helpful for the students to have access to the written passage.

If there is time in the lesson, questions should not only be factual, but also of the inferential and opinion type. (These are discussed in the chapter on Reading and Word Study.) This technique not only gives the students more opportunity to talk but also relates new information to the students' own world and experience, and so makes the new language more real to them. These discussions can be very useful in imparting cross-cultural information and teaching behavior appropriate to the culture of the target language.[34] It is easy, however, to go off on a tangent, so these discussions should be planned carefully and scheduled into the day's lesson plan.

Step 3. Identification of the Pattern

Next, the students need to identify the target pattern they are about to learn. The simplest way is for the teacher to write on the blackboard one example from the dialogue and then have the students find the other occurrences of the same pattern. This technique serves to focus the students' attention on the specific teaching point as well as on the context and form of the new pattern. If there is only one example of the pattern in the introductory passage, the teacher can make up another example (with vocabulary the students already know) for the board and then let the students discover the example in the text. They should identify the place in the dialogue where the pattern occurs by line or paragraph and then read their example. This gives slower students a chance to find the patterns as they are called off even if they have not been able to discover them for themselves.

As each new pattern occurs in the lesson, this procedure should be repeated. The class returns to the introductory material and identifies the next pattern before they go on to mechanical drills. It is important that the students are consciously aware of the particular pattern they are working on.

Sometimes the students will identify the wrong pattern. They might for instance include the continuous form (she has been writing) with the simple present perfect (she has written). It is

---

[34] The discussion following a dialogue on bargaining for a car revealed not only that bargaining in the U.S. is possible, but that it is often done by men, whereas it is a woman's job in many other countries.

important in such cases that the teacher pause for a moment, put both patterns on the board, and have the students point out how the two patterns differ. Such a procedure should not take more than two to three minutes but it is important because it serves to avoid later confusion.

Step 4. Formal Explanation

It is a moot point whether the formal explanation should precede or follow the mechanical memorizing drills. By formal explanation we mean an analysis of the particular linguistic forms and characteristics of a structural pattern, such as word order, concord agreement, shape and combination of forms—whatever the particular characteristics of the pattern the students must learn if they are to use the pattern correctly. One may either begin with mechanical memorizing drills and then have the students themselves state the rule, i.e., give the formal explanation, or one may begin with a formal explanation before doing any drilling. The decision depends on the nature and complexity of the pattern, the aptitude and proficiency of the class, and on the sequencing of the structures in the materials.

The formal explanation should be as simple and graphic as possible, and when possible, include a contrast to a similar previously learned pattern. For example, if the class have already learned third person singular simple present and they are now working on the plural, the teacher writes on the board:

```
The boy    works  at the service station.
The boys   work   at the service station.
```

and asks the class how the two patterns differ. The students are likely to answer that one pattern is singular and the other plural. Then in order to focus on the formal difference, the teacher can ask: "How do you know?" "What happens to the verb when the subject is plural?" etc. The students must be made consciously aware of the differences between the patterns they are studying, and an efficient way to achieve this purpose is to have the students themselves give the rule. In beginning homogeneous classes, this discussion can be done in the native tongue; with heterogeneous classes, it has to be done in the target language, but if the students supply the rule, the teacher will know that the students have understood and, furthermore, the explanation is likely to be in such simple language that the other students will be able to follow.

Following the formal analysis of such contrasting patterns, it is sensible to do a testing drill of the discrimination-pattern recognition type as is listed on page 16 before continuing with drills which require the students to produce the pattern. This type of drill assures the teacher that the students have in fact understood the rule, and prepares the students for further practice.

The linguistic terminology of the formal explanation is not important. Class I words, nouns and NP's will do equally well; what is important is that the teacher and students share a set of commonly understood labels which they can use to refer to the linguistic forms and their categories. Our preference is for the terminology which the students already know from a study of their mother tongue or foreign languages, which for most parts of the world means the terminology of Latinate grammars. Using such a terminology does not mean that one has to subscribe to the same linguistic analysis.

There are two main points to remember about the formal explanation: (1) it should not be missing from the lesson, and (2) it should be brief. It is perfectly possible to make such explanations in two to three minutes of class time, and the teacher should always be aware of the lesson plan at this point of the lesson as it is very easy to waste time here.

And this leads us to a final remark about linguistic explanations. Students ask questions for many reasons, many of which have nothing to do with finding an answer. They ask questions to get the teacher off the track and get a breathing spell, and they also ask questions to "test" the teacher's knowledge of the target language. Many teachers are flattered when students ask questions which seemingly reflect an interest in the subject matter and are delighted to impart knowledge to a potential polyglot. Many a young teacher is challenged by such questions and feels compelled to offer an explanation far beyond the student's competence in order to prove his own expertise in the language. It is difficult but essential to learn to say "I don't know. I'll look it up and answer your question tomorrow," or "You don't need to know that but I'll be glad to tell you after class." The necessity for linguistic explanations should not be taken as an excuse for long digressions.

Students also have to learn that much in language is arbitrary and has no reason or rule. We had one group of students that insisted that the teacher give them the rule for *in* in English and refused to believe that there was no such rule. They simply had to be convinced that there are aspects of language which are primarily mastered through memorization and practice.

Step 5. Mechanical Drills

The purpose of mechanical drills is to help students learn the forms of the new pattern and all procedures follow from this objective.

Mechanical drills should be drilled at a rapid pace (they are also fluency practice) with the books closed. The purpose is to memorize the pattern and they won't do that if they can simply read from the text. If students have great difficulty with a pattern, the model sentence may be left on the board for the first few drills, later to be erased. A drill should have from seven to ten items each, and should take no more than two minutes. A simple substitution drill should take no more than seventy seconds or the pace will begin to drag and the students lose interest. With complex patterns and increased length of utterance, the time per drill will be somewhat longer. Mechanical drills are inherently boring, and should be abandoned as soon as the students have learned the pattern. They should certainly not be overdrilled. In the classroom a two phase drill is quite sufficient; the teacher gives the cue, the students respond, and the teacher gives the next cue without repeating the students' response. A three phase drill increases the ratio of teacher talk, achieves nothing if the students' answer already was correct, contributes to boredom and slows down by one-third the number of drills which can be done. Mechanical drills should always be done chorally (or by rows in large classes); this technique assures maximum participation. The students will get individual practice later with the meaningful and communicative drills which cannot be done chorally.

Mechanical testing drills lend themselves very well to homework as they by nature test how well students have learned the formal aspects of a pattern. Written homework reinforces the oral classroom work; it provides an alternative mode of presentation for students with poor auditory memory and allows the students themselves to evaluate how well they have mastered the pattern. But written homework should not be given in such amounts that it becomes busy work. An assignment of two or three drills per pattern is more than ample.

Step 6. Functional Explication

To learn the linguistic forms of a pattern is not enough; next students need to learn when to *use* the pattern. The troublesome part of learning the present progressive in English is not the particular form of *I am going* but when to use it and when not to.

At the very beginning levels, when the students have very few structures at their command, the functional explication will be very limited and may well coincide with the formal analysis. But at later stages it is helpful to separate the two, so the students won't have to struggle with learning a new structure at the same time as they must think of when to use it. It is the old principle of not teaching two things at the same time.

For example, once the students have learned the present continuous (the boy is working), that structure must be contrasted with the function of the simple present. The process of explanation is much the same as with the formal analysis: contrasting structures are put on the board and students are asked how they differ in meaning:

(Previous pattern)	The boy	is working	now.
	The boy	works	every day.

Our students readily come up with the generalization that the distinction is between "at this moment" versus "always, usually," which is all the terminology needed to express the difference between the immediate versus habitual present. If the previous structure has been mastered, and the new structure is carefully presented in context, the functional explication should take no more than a minute or two, but is a vital step without which none but the most able students will be able to progress toward communication.

Step 7. Meaningful Drills

There is a great difference in difficulty between mechanical and meaningful drills, and meaningful drills often sound very raggedy and halting after the rapid pace of the mechanical drills. Students are now concentrating on meaning rather than on form, concentrating on an answer which is true rather than correct. There still is a correct answer, and the teacher should insist on it, both in form and content.

It is helpful if the drills immediately following the functional explication concentrate on the contrasting structures to assure that the students have learned the rule and to reinforce that rule. The teacher may begin with a discrimination-pattern recognition drill in the form of questions, the answers to which the class knows. Such a drill can either be based on the introductory passage:

Does Bill take a street car to school?	S:	Yes.
Is he taking a street car right now?		No.
Does Bill work at a gas station?		Yes.
Is he working at a gas station now?		No.
etc.		

or on the class situation:

Does José speak Spanish?	S:	Yes.
Is he speaking Spanish now?		No.
Does Alicia take the bus to school?		Yes.
Is she taking the bus now?		No.

where the names refer to the students in the class.

This type of drill is then followed by drills in which the students produce the contrasts, as in this correlative substitution drill where the time words are used as cues:

Repeat:	Bill works downtown every day.		
Substitute:	now	S:	Bill is working downtown now.
	tomorrow		Bill is going to work downtown tomorrow.
	every day		Bill works downtown every day.
	next week		
	on weekends		
	every Saturday		
	etc.		

(Note that the students already know the *going to* future.)

Most frequently meaningful drills cannot be done chorally as there is more than one correct answer, as in this drill which is based on the classroom situation and the students themselves.

T:	What is ( ) doing now?	S:	She's (studying English.)
			She's (looking out the window.)
			She's (thinking about lunch.)
			etc.
	What does ( ) do every day?		He (goes to class)
			He (studies English.)
			He (writes to his girl friend.)
			etc.

The pattern is controlled, but there is no way the teacher can predict exactly what the student will reply. He can, however, insist on a full statement answer; the students still need practice on the form of the pattern.

These drills will, as we said, seem halting, but if the pace breaks down completely it is probably because the students have not sufficiently memorized the forms of the pattern. The remedy then lies in going back to more mechanical drills—the language laboratory is a good place for remedial drilling—rather than in going over the explanation again.

Step 8. Communicative Drills

The purpose of communicative drills is only partially to teach grammatical patterns. The purpose now includes teaching the *use* of language for communication, where the focus is on *what* is said rather than on *how* it is said.

The simplest way to construct communicative drills is simply to instruct the students to answer truthfully in question-answer or rejoinder types of drills. The one necessity for communicative drills is that the students contribute new information to the class. In the following drill, the student may or may not give an answer which includes the teaching point (BE + adjective):

> T: Describe the weather S: (It's beautiful.)
> in your country. (Wonderful.)

But all that is necessary is that the students respond conversationally and grammatically in an appropriate fashion; that is, after all, what we are trying to teach them in these drills. In our experience, these are the drills which the students like best and which they have most fun doing.

It may seem obvious to an experienced teacher, but we would like to emphasize the importance in these drills for the teacher to listen to and react to what the students say. In a real act of communication one reacts to provocative statements, and so it should be in the classroom. For example, in a class we observed once, a student replied to another's question: "I drive a Rolls Royce all year." We could see raised eyebrows on the part of the other students, but the teacher went right on as if this had not been heard. While it is possible that this student came from a wealthy family, it is also possible that she was answering the first thing that came into her head. Such random answers defeat the purpose of the communicative element in this stage of drilling, and the teacher should gently insist that students answer truthfully. In order to do so, he must listen to the student's answer. More important, on the interpersonal level, the students must feel that what they have to say is of significance to someone, and the teacher, by reacting, sets the tone and atmosphere in the classroom.

It is also important to point out that there may be times when the answers to communicative drills seem to create embarrassing situations. For example, in class once a student's response to the question whether he had ever been in an accident was: "Yes. I was driving and my best friend was killed." At such times the best reaction is the same form of sympathetic response one would make outside of the classroom: "How sad," or "How awful for you," and then change the topic.

Communicative drills are still only drills and students need to go beyond them to real interaction activities. These we discuss in the chapter on communicative competence.

CONDUCTING AND CORRECTING DRILLS

The main aim in conducting drills is to get students to practice with a minimum amount of teacher talk. The simplest way we have found to get a class to do a drill is this: The teacher models the first two or three items. He reads (or speaks) the cue, pointing at himself. He then reads the response, pointing at the students. His gestures will indicate who is to say what. With a class that is learning to drill, the teacher may preface the cue with "I say" and the response with "You say." The teacher returns to the *initial* cue and the class repeats the response which they have already heard. Then the teacher gives the next cue and they continue the drill. This technique to begin the drill by repeating the examples is very helpful in keeping everyone together and helps the slower students figure out how the drill goes.

You frequently hear teachers introduce drills with directions like "I am going to make a statement. The first student will make it into a question and the student next to you will answer it." This kind of direction serves no purpose whatsoever and it wastes time and increases the ratio of teacher talk. Students know how to drill from the examples they hear, not from verbal directions.

The pace of a drill should be brisk. The best way to do this is to give the next cue just as the students are finishing the response to the previous one. Caution is needed, though, because if the cue is given too soon, the students will be confused and forget what they are saying. It usually helps the pace if the teacher stands up to direct the drill. If the pace is very bad in a meaningful drill, it may be because the students have not sufficiently learned the forms of the pattern. As we pointed out earlier, the remedy then lies in going back to more mechanical drills, rather than in changing the pace of the cueing.

In calling on individual students, the use of gestures keeps the pace up, and it also keeps the students' attention on the teacher at all times. With a very eager class, it is helpful if the teacher mentions the name of the student to be called on *before* the question: "Mustapha, when did you . . .?" This will keep others from answering before the question is completed. The reverse is true of a sluggish class; by mentioning the name first, the other students know they will not have to answer and so they stop listening. There the name should be given *after* the cue.

The teacher should use a normal rate of speech. If he slows down, it distorts his intonation, but worse, it makes the students incapable of understanding anyone outside the classroom since they will have had no practice in listening to normal speech. If students obviously don't understand, the teacher may well have to slow down in, for example, a formal explanation, but what he must remember to do is to repeat the explanation at normal speed. Students who are not used to teachers who speak at normal speed will complain bitterly in the beginning, and the teacher should take care to explain to them—in the mother tongue if necessary—why he won't slow down and that he will be glad to repeat everything until they do understand.

Correcting Mistakes in Drilling

Techniques for correction vary with the class of drills and the nature of the mistake, but the most important point that the teacher must learn is not to correct every mistake the student makes. In mechanical drills, all mistakes on the new pattern and those of last week should be corrected. The students are working on internalizing new forms and obviously they must learn correct forms. The teacher simply supplies the correct form and the student repeats. For example, in a transformation drill on irregular past participles, the teacher cues *He went*, the student responds *he has went*, the teacher says *gone* and the student repeats, *he has gone.* At this stage, it is time consuming, confusing and just not productive to have the student correct himself. Nor is it very productive to have other students do the correction; it provides an atmosphere of oneupmanship and competition, but more importantly the student needs a clear model which the teacher can best provide. Having other students correct will also break up the pace of a drill very badly.

Pronunciation errors should not be corrected in grammar drills any more than grammar mistakes should be corrected in pronunciation drills. An exception to this is the type of pattern where grammar and pronunciation intersect as in the /-t -d -id/ pronunciation of the past-*ed* and-*d* forms.

At the mechanical skill stage of learning a structural pattern, the mistake is most likely due to a faulty knowledge of the rule or form of the pattern. That is a competence error and is, as we said, best corrected by supplying the student with the correct form.

At the meaningful drill stage, the students' mistakes are more likely to be performance errors or slips of the tongue—that is, they know the rule but misspeak. The emphasis now shifts from supplying them with the right form to getting them to self-monitor their speech, to correctly apply the rules which they know. The teacher calls attention to the mistake, but the students themselves do the correction. The teacher can use gestures (a raised eyebrow, a headshake) to indicate a mistake. If the required response is long, a nonverbal signal probably is not clear enough to focus the students' attention on the mistake and they are likely to make an additional mistake by changing a correct form rather than the incorrect one. The teacher can indicate the mistake in three ways. For instance, in a drill on the present tenses, the student says: "He is working every day." The teacher can (1) repeat the incorrect word with an incredulous expression and question intonation, here *is working???* thus signalling "You can't really mean to say this;" or he can (2) repeat the word that triggers or co-occurs with the correct response, usually the cue, here *every day*, which signals the habitual present; or, finally the teacher can (3) simply mention the label for the grammatical category the student has wrong, here *habitual present.* Which of these is the best technique depends on the nature of the pattern and the mistake. In the example above, we would prefer the second alternative because it is the relationship of *every day* and the habitual present one is trying to teach.

In communicative drills the emphasis is on the message, and most errors should be ignored except serious errors on the teaching point or those which interfere with communication. At this stage there is typically a lot of peer teaching; the students help each other with vocabulary items and structures in order to get meaning across. This is exactly the kind of communicative atmosphere one wants to encourage. The teacher should serve primarily as a resource person, helping the students when they get stuck and turn to him for help. Mistakes should be dealt with as quickly and unobtrusively as possible by supplying the correct form.

Natural conversational reaction at this stage can help the student who has failed to grasp the function of the pattern. In a communicative drill on the present perfect continuous, the teacher asked a student what he had been doing all morning. Instead of something like the expected "I've been sitting in class," the student replied, "I've been sleeping all morning." The teacher responded, "Really? Are you sleeping now?" The student immediately corrected himself with a look of new understanding.

CONCLUSIONS

In this chapter, we have attempted to deal with the theoretical concerns of sequencing the activities of a grammar lesson, the practical concerns of supplementing such a lesson and the problems of conducting a grammar lesson in the classroom. The discussion reflects the problems we have faced in our teaching and questions frequently raised in teacher training classes.

APPENDIX

The sequence of structural patterns follows that of Bruder, *MMC–Developing Communicative Competence in English as a Second Language.*

BE (present)–statements and questions
    Third person singular + BE + adjective (The boy is tall.)
        Subject pronouns (He/she/it is tall.)
    Questions and affirmative short answers (Is the boy tall? Yes, he is.)
        Negative and short answers. (The boy isn't short. No, he isn't.)
    Third person plural + BE + adjective (The boys are tall.)
        Subject pronoun (They are tall.)
    Questions and affirmative short answers (Are the boys tall? Yes, they are.)
        Negative and short answers. (The boys aren't tall. No, they aren't.)
    X + BE + noun phrase (3rd person)
    Singular (The boy is a student.)
    Plural (The boys are students.)
    Adjective + noun (The tall boys are good students.)
    Second person–singular plural
        Statement (You're a good student. You're from Latin America.)
        Question (Are you a graduate student?)
        Negative (You aren't lost.)
    First person–singular/plural; Negative, (I'm from the United States. We're confused. I'm not a student.)
    Alternative questions–all persons (Are you from Canada or the United States?)
    WH questions
        Who/what in subject position (Who is last? What is confusing?)
        Where are you from?
    Alternate negative forms (He's not.)
    Present continuous
        Statement (He's talking to the students.)

Question and short answers (Are you taking the same classes? No, we aren't.)
Negative statement (I'm not living in the dorms.)
WH questions
  Who   (Who is coming with me?)
  What (What are the people doing?)
  Where (Where are you going?)
BE—tag questions
  I. (It isn't crowded, is it?)
  II. (You're taking engineering, aren't you?)
"Going to" future
  Statement (I'm going to look for a new coat.)
  Question (Are you going to buy a camera?)
  Negative (I'm not going to buy anything.)
  WH questions (What are you going to buy?)
Possessive adjectives and pronouns
  Adjectives (Where are my gloves?)
  Pronouns (Are these yours?)
  Whose (Whose gloves are on the seat?)
Demonstrative adjectives and pronouns
  Adjectives/pronouns (I want these books; he wants those.)
  Which (Which camera are you going to buy?)
Simple present tense
  Third person singular
  Statement (He lives with his family.)
  Interrogative and short answers (Does he drive. . . ? Yes, he does.)
    Negative (He doesn't drive to school.)
  Third person plural
    Statement (The boys study hard.)
    Interrogative and short anwers (Do they. . .? No, they don't.)
    Negative statement (The girls don't drive to school.)
  First and second person (We commute to school.)
  WH questions
    Who (Who studies English?)
    What (What does it mean?)
    Where (Where does the student live?)
    When (When does he study?)
  Tag questions
    I. (He doesn't drive, does he?)
    II. (They speak English, don't they?)

Indefinite pronouns (*every/no* in subject position)
  Statements (Everyone knows that. No one is here.)
  Yes/no questions (Does anyone have change?)
Count/noncount nouns
  some/any
    Affirmative (He needs some advice.)
    Interrogative/negative (He doesn't have any money.)
    Expressions of quantity
    a lot of (a lot of things/money)
    much/many (not much beer/not many ideas)
    a little/a few (a little beer/a few ideas)
    WH questions (How much beer. . .? How many ideas. . .?)
Request/suggestion forms
  Request (Please give me some advice.)
  Suggestion (self included)
    Let's (Let's go to the movies.)
    Shall (Shall we go?)
    WH + shall (Where shall we go?)
Indefinite pronouns (*every/no* in object position) (He likes
  everything; we don't like anything.)
Postnominal prepositional phrases (the man with the beard)
Irregular nouns (child-children)
Frequency adverbs
  With affirmative verbs (We always have music at parties.)
  Yes/no questions (Are you ever late for class?)
  Negative statements (He's never late.)
  WH question (How often do you have parties?)
Indefinite pronouns
  (one/ones) (I don't like this car, I'm going to get a new one.)
BE—past tense
  Affirmative (I was an hour late.)
  Yes/no questions (Were you in class?)
  WH questions (Where were you?)
Time expressions
  Responses to *when* (I was in Paris *in* January/*on* June 27/*during*
    the summer.)
  Reponses to *how long* (I was in Paris for three weeks.)
Past continuous tense (Everyone was leaving.)
Tag questions—BE—past
  I. (Bill wasn't driving, was he?)
  II. (You weren't late, were you?)

Place expressions (*in* Boston/*on* Main Street/*at* 381 Smith Street)
Simple past tense—regular verbs
   Affirmative (I called my friend in California.)
   Interrogative and short answers (Did you learn the dialogue?
      No, I didn't.)
   Negative statements (I didn't need any help.)
   WH questions
      What (subject), *Where*, etc. (What happened? Where did he
         play tennis?)
      Who (object) (Whom did she call?)
Modal verbs
   Can
      Affirmative (We can leave now.)
      Negative (I can't find the book.)
      Interrogative—(Can you do it? When can you do it?)
   Will
      Affirmative, negative, interrogative (I'll do it tomorrow.)
      Request form (Will you help me, please?)
   Should—all patterns (You should open a bank account.)
Articles
   a/the (He needs a car. I used the car yesterday.)
   no article/*the* (He goes to church on Sunday. The church is
      beautiful.
Indefinite adjectives and pronouns—*other*
   Adjective (The other man is a lawyer)
   Pronoun (Some books are cheap; others are expensive.)
Personal pronouns—object (Bill can see us tomorrow.)
Past tense—irregular verbs—1 (past tense form same as past
      participle)
   Verbs with / ɔ / (*caught*); *make, have*
      Statement (She made a cake.)
      Negative (She didn't have time.)
      WH (When did she teach the class?)
   Verbs with (/ ɛ / (*read*); final consonant change (meant)
   Unpredictable change (*found, sat*)
Possessive forms
   's
      Names (Mrs. Brown's car. . .)
      Nouns (My roommate's brother. . .)
   of the (the top of the table)

Prearticles (quantifiers)
  Count nouns (many of my friends)
  Noncount nouns (a little of her time)
BE (past + *going to* + verb (I was going to study, but I went to a movie.)
Past tense—irregular verbs—2 (all principal parts are different) (We drove the car home.)
Adverbs—*here/there*
  Location (Where's the letter? Here it is.)
  Pronouns (When were you in Paris? We were there last year.)
Modal verbs (all patterns)
  Ought to (He ought to pay the bill.)
  Might (We might not finish in time.)
  Have to (Do we have to leave now? Yes, we do.)
Used to + verb (I used to live in Boston.)
Past tense—irregular verbs—3
  verbs with all principal parts the same (*cut*)
  come, run (present and past participle the same)
Tag questions—past tense
  I. (You didn't sell the car, did you? No, I didn't.)
  II. (He found the money, didn't he? Yes, he did.)
Substitute subject—*there* (There's a phone call for you.)
Verb + indirect object + direct object (The doctor sent us a bill.)
Reflexive pronouns—indirect object (I was going to buy myself a car.)
Comparison 1 (noun comparison)
  Like (My room is like a prison.)
  The same as (Autumn is the same as fall.)
  Different from (A dictionary is different from an encyclopedia.)
Manner expressions
  How (How did she study?)
  -ly (She studied quietly.)
  By + noun/verb-*ing* (She studied by remote TV./ She studied by watching T.V.)
  With/without + noun (She studied without books.)
Substitute subject—it
  Introducing time, weather, people (It's cold. It's John at the door.)
  Replacing a noun phrase (It's fun to bargain for a car.)
Modal verbs (all patterns)

May
> Possibility (We may not go to class today.)
> Permission (The child may not play in the street.)

Must
> Necessity (Must the children go to bed now?)
> Deduction (Someone is coming. It must be the mailman.)

Ago with past tense (He bought the car a week ago.)

Present perfect tense
> Irregular past participles. (He's written four letters this week.)
> Interrogative and negative. (Have you heard. . .? No, we haven't.)
> Immediate past action (I've just seen Bill.)

Present perfect continuous (She's been studying for four years.)

Since with present perfect. (He's been here since Thursday.)

Already/yet (We haven't seen the movie yet.)

Tag questions—present perfect
> I. (They haven't left yet, have they? No, they haven't).
> II. (He's already done it, hasn't he? Yes, he has.)

Why + reason responses
> *Why* (Why did he go downtown?)
> *In order to/for* (. . .in order to buy a coat/ . . .for a coat.)
> *Because* + clause (. . .because he wanted a coat).

Agent nouns (*teacher* etc.)

Noun + noun modification (English teacher)

Conjunction (*and/or/but*) (a desk and a chair)

Relative clauses
> Subject (We saw the man who won the prize.)
> Object (She called the people whom she expected for dinner.)
> Possessive (I saw the girl whose friends are in jail.)

Before/after/until + phrase (I'll tell you after class.)

Too/enough
> *Too*
>> Adverb/adjective modification (This book is too expensive.)
>> Noun modification (We have too much advice.)
> *Enough*
>> Adverb/adjective modification (The exam was easy enough.)
>> Noun modification (He didn't have enough time.)

Subordinate clauses
> *Before/after/until* (I'll do it before I go to class.)
> *While* (I'll get some sleep while you're reading the paper.)

When/where (I'll see him when I go to New York.)
Conjunction
    And. . .too/and. . .either/but (I like sports and Charlie does too.)
    Alternate expressions (I like sports and so does Charlie.)
Modal verbs (all patterns)
    Could
        Past ability (I couldn't speak English a few months ago.)
        Polite request (Could you get me some cigarettes, please?)
        Present or future possibility (I could help you tomorrow.)
    Would
        Polite request/invitation (Would you get some stamps, please?)
        Expressions of desire or preference (I'd rather have tea.)
Verb + *to* + verb (The boys want to leave.)
Two word verbs—Nonseparable (We listen to the news every day.)
Comparison 2
    Nouns (This book was the same price as that one.)
    Adjectives and adverbs (This book was as expensive as that one.)
X + WH + statement (I don't know when I'll go to Boston.)
Comparison 3 (*-er. . .than/more. . .than)*
    (This book is cheaper than that one.)
    (That book is more expensive than that one.)
Comparison 4 (*the. . .-est/the most* X)
    (This book is the cheapest.)
    (That book is the most expensive.)
Negative questions (Isn't it the same in your country?)
Past perfect tense
    Simple past perfect (I'd been in Paris a week before I saw him.)
    Past perfect continuous (He'd been reading for an hour when we called.)
Verb + direct object + *to* + indirect object
    Statement (She read the letter to the boys.)
    WH question—*who* (Who did she read the letter to?)
Reflexive pronouns
    with *by* (He likes to study by himself.)
    Emphatic (He should do it himself.)
If clauses
    Request (If you have time, I'd like some help.)
    Habit (If I can't get to sleep, I read for a while.)

Generalization (If you've seen one city, you've seen them all.)

Modal verbs

Perfect modals

Must (John must have been sick; he wasn't at the party.)

Could (We couldn't have gone with you; we didn't have any money.)

Should (Bill shouldn't have gone to the movies; he missed an important telephone call.)

Would (I would have gone to the party, but I didn't have anything to wear

Perfect modals—continuous (Jane must have been studying.)

Verbs + direct object + for + indirect object

Statement (She answered the questions for her friend.)

WH question—*who* (Who did she answer the questions for?)

Verb + noun phrase + *to* + verb

(The teacher reminded the students to do the work.)

Two word verbs—separable (She looked the word up.)

If clauses—condition 1 (If I finish my work, I'll help you.)

Adjective phrases (It's hard for us to meet Americans.)

Passive voice 1 (French is spoken in Canada.)

If clauses—condition 2 (If I were rich, I'd go to Europe.)

Have—causative (Where can I have my hair cut?)

Passive voice 2

Present perfect (I haven't been asked to help.)

Future (The new students will be given an advisor.)

BE + *used to* + noun phrase (We're used to the food here.)

2
Speaking

COMMUNICATIVE COMPETENCE[1]

Generally communicative competence is taken to be the objective of language teaching: the production of speakers com-

This chapter is based on a paper by Christina Bratt Paulston, "Developing Communicative Competence: Goals, Procedures and Techniques" written for the Defense Language Institute, Lackland Air Force Base, Texas. Permission to quote is gratefully acknowledged.

[1] It is customary academic procedure to acknowledge with thanks the help one has received from one's colleagues in the writing of a paper. In this case there simply would have been no paper without the help of Dale Britton, Barry Brunetti, John Hoover, Judy Kettering and Howard Lagoze, instructors in the English Language Institute of the University of Pittsburgh, whose zeal and enthusiasm have served as steady encouragement in our joint endeavor to break new grounds in language teaching. I thank them for their basic contribution to the paper and reserve for myself whatever flaws remain.

Thanks are also due to Michael Knight, David Jones and Ingrid

petent to communicate in the target language.[2] As Francis Johnson has pointed out, communication "requires interpersonal responsiveness, rather than the mere production of language which is truthful, honest, accurate, stylistically pleasing, etc., those characteristics which look at language rather than at behavior, which is the social purpose of language. Our end product is surely getting things done, easing social tensions, goading ourselves into doing this or that, and persuading others to do things. Communication arises when language is used as such interpersonal behavior, which goes beyond meaningful and truthful manipulation of language symbols."[3]

It is when we try to isolate the skills we need for efficient communication that we find divergent opinions. It is rather typical of language teachers that they tend to equate communicative competence with the ability to carry out linguistic interaction in the target language—Rivers is a good example of this approach.[4] But efficient communication also requires that speakers share the social meaning of the linguistic forms, that they have the same social rules for language use.[5] Dell Hymes, the anthropologist, argues that communicative competence must include not only the linguistic forms of a language but also a knowledge of when, how and to whom

---

Freebairn-Smith, of the Folkuniversity of Stockholm, who first introduced me to role play.

Sarah Thomason read an earlier version of the paper which much benefited from her comments for which I am grateful.

[2] Christina Bratt Paulston, "Linguistic and Communicative Competence," *TESOL Quarterly,* 8, no. 4 (December 1974): 347-362.

[3] Frank Johnson, personal communication, July 31, 1970.

[4] Wilga Rivers, "From Linguistic Competence to Communicative Competence," *TESOL QUARTERLY* 7, no. 1 (March 1973): 25-34.

[5] Susan Ervin-Tripp, *Language Acquisition and Communicative Choice* (Stanford, California: Stanford University, 1973): and John Gumperz, *Language in Social Groups* (Stanford, California: Stanford University, 1971). See also the book review of the latter by Allen D. Grimshaw in *Language Sciences* no. 27 (October 1973), pp. 29-35. Two articles have appeared in the *TESOL Quarterly* which attempt to make this body of knowledge relevant to the field of TESOL: Ulf Hannerz, "The Second Language: An Anthropological View," *TESOL Quarterly* 7, no. 3 (September 1973): 235-248; and Allen D. Grimshaw, "Rules, Social Interaction, and Language Behavior," *TESOL Quarterly* 7, no. 2 (June 1973): 99-115.

it is appropriate to use these forms.[6] I have come to think that it is every bit as important in second language teaching (as opposed to foreign language teaching), to teach the appropriate forms of social usage as the linguistic forms themselves. Let me give you some examples. We all teach the WH questions early in the curriculum, but we don't teach the questions you can and cannot ask. If you were to ask me how much money I make, I would probably consider you drunk, mad or shockingly boorish. Yet it is a highly polite question in many Asian countries. The social meaning of the equivalent linguistic forms varies from culture to culture.

Communication includes nonverbal behavior as well, of course; as often mentioned, eye contact behavior carries the meaning of honest dealings in Anglo culture while it is rude and disrespectful in Hispanic and many other cultures. We probably all know that, but how many of us have taught "proper" (and I'll come back to that) eye contact behavior to our students? There are very strong constraints on teaching adults to behave. Sociolinguistic rules, it is felt, should be learned in childhood, and teaching adults such rules implies that they were not properly brought up. Obviously, however, there is nothing inherently more proper about one set of behavior vis à vis another *except* in cultural appropriateness. On a superficial level, communicative competence may simply be defined as tact and good manners and people not sharing that system will consider others rude and tactless. We do our students a disservice if we don't teach them the social rules along with the linguistic rules as long as we remember not to imply any moral superiority of one rule over the other.

Occasionally, faulty rule sharing will lead to complete breakdown in communication. Here is an example from my recent stay in

---

[6] Dell Hymes, "The Anthropology of Communication," *Human Communication Theory*, F. Dance, ed. (New York: Holt, Rinehart and Winston, 1967); "Models of the Interaction of Language and Social Life," *Directions in Sociolinguistics*, John Gumperz and Dell Hymes, eds. (New York: Holt, Rinehart and Winston, 1972): "Editorial Introduction," *Language in Society* 1, no. 1 (1972): 1-14; "Introduction" in *The Function of Language in the Classroom*, Courtney Cazden, Vera John and Dell Hymes, eds. (New York: Teachers College Press, 1972), pp. xi-lviii; "On Communicative Competence" in *Sociolinguistics*, J. B. Pride and J. Holmes, eds. (Harmondsworth, England: Penguin Books, 1972), pp. 269-293.

Sweden, where I was born and raised. We (my American husband and children) celebrated Thanksgiving by having my immediate family (Swedish) and friends for a traditional turkey dinner. I was busy in the kitchen and came belatedly into the living room just after my sister-in-law had arrived. In impeccable Swedish I asked her politely, "Do you know everyone?" Any native American would correctly interpret such a question to mean that I wanted to know if she had been introduced to those guests she had not previously met. She looked at me sourly and said, "I don't know everyone, but if you are asking me if I have greeted everyone, I have." Fussed as I was, and in such an archetypical American situation, I had momentarily forgotten that proper Swedish manners demand that guests do not wait to be introduced by a third party, but go around the room, shake hands with everyone and say their name aloud to those they have not previously met. Any child knows that, so my sister-in-law felt that I had reprimanded her for bad manners, for faulty sharing of a systemic set of social interactional rules. Clearly, the meaning of an interaction is easily misinterpreted if the speakers don't share the same set of rules. Hence the necessity for teaching those rules.

This anecdote also illustrates another aspect of communicative competence: it is easier to keep one's linguistic codes separate than one's social codes as one is often not aware of the social codes on a conscious level until they are violated. It is much easier to be bilingual than bicultural.

Communicative Competence: Goals

It is important to be clear about the goals of teaching communicative competence because the techniques and procedures of teaching follow from these goals. Linguistic competence forms part of communicative competence, so our students need to acquire a basic knowledge of linguistic forms, the skill-getting stage in Rivers' model.[7] The regular course work as outlined in the previous chapter serves perfectly well for this stage. The teaching points here can be broken down to specific sounds, grammar patterns and vocabulary items in the traditional skills of listening, speaking, reading and writing.

[7] Wilga Rivers, "Talking Off the Top of Their Heads," *TESOL Quartery* 6, no. 1 (March 1972): 71-81.

But learning specific sounds and patterns does not necessarily entail the ability to use them, and our students need practice in using the linguistic forms for the social purpose of language, as Johnson describes it. In "Talking Off the Top of Their Heads," Rivers discusses the need for students to use language for the normal purposes of language: establishing social relations, seeking and giving information, etc.[8] There is experimental evidence[9] that this is a necessary step in efficient language learning, and so it must be incorporated in the teaching process as well. One needs to be certain that such interaction activities form part of the curriculum on a frequent and regular basis, in beginning as well as in advanced courses.

There are two basic classes of communicative interaction activities, depending on the teaching point, and there is room for both in the curriculum. In one kind of exercise, the teaching point is simply to get meaning across, to be able to communicate some referential meaning in the target language. These I have called exercises in communicative performance,[10] and they are excellent and necessary for developing linguistic competence. In the other type of exercise the teaching point is getting meaning across in a socially acceptable way, and typically these exercises contain culturally relevant information—social interactional rules—in what I at times call a contrastive Emily Post approach to language teaching. I would call only the latter activities for developing communicative competence.

I will discuss procedures and techniques with each specific type of interaction activity, but there is one set of procedures which holds for all of the communicative interaction activities, and which I cannot emphasize strongly enough. There should be *no* correction from the teacher during these activities. If the basic teaching point is getting meaning across, the students have achieved the objectives of the exercise if they succeed in doing so. It is inhibiting, hampering,

---

[8] Ibid, p. 76.

[9] See for example Sandra Savignon, "Study of the Effect of Training in Communicative Skills as Part of a Beginning College French Course on Student Attitude and Achievement in Linguistic and Communicative Competence" (Ph.D. dissertation, University of Illinois at Urbana, Champaign, 1971).

[10] For a discussion of communicative performance, see Paulston, "Linguistic and Communicative Competence."

and frustrating beyond belief to be consistently checked and corrected when one is struggling with ideas in another language. On the other hand, the teacher should help with vocabulary, grammar, and pronunciation when the students ask him, as they frequently do. The students should very early on be taught phrases for talking themselves out of trouble; phrases like "How do you say this in English?" "Is that right?" "What's the word for the thing that . . .?" are very useful to know.

What the teachers in the Institute do is to write down the worst horrors they hear, and then the class spends five or ten minutes after the exercise in a friendly postmortem. We concentrate on clearing up idiom and vocabulary confusion, and it is elementary psychology but nevertheless effective to point out *good* word choices and expressions too. Once in a blue moon you run across a student who insists that the teacher correct his every mistake; you are likely to lose his confidence if you don't, so the easiest way out is to tape his performance and then go over it with him outside of class. But it is too inhibiting, time consuming, and inefficient to tape record these activities for correction purposes as a standard procedure for the whole class.

COMMUNICATIVE INTERACTION ACTIVITIES

In the Institute, we use four basic types of activities in various combinations for developing communicative competence: social formulas and dialogues, community-oriented tasks, problem-solving activities, and role play. There are surely others, but we have not thought of any. I am deliberately excluding from this discussion exercises in communicative performance, such as games and charades, although we use them too.

1. Social Formulas and Dialogues

In her *Interaction Activities* Judy Kettering has one unit on "Establishing and Maintaining Social Relations" which covers such speech encounters as greetings, partings, introductions, excuses, compliments, complaints, hiding feelings, etc. It is very difficult to lie, to complain and to turn someone down for a date in another language, and our students need to be taught how to do this in an appropriate manner. These are exercises deliberately designed to develop communicative competence, as you can see from this section on "Excuses and Apologies":

EXCUSES AND APOLOGIES[11] (abbreviated)

I. Phrases

    A. Formal

        1. Excuse me, please.

          Pardon me.   Of course.

          I'm very sorry.   Certainly.

          I'm sorry.

          I beg your pardon.

        2. Excuse me for being late.   { That's quite alright. }

          I'm sorry I'm late.

          Excuse me for a moment please. { Think nothing of it. }

        { I'm sorry I forgot to } { call.

        { I'm sorry I didn't } { come.

                             answer your letter.

                             inform you.

          I'm sorry, but I must leave early.

    B. Informal

        2. Sorry I'm late.   { It's O.K.

                  { call.

          Sorry I forgot to { write.   { Don't worry.

                  { come.   Sure.

                  { tell you.

          Just a minute. I'll be right back.   { It's alright.

II. Dialogues

    A. Formal

        2. A: Miss Larson?

          B: Yes?

          A: Please excuse me for losing my temper in class yesterday.

          B: That's quite alright. Was something troubling you?

          A: Yes. I had just gotten a letter from a friend of mine and I guess I was more upset than I thought.

    B. Informal

        1. A: How was your vacation, Maria?

---

[11] Judy Kettering, "Interaction Activities," mimeographed (Pittsburgh: English Language Institute, 1974), p. 36 (in abbreviated form).

B: I had such a good time, I hated to come back.

A: Did you get my postcard?

B: Yes, thanks. And I meant to write to you too but I was just so busy! I'm sorry.

A: That's O.K. I knew you probably didn't have much time.

3. A: I'm glad you're still here! Sorry I'm so late.

B: Don't worry. The bus hasn't come yet.

A: I was just walking out the door and the phone rang. It was my mother and . . . well, you know how my mother talks!

B: I'm surprised you aren't later!

III. Situations

A. Structured
1. A: How was your vacation?
   B: Great. Hey, thanks for the postcards.
   A: Sure. But I didn't get any from you!
   B:

B. Semistructured
1. A: Hey, where were you last night?
   B: I was waiting for you to call to tell me what the address was.
   A:
   B:
2. A: What'd you get so angry at me for this morning?
   B:
   A:
   B:

C. Unstructured
1. You're in class and suddenly you don't feel well.
4. You are at a friend's house for dinner. You must leave early to study for a test for the next day.
6. You told Fred you would come over to study with him last night, but you forgot. He sees you and asks you why you didn't come.

In all of these activities, there is a progression from tightly controlled language use, where the student is learning the social formulas, to a situation where he can use them. The phrases and the dialogues lend themselves well to work in the language laboratory, but it is important that the teacher spends some time in the initial presentation of the section in explaining the meaning, the connotations and the sorts of situations in which you would use the various expressions, an introductory mixture of Emily Post and socio-linguistics as it were. I was amazed to see the eagerness with which our students received this information; it clearly filled a definite need. Note section IB. In all of these encounters, the students are taught a formal and an informal way for apologizing, saying thank you, etc. I doubt that one can systematically teach register variation in all areas of language, but we *can* teach our students to be sensitive to levels of style so that noting such levels becomes part of their language learning strategies.

Although the dialogues can be assigned to the lab, they lend themselves well to pupil-to-pupil work, where the whole class is divided into pairs working simultaneously. The students in each pair take turns reading from the printed dialogue while the other answers from memory until they can run through both parts of the dialogue without looking at the text. This old technique is a remarkably quick way for a class to memorize brief dialogues.

The situations (from structured to unstructured) take on aspects of play-acting or role play and are more effective with an audience. The unstructured situations lend themselves particularly well to role play and are best handled as such. (See discussion under role play.)

2. Community-oriented Tasks

Community-oriented tasks are sets of exercises which compel the student to interact with native speakers outside the classroom. The teaching point here is twofold: (1) communicative participation in the community in what Stevick would call "real" situations [12] and (2) (and this is what assures their success) the collection of highly relevant and needed information. Here are two examples (all place names should of course be changed to local references):

THE BANK [13]

1. What is a checking account? A savings account?
2. Can you take money out of a savings account at any time?

---

[12] Earl Stevick, *Adapting and Writing Language Lessons* (Washington, D.C.: Foreign Service Institute, 1971).

[13] Kettering, p. 59

3. What is interest? What bank gives the highest interest rate in Oakland? What is "compounding" of interest? What is the difference between interest compounded daily, monthly, quarterly, bi-annually, annually? Which gives you the most money?

4. What does "withdrawal" mean? "Deposit?"

5. What is 24 hour banking? Does the Oakland Pittsburgh National Bank (next to the Book Center) have 24 hour banking?

6. How do you open an account?

7. If you take out a loan, do you want a high interest rate or a low interest rate? Why?

8. There are three types of checking accounts:
   a. minimum balance
   b. 10¢ a check
   c. free checking

   What are the differences between these three kinds?

   Advantages and disadvantages?

9. What happens if you "overdraw?"

10. What other services do banks provide besides the above?

THE AUTOMOBILE[14]

1. What are Service Stations?
   What is "regular" gasoline? "super?" "low-lead?"
   How much does each cost per gallon?
   How much does a quart of oil cost?

2. How often must you have your car inspected? How much does it cost?

3. What is a "tune-up?" How often should your car be "tuned up?" How often should you change oil? What must you put in the water in your car in the winter?

4. Do you need a U.S. driver's license to own a car? Where do you get a driver's license? What tests do you have to take to get a license? How long is a license valid? How much does it cost?

5. What is automobile insurance? What are the differences between the following kinds of automobile insurance?
   a. comprehensive
   b. collision
   c. uninsured driver

---

[14] Ibid, p. 60.

Why is it a good idea to have insurance? Where do you get insurance?

6. Buying a car
   a. What is a warranty?
   b. Is the purchase of a car taxable?
   c. Can you usually trust car salesmen? Why or why not?
   d. What is a "test drive?"
   e. What is car registration? Where should it be kept?
7. If you get stuck on a highway or freeway (your car breaks down), what should you do?
8. What is AAA? What services does it offer?

The assignment is handed out in class and the topic explained in general terms. Then it is up to the students to find the answers outside of class. After a reasonable amount of time, they report their findings to the rest of the class. An alternative to oral reports is to have them act out their answers in a role play, like this one:

ROLE PLAYING: THE BANK [15]

Situation

Alfred Newman has just moved to Pittsburgh and has gone to the Pittsburgh National Bank to open both a checking account and a savings account. He must answer questions asked by a bank employee who types out the information. He has a check for $5000 which he wants to put in the savings account and his first pay check for $289.35 with which he will open the checking account.

Roles

Alfred Newman—young man who has just moved to Pittsburgh
Tilda Thompson—bank employee

Useful Expressions

Alfred   "I just moved to Pittsburgh."
          "I would like to open a bank account."
          "I have two checks to deposit."

---

[15] Barry Brunetti and John Hoover, "Roleplay: The Bank," mimeographed (Pittsburgh: English Language Institute, 1974).

Tilda   "Good morning. May I help you?"

"I need your name, address, etc."

"Let me have your checks and I'll deposit them for you and bring your receipts."

"What type of checking account do you want?"

Information Necessary to Open Bank Accounts

A. Checking account
1. Name, address, phone number.
2. Occupation and employer.
3. Individual or joint (with wife, parent, etc.) account.
4. Type
   a. Regular—no minimum balance, free checks.
   b. Deluxe—personalized checks, service charge for each check deducted from balance each month (10¢ per check). $300 minimum balance.

B. Savings account
1-3. Same as for a checking account.
4.   Social Security number.
5.   Pays 5 percent a year interest.

(For a discussion of techniques of role playing, see below.) The role play should then be followed by a discussion session where the students may ask questions on matters that seem unclear to them. It is absolutely vital that the topic is relevent to the students' needs. The automobile exercise is of no use to students who have no intention of driving or buying a car, but it is one of our most successful exercises with those students who do. These exercises may be given as group or individual assignments, depending on such factors as the length and complexity of the assignment, and the number of students in the class. Some of Kettering's other exercises are on the supermarket, telephone installation, looking for an apartment, hospital facilities, etc. These may not be typical of your students' needs, but they are of basic importance to our students and these exercises serve their purpose very well. Simply look around you, think of what your students need to know, and then write out the questions for them to find out; that's all, and you have yourself a perfectly good community-centered task.

3. Problem-solving Activities

These exercises are just what they sound like; the students are presented with a problem and some alternative solutions from which they have to choose one. The following exercise, again from Kettering, contains directions for use as well:

A CAMPING TRIP[16]

You are going on a three day camping trip up in the mountains. You will carry *everything* you need for the three days on your back. Since you are going into the mountains, it will be cold. This kind of trip is called a pack trip because you walk and carry everything you take with you on your back in a bag called a "pack." You have decided that you can't carry more than 25 pounds on your back comfortably. You made a list of things you want to take with you but they add up to more than 25 pounds. Now you have to read your list and include only the most important items. Remember they cannot add up to more than 25 pounds including the pack. Also remember that you will not see anyone for the three days and must include everything you need in order to survive.

You must come to a decision in your groups (and be sure you add up weights so they don't total more than 25 pounds). You must be able also to tell why you chose each item. There is no one correct list although certain items must be included on each list. When you have finished your list, choose a representative from your group to present your list to the other groups. You may challenge or be challenged by another group to tell why you chose an item so be sure you can justify each item.

If you don't understand the meaning of any item, you may ask your instructor.

List

6 lb.	sleeping bag	3 lb.	extra pair of shoes
3 lb.	pack	6 lb.	water container (full of
1 lb.	pillow		water)
6 oz.	small book to record	4 lb.	camera
	what you see	6 lb.	3-day supply of food
8 oz.	swimming suit	12 oz.	plate, fork, knife,
4 oz.	dish soap		spoon

---

[16] Kettering, p. 82.

4 oz.	tooth paste		12 oz.	insect repellent
2 oz.	tooth brush		2 lb.	extra set of clothing
1 lb.	pot to cook in		3 lb.	fishing pole
1 lb.	flashlight		6 oz.	towel
1 lb.	rain jacket		1 oz.	matches

16 ounces = 1 pound; oz. = ounce; lb. = pound

I used this exercise when I last taught in Sweden and it was my first successful effort at getting my students to talk freely. They protested at once that one should not go alone into the mountains, laughed aloud at the notion of a swimming suit, pointed out to me who had not thought of it that you don't need any insect repellent when it is cold in the mountains because then there are no insects. My quiet Swedes became positively talkative, illustrating a basic principle of these exercises—the closer you can come to the students' interests and prior experience, the more successful the exercise will be. Being Swedes, all of my students had been on camping trips, and they knew what they were talking about.

These exercises may seem to be ideal for developing communicative competence, but most of them are communicative performance exercises for developing linguistic competence and carry no sociocultural information. The teacher can of course sum up the discussion with a comment on the relative acceptability in our culture of the various alternatives, but he should recognize that these activities tend to confirm the cultural bias of the students. I tried one activity called "Dinner at an American Home" in which as a guest you are served liver which you hate.[17] What to do? Of the listed alternatives, the Swedes settled on the same rule I have: Eat it and pretend you like it. The Finn, however, said she would say nothing but not eat it; the Colombian said she would say her doctor had told her not to eat liver; and the German stated emphatically that she would tell the hostess that she didn't like liver. We had a nice discussion about cultural relativity, but I failed to convince them that it might be considered that in Sweden my rule was possibly a more viable alternative.

I prefer to hand these exercises out in class on the same day I intend to do them rather than have the students read them through

---

[17] Ibid, p. 76.

at home. Although I waste time going through the problem, explaining words and such, the interest level of the group seems much higher when they can get at the problem immediately. Experiment with your classes and see which works best for you. If you are pressed for time, by all means have your students prepare at home.

Francine Shumann suggests an exercise which is a combination of the community-oriented task and problem solving.[18] Give the students a suitable Ann Landers problem but with her answer removed, then send them out in the community to ask Americans what their suggested solution for the problem would be. The next time the class meets, they all compare notes and finally Landers' answer is read. There is a lot of cultural information in such an activity.

Most of the problem-solving activities involve group work, so you need to give thought to a few basic considerations. How large should a group be? Well, it depends partly on the size of the class, but ideally I would not have more than four or five in a group. How will you group the students: the talkative ones in one group and the quiet ones in another, or all mixed up? Expert opinion can be found in favor of every possible alternative, but I prefer a mixed bag myself. Should the groups be fluid or permanent? It is a temptation to have permanent groups because it is convenient, lends itself to competition and saves time. But members in a set group will quickly establish set patterns of relationships, the opposite of what one wants in these activities where there should be as much talk as possible in reaching an agreement. Switch the groups around, and change the group leaders as well.

As a final remark on problem-solving activities, I'd like to qualify an earlier point. I said that the teacher should not correct, but there is normally a lot of peer teaching and correction in these activities and that is as it should be. It will seem like correction to the teacher, but actually the students only help when someone gets stuck or if they don't understand. The emphasis is on getting meaning across, not on linguistic forms.

---

[18] Francine Schumann as cited in John H. Schumann "Communication Techniques for Intermediate and Advanced ESL Students" (Paper presented at the TESOL Convention, Denver, March 7, 1974).

4. Role play

Role plays are exercises where the student is assigned a fictitious role from which he has to improvise some kind of behavior toward the other role characters in the exercise. I am not considering the acting out of set dialogues or plays as role play nor the acting out of dialogues and plays written by the students themselves. In some role plays, as in the one on opening a bank account above, the student may simply be assigned the role of playing himself, but then you have a simulated situation rather than real role play. The two basic requirements for role play, as I see it, are improvisation and fictitious roles.

Role play can be very simple and the improvisation highly controlled, or it can be very elaborate. Which you should choose is primarily a matter of student proficiency. Certainly role play can be used in beginning classes, as well as in advanced ones.

The format of a role play consists of three basic parts: the situation, the roles and useful expressions. Occasionally a section on background knowledge is needed for advanced role play. The *situation* sets the scene and the plot, i.e., explains the situation and describes the task or action to be accomplished—again the task can be very simple, such as a telephone call, or very elaborate, as settling a complex business deal. The situation is a good place to introduce specific cultural information if that is part of the objective of a given role play.

The *roles* section assigns the roles, the list of characters. The roles should all have fictitious names; it aids the willing suspension of disbelief. Here you need to include such information as personality, experience, status, personal problems and desires, and the like. A role can be very simple, merely a skeleton name and status, or quite elaborate. But role descriptions should not be overly elaborate—unlike the situation, which may very well be—because then the playing of the role becomes a matter of clever acting and that is not the objective. On the contrary, it is inhibiting and counterproductive. You want the student himself to create the personality through hints of background or behavior like "educated in a convent, strong moral views " about the applicant for a job as marriage counsellor or "very particular, constantly mentions things she doesn't like" about the woman buying a house. I get a strong impression of their personalities from just those snippets of characterization.

Useful expressions contains the linguistic information, primarily expressions, phrases and technical vocabulary (an efficient way to teach vocabulary). Grammar patterns which are necessary also fit in here, e.g., WH questions for an interview situation. We try to incorporate as much sociolinguistic information as possible in this section. In a role play about a car accident, developed by Britton and Lagoze, the wife of one driver is angry both with the police and with the young boy who hit their car. [19] It can be useful to know how to express anger with a policeman in an acceptable manner, and in this section we deliberately try to incorporate register and mood variation in language. And a word of caution when you write your own role play; be careful not to have your men talk like women and vice versa. In a section on compliments, Dale Britton had written as a sample expression "What a lovely dress you are wearing" which was fine with me, but the male instructors rejected it out of hand as woman talk—they'd never say that. Language is much more marked for sex than we are consciously aware of.

Background knowledge is occasionally an essential section. It is no good at all to ask students to act out roles which demand a general knowledge they don't have. In order to act out a school board meeting on open classrooms, a town meeting on local industrial pollution or a newspaper interview on the problems of the aged, the students must have subject matter information prior to the role play. It need not be complicated at all—a short reading assignment, a lecture by the teacher or, always appreciated, a guest lecture or a film—but some source of knowledge is necessary or the role play won't come off.

But enough of talking about role plays; let's look at one. Here is a role play by John Hoover, still in experimental stage:

ROLE PLAYING: BUYING A HOUSE [20]

Situation

Mr. and Mrs. Smythe are interested in buying a house in Pittsburgh, as Mr. Smythe's company has transferred him from the San Francisco office. They are being shown a house in Shadyside by the real estate agent. The Smythes have three children aged four, twelve and fourteen, two dogs and two cars. The house they are looking at is a four bedroom

---

[19] Dale Britton and Howard Logoze, "Role Play Activities for TESOL," mimeographed (Pittsburgh: English Language Institute, 1974).

[20] John Hoover, "Role Play: Buying a House," mimeographed (Pittsburgh: English Language Institute, 1974).

home with a small yard and a single garage. Between them, the couple must decide whether they will buy the house or not.

Roles

Mr. Smythe—very anxious to find a house because this is the tenth one he and his wife have looked at. He's desperate and willing to compensate for any deficiencies. He wants to buy this house.

Mrs. Smythe—very particular about what kind of house they buy. She does not want to buy this house and constantly mentions things she doesn't like about it.

Fred Fraudly—real estate agent, very anxious to sell the house to the Smythes because he gets a big commission if he does. He refutes all of Mrs. Smythe's complaints about the house and tries to convince the couple to buy it.

Useful Expressions

Mr. Smythe (to his wife)	"There's nothing wrong with this house—let's take it."
	"I'm tired of looking."
	"Don't be so picky. We can fix that."
Mrs. Smythe (to agent)	"What's the matter with the_____."
	"The_____is all wrong."
	"There's no_____."
	"The_____ is too_____ ."
Fraudly	"You won't find a better deal anywhere."
	"There's a_____within walking distance."
	"We'll give you easy terms with only $_____down."

Topics for Discussion

1. Age of house and type of construction
2. Floor plan
3. Number and size of rooms
4. Yard area and landscaping
5. Neighborhood—facilities, transportation, shopping, etc.

Vocabulary

basement	built-in cabinets	storage area
attic	double garage	mortgage
closet	central heating and air conditioning	down payment

We worried about whether there were enough vocabulary items and added some. Can you think of some to add? I think the role descriptions are very good; they give me a general strategy for the characters. You could add roles by having the children participate, and if you changed the number of bedrooms to three, you would add conflict because two boys would have to share a room. Conflict is highly desirous in role play as it motivates the characters to talk. Change the ages of the children to ten, twelve and fourteen, and the conflict grows sharper. But you get the idea of beginning with a general situation and then continuing to tinker and play with it.

Once you have a role play what do you do with it? Well, the procedures vary somewhat from play to play but these are basic guidelines. Depending on the type and level of class, we do a role play once a week or every other week. The role play is handed out in the beginning of the week, the situation and the rest of the information is gone through and explained, and then roles are assigned. It doesn't work very well to ask for volunteers; no one wants to volunteer for nasty characters and it wastes a lot of class time, so we tend just to assign roles. The students take home the role play exercises, learn the useful expressions and think about what they might say on their own. When they perform the role play in class, they stand up and walk about, and they are not allowed to have the written copy in their hands. Occasionally the teacher takes one of the roles to keep the play moving; this is useful especially in the beginning when the students are learning to do role plays.

In role plays which contain only a few roles, it might seem like a good idea to have several groups do the role play simultaneously as group work, but this doesn't work. I don't know why, but it seems that successful role play requires an audience even if it is only the rest of the class. If such work is treated as rehearsal, and the groups later perform for the whole class, it will work well enough for elementary role plays which are strictly controlled with improvisation at a minimum, as in this very simple exercise. After we had worked through a dialogue and drills on the grammar pattern—modals in polite requests—each pair of students was given a set of cards but each student only saw his own card. One card would say:

> You are in London on a business trip and you have Saturday free. You want to visit the British Museum but you don't know if it is open on Saturday. You also want to know how much the entrance fee is. Call up and find out.

The other card said:

> The British Museum is open Monday through Saturday, 9:00 AM to 5:00 PM. There is no entrance fee.

The students then had to pretend to call up their partners and request whatever information the card instructed them to (each set was different). The person who answered was not to give more information than he was asked for, so he couldn't just read off his card. It may seem to you that this exercise is so simple it is not worth doing, but to a beginning class it is difficult and challenging enough. A role play like this lends itself perfectly to be followed by an out of class community-oriented task where the students have to call up a native speaker in a real situation for some piece of information. It will have students practicing telephone dialogues with a vengeance—my students certainly did.

In some exercises, part of preparing for the role play involves acquiring some background or technical knowledge, and it is an excellent way of coordinating lectures for aural listening comprehension or reading assignments with the rest of the class work. In preparing for this role play in an advanced class, the students read an assignment on new ideas in education:

ROLE PLAYING: A JOB INTERVIEW[21]

Situation

> Two elementary school teachers are applying for a teaching position in Langton School. One teacher is young, just out of college. The other is an older teacher with many years of experience. The principal, Harry

---

[21] Dale Britton, "Role Play: A Job Interview," mimeographed (Pittsburgh: English Language Institute, 1974).

Smith, interviews one teacher at a time (the other teacher leaves the room), in order to decide which one is best suited for the position. Each teacher tries very hard to convince the principal that she is the best one for the job.

After the principal has made a decision the class discusses his decision. How many agree with his choice? Disagree and why?

Cast of Characters

Miss Margaret Johnson—Young, just out of college; has completed all the required education courses along with practice teaching. Is acquainted with all the new ideas in education and is eager to put ideas into practice. Emphasizes her degrees and courses.

Mrs. Cora Abernathy— Older teacher; has taught elementary school for twenty years. Loves children; is dedicated. Emphasizes her experience.

The Principal— Decides which teacher is best suited for the job.

Information that the Principal Should Get From the Two Applicants

I. Qualifications
   1. Education (college, refresher courses, in-training courses)
   2. Experience (number of years, city, kind of school)
II. Personal Information (this information gives the principal a picture of the person, not just the worker)
   1. College graduation date
   2. Health
   3. Community activities
   4. Interests
   5. Marital status
III. References (the principal asks for the names of people he might contact who would be willing to vouch for the teacher's ability and character, for example, a former principal, a college professor)
IV. Salary
V. Questions to help the principal determine if the applicant is suited for the job.

   Examples

"Do you like teaching?"

"What are your feelings about the open classroom?"

"What would you do if your class had a number of slow learners?"

"How should children be punished for misbehavior?"

"Do you believe in screaming at the children to get their attention?"

"What are your feelings about homework?"

"Why do you think you would be good for this job?"

Such interviews may be made much more structured, as in this example from *Lifeline* by David Jones et al, where no prior reading is necessary:

A JOB INTERVIEW[22]

Interviewers

You will have the applicant's application form in front of you, so look through it quickly and ask any further questions you think necessary on education, qualifications or previous experience, for example. See which of the choices the applicant has marked, and find out whether this priority would have any effect on doing the job applied for. (Ask for example if the fact that the applicant did not mark "the offered salary is attractive" means that she isn't interested in money at all! And so on). Remember that you will only have a short time for the interview, so try and make all your questions to the point. Give hypothetical situations that might arise in the job, and ask what the applicant would do.

Interview for secretary/personal assistant

Apart from the basic requirements for the job, you must be satisfied that the applicant can work independently and be a genuine personal assistant. Question the applicants closely on previous jobs to check on this point; also see their reaction to hypothetical situations: e.g., "What would you do if your boss had an important meeting the next day, but had left some vital papers

[22] David Jones et al, *Lifeline* (Stockholm: Kursverksamheten vid Stockholms Universitet, 1973).

in a town 100 miles away?" or "what would you do if two important clients had by mistake been given the same time for appointments, and arrive at the same time?" Check on the question of travel at short notice.

Secretaries/personal assistants

> *Barbara Arrowsmith.* 26 years old. Comprehensive school, good certificate in shorthand/typing from secretarial college. Several previous secretarial jobs, but only the last one involved a lot of real responsibility—as senior secretary in a small publishing company. Did French as part of her secretarial training but hasn't had occasion to use it for the last five years. Has only been abroad a few times, and the travel part of the job is a big attraction (although her fiance is against her applying for the job just because of this aspect). Believes that the best technique in interviews is never to disagree with anything the interviewer says, and to be as polite and flattering as possible.
>
> *Gillian Henderson.* 28 years old. Grammar School qualifications (A levels) in German, History and Economics. Secretarial skills self-taught, but has found them adequate so far in a variety of jobs—bank clerk, reporter for local paper, only secretary for underground newspaper (run by her ex-husband), courier for travel agency, researcher for author, unpaid assistant to organizer of a charity. Has lived abroad and speaks good German with some Finnish and Greek. Is used to taking responsibility and working independently, but has little idea of what would be involved in such a secretarial job. Believes that the best technique for interviews is to dominate as much as possible.

Howard Lagoze developed a role play in the format of a radio talk show, which required the students to listen to the radio at home. The teacher plays the commentator in order to keep up the pace, but with a fluent class that is not necessary. The students are assigned a variety of preposterous opinions on topics from the death penalty to streaking; they prepare some kind of telephone call at home (not allowed to read from notes), and act it out the next time in class. The class I saw had a rollicking good time doing it, got good practice in arguing a point and finished the role play with a discussion on the social values of talk shows where the students contributed observations on talk shows in their own countries. There was a marked difference in the various cultural approaches of dealing with the same phenomenon—a teaching point in itself.

An occasional procedural problem in role plays is that one student will hog the show. When students are trained to do role play they should learn that whoever plays chairman, judge, commentator, principal or whatever role is in charge of the proceedings has as his responsibility the task of keeping any one person from talking too much. It is an infrequent problem.

In some role plays not all players know the task or strategy of the other players, and the actual role play is preceded by "secret" group work. Oxford University Press' *The Bellcrest Story* is of this order, with many company board meetings and business deals.[23] I'll finish by telling you about one that our students do, again written by Dale Britton. It is a courtroom scene; some students have been charged with violations such as screaming and hollering in front of the university dormitory at 2:00 A.M., kicking dogs or turning over park benches—all actual suits, by the way. Some students are counsel for the defense, others for the prosecution, and the rest are witnesses. They then go into group work, planning their defense and prosecution, respectively, of their various cases, but no group knows what the others are planning. They get a lot of legal information, not at all useless for foreign students, in the process. The day I visited a class doing this role play, the young man charged with screaming and hollering claimed in his defense that he had been attacked by two men who tried to kidnap him while he was on his way home from the computer center, where he had been working, and that he had screamed for help. Subsequent witnesses brought out the fact that he was the son of wealthy parents and a man of staid and studious character. An eye witness attested to having seen two men fleeing as the police officer approached to make the arrest. The witnesses were subjected to a very tough grilling by the counsel for the prosecution—incidentally a very shy Thai student who rarely spoke in class—but to no avail. The witnesses could not be shaken, and they improvised right along to meet the many questions, designed on the spot to trip them up. The judge's verdict of not guilty was greeted with cheers by the class.

---

[23] Oxford University Press, *The Bellcrest Story* (London: Press, 1973).

I hope you get the same feeling I had in watching these students, that they were having great fun and that they were very pleased with themselves in being able to follow and handle unexpected arguments in a language they were far from fluent in. As they were struggling with the language in proper court procedure— they knew more about it than I did—they were also processing rules and beliefs of our judiciary system which are basic to our cultural values. I suppose you might say they were wasting time, they weren't studying grammar or vocabulary or learning reading skills, but I would say that all the study of English skills is a waste of time if we don't also teach our students how to function in our culture with those skills.

3
Pronunciation

INTRODUCTION

The acquisition of a good pronunciation in the target language is commonly held to be the most difficult of all tasks in language learning. It is a matter of physical fact that after the age of puberty virtually no one can acquire a native pronunciation. This chapter begins with a discussion of feasible goals and objectives, followed by a brief outline of linguistic aspects of phonology for teachers who have had no training in linguistics. The major part of the chapter is devoted to techniques of teaching pronunciation—articulation, stress and intonation—at various levels of proficiency.

GOALS AND OBJECTIVES

In many parts of the world, English is taught, much as Latin is in the United States, strictly as a reading course. Obviously it would make little sense to spend a large proportion of class work on pronunciation in such a course. Our concern here is with courses which have as their major goal communication, oral as well as written, with other speakers of the target language. With such a goal, it is obvious that considerable energy has to be expended on practicing and learning the sound system of the target language or the students will not be understood. We have all met fluent and rapid speakers we could barely understand, correct though they may have been in syntax. One objective in teaching pronunciation is not to let the student's fluency outrun his comprehensibility.

Accentless speech is simply not an attainable goal for our adult students, nor do we attempt to get them to sound "near native," whatever is meant by that expression. Our goal is based on pragmatic concerns; we want our students to understand and to be understood.

Comprehensibility as a criterion for the goal of teaching pronunciation has its difficulties. It is influenced by such variable factors as willingness to understand, quietness of surroundings, familiarity and experience with the speaker, etc. It should be recognized that comprehensibility is a very subjective criterion.

We should also make clear here that pronunciation practice cannot in any real sense be divorced from listening practice. In this book the two skills are treated separately, but in actual classroom practice listening and speaking should be coordinated.

Chastain is right in thinking that too much importance has been placed on correct pronunciation in beginning classes. The teacher's job is to get "the students' speaking ability to the point at which they can concentrate on the message rather than on the code."[1] This is the counterpoint of Hockett's "a good pronunciation of a foreign language is one which will not draw the attention of a native speaker of that language away from *what* we are saying to the *way* in which we are saying it."[2] Our goal then in teaching pronunciation is the production of a sound system which does not interfere with communication, either from the speaker's or the listener's point of view.

For a beginning student, adequate pronunciation will include control of the segmental phonemes, statement and question intona-

---

[1] Kenneth Chastain, *The Development of Modern Language Skills: Theory to Practice* (Philadelphia: Center for Curriculum Development, 1971), p. 202.

[2] Charles F. Hockett, "Learning Pronunciation," in Croft, ed., *Readings on English as a Second Language* (Cambridge, Massachusetts: Winthrop Publishers, 1972), p. 62.

tion for simple utterances, and stress and rhythm patterns for simple utterances. At intermediate and advanced levels pronunciation practice should concentrate on the allophonic variants, intonation patterns of complex sentences, contrastive stress patterns, and the affective devices by which native speakers indicate anger, amusement, sympathy, etc.

Children learn pronunciation by imitation, and for adults as well imitation remains the basic technique of learning the sound system of the target language. But perfect mimics are very rare, and most adult learners benefit from specific linguistic explanation about the sounds with which they are having difficulty. What follows is a brief discussion of some linguistic aspects of the sound system of English in order to facilitate such linguistic explanations for the teacher. If the reader knows the difference between a phoneme and an allophone, however, skip ahead to page 90.

DISCUSSION OF PHONOLOGY

While all human vocal organs are structurally very much alike, each language has its own system of combining the noises produced by the vocal tract, and it is this difference in the sound system which gives each language its particular quality. The elements of the sound system we will be concerned with are phonemes and allophones, intonation, and stress and rhythm.

Phonemes and Allophones—Segmental

A phoneme is the smallest unit of sound in a language which carries distinctive meaning; the words *pin* and *bin* mean different things in English because /p/ and /b/ are separate phonemes. Sets of words which are distinguished by only one phoneme are called minimal pairs, triplets, etc. (*pin, bin, tin, din*). These sets are very useful in presenting the sounds to foreign language students.

Linguists can identify differences in the pronunciation of sounds which native users of the language do not perceive as different. The /p/ in *pin* is pronounced with a puff of air (aspiration), whereas it is not followed by a puff of air when it follows /s/, as in *spin.* So we say that in English the phoneme /p/ has an allophone [p^h] (the h represents the aspiration) when it comes at the beginning of words.

In some languages the addition of aspiration to a sound will change the meaning. In Thai for example the words /tii/ and /thii/ mean "hit" and "an occasion," respectively; /t/ and /th/ are two separate phonemes in Thai. One of the most difficult things in learning the sounds of a new language is hearing and producing sounds which are phonemic in the new language but allophonic in one's native tongue. Native speakers of English produce both [th] *tear* and [t] *stare* with no difficulty but presented with the Thai words above, they hear the unaspirated one as /d/ because unaspirated /t/ does not occur initially in English, but /d/, which is unaspirated, does as in, *dare.* We hear the sounds of a foreign language in terms of our own phonemic, i.e., meaningful, system; unaspirated /t/ is not distinctive in English, so we hear the closest meaningful sound /d/. This presents a further problem because /d/ is also a phoneme in Thai:

	Thai	English
Phonemes	t th d	t d
Allophones		th

The articulation of a sound is described in terms of the shape of the vocal tract. Articulation is broken down for consonants into the *point* of articulation (where in the vocal tract the air is obstructed) and the *manner* of articulation (how the air is obstructed). Description also includes whether the vocal cords are vibrating; if they are, the sound is described as "voiced" (VD); if they are not the sound is described as "voiceless" (VL). The diagram (page 85) shows the vocal apparatus with the main articulators. The words in parentheses are those used in the linguistic description of the sound (see chart, page 85).

Consonants

Because the spelling systems of many languages do not represent all of the sounds of the language, linguists use a special notation system, commonly referred to as a phonetic alphabet, where one symbol stands for one specific sound. We have used the system of Fries and Pike.[3] The table (page 86) classifies English consonant phonemes as to place and manner of articulation.

---

[3] Kenneth L. Pike, *Phonemics: A Technique for Reducing Languages to Writing* (Ann Arbor: The University of Michigan Press, 1947).

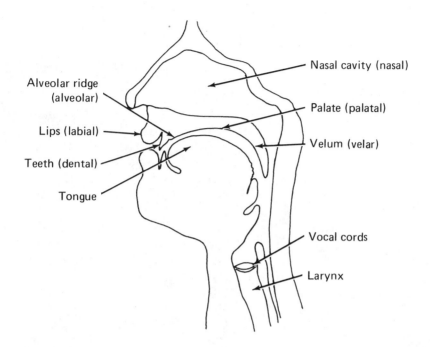

		Front of mouth					Back of mouth	
Point of articulation		Labial	Labio-dental	Dental	Aveolar	Palatal	Velar	Glottal
Manner of articulation								
Stops	VL	p			t		k	
	VD	b			d		g	
Fricatives	VL		f	θ	s	š		h
	VD		v	ð	z	ž		
Affricates	VL					č		
	VD					ǰ		
Nasals	VD	m			n		ŋ	
Liquids	VD				l,r			
Glides	VD	w				y		

Key Word List

Phoneme	Position in a Word		
	Initial	*Final*	*Medial*
Stops			
p	*p*in	ri*p*	ri*pp*ing
b	*b*in	ri*b*	ri*bb*ing
t	*t*in	righ*t*	a*tt*ack
d	*d*in	ri*d*e	a*d*ore
k	*k*in	rac*k*	ra*k*ing
g	*g*un	ra*g*	la*gg*ing
Fricatives			
f	*f*an	lea*f*	laug*h*ing
v	*v*an	lea*v*e	lea*v*ing
θ	*th*in (thigh)	brea*th*	e*th*er
ð	*th*en (thy)	brea*the*	ei*th*er
s	*s*ue	ic*e*	cea*s*ing
z	*z*oo	eye*s*	sei*z*ing
š	*sh*ine	hu*sh*	blu*sh*ing
ž	–	rou*ge*	mea*s*ure
h	*h*unt	–	–
Affricates			
č	*ch*ar	bea*ch*	rea*ch*ing
ǰ	*j*ar	ju*dge*	bu*dg*et
Nasals			
m	*m*e	ru*m*	swi*mm*ing
n	*kn*ee	ru*n*	ru*nn*er
ŋ		ru*ng*	ha*ng*er
Liquids			
r	*r*ed	hea*r*	mi*rr*or
l	*l*ed	hea*l*	mi*ll*er
Glides			
w	*w*et	bo*w*	bo*w*ing
y	*y*et	bo*y*	bo*y*ish

Definitions—Manner of Articulation

Voiced-Voiceless (VD/VL) In some consonants, the only difference is in the activity of the vocal cords. In voiced consonants they vibrate; in voiceless ones they don't. One can feel the difference by putting the fingers around the throat in the area of the larynx and saying alternately *ssss-zzzz-ssss*. The vibration with *zzzz* is the vibration of the vocal cords.

Stop The stream of air is cut off completely at some point in the vocal tract. Say *pin, tin, kin* and notice that the air is stopped first at the lips (labial): /p/; then behind the teeth (alveolar): /t/; and lastly in the back of the mouth (velar): /k/.

Fricative The stream of air is impeded, but not cut off entirely. Say *fin, thin, sin* and *shin* and notice that the air is impeded first by the teeth on the lower lip (labio-dental): /f/; the tongue between the teeth (dental): /θ/; the tongue behind the teeth (alveolar): /s/; and and last the tongue in the middle of the mouth near the roof (palatal): /š/.

Affricate The stream of air is first stopped and then released as in fricatives. Say *char* (/č/). It begins with the tongue in position for /t/ and then moves to position for /š/. In *jar* (/ǰ/) the tongue starts in position for /d/ and then moves to position for /ž/.

Nasals In nasal sounds, the air passes through the nasal cavity. Say *Kim, kin, king* and note where the air is obstructed at the end of each word. (/ŋ/ only occurs in syllable final position in English, so we use the final sounds for comparison).

Liquids The passage of air is obstructed in the middle of the mouth and air escapes around the sides of the tongue. Say *red, led* and note the position of the tongue vis à vis the alveolar ridge.

Glides Say *wet, yet.* There is very little restriction with these sounds. They are also sometimes called semivowels.

Note that the voiced-voiceless distinction is important only for the stops, fricatives and affricates; all other consonants and all of the vowels are voiced in English.

Minor Consonant Features

Certain allophonic variations are important to intelligibility and should be learned for production at the intermediate stages.

Aspiration The voiceless stops /p, t, k/ are aspirated (followed by a puff of air) when they are at the beginning of a word and followed by a vowel: *pit, tip, kin.* This does not make a phonemic (change of meaning) difference in English, but native speakers will perceive the unaspirated stops as /b, d, g/. *Pig* could thus be mistaken as *big* and the students will be more easily understood if they learn to add the "puff of air."

Unreleased Stops Stops in final position are often unreleased, i.e., not clearly pronounced at the ends of words (*pet, stub*). It is not necessary for the students to master this feature, because they will be understood if they pronounce the stops in the same fashion in all positions. They will need practice, however, in order to be able to understand native speakers.

Flapped /t, d/ In the middle of words, /t/ and /d/ are pronounced very fast and very much alike (*bitter/bidder, writer/rider*). The students should have this information and be given exercises which emphasize the context, so that they can understand native speakers.

Liquids The liquids have different tongue positions depending on whether they are at the beginning or at the end of a word following a vowel. Say *red/tar* and *large/call* and notice the position of the tongue in each case. If the students have difficulty with these sounds, it may help to point out to them the proper tongue position.

Vowels

When we talk of the vowel system we are discussing sounds where the flow of air is relatively unobstructed through the oral cavity. It is the shape of the oral cavity and the movement of the tongue (upward-downward and forward-back) in the mouth which give the vowels their characteristic quality. Say *Pete, pit, pate, pet, pat, pot, putt, Paul, pole, pull, pool* and notice how the tongue and jaw tend to lower and then rise again after *pot.* The charts below show the vowels of English and the relative position of the tongue and jaw for their articulation.

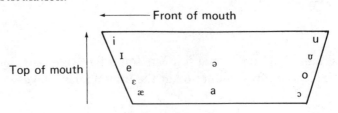

Key Word List

Phoneme	Example
i	p*ee*l, P*e*te
ɪ	p*i*ll, p*i*t
e	p*ai*l, p*a*te
ɛ	p*e*ll (as pell mell), p*e*t
æ	p*a*l, p*a*t
a	p*o*t
ə	p*u*tt
ɔ	P*au*l
o	p*o*le
ʊ	p*u*ll
u	p*oo*l

Diphthongs	
aɪ	p*ie*
ɔɪ	p*oi*se
aʊ	p*ou*t

Compared with many other languages, English has a large number of vowel sounds. The students will need many exercises and a greal deal of practice before they will be able to hear the distinctions.

Minor Vowel Features

Tense/Lax When the vowels /i, e, ɔ, o, u/ are pronounced, the muscles in the jaw are tightened or tense. When the other vowels are pronounced, these muscles are relaxed. When saying /i i i i i/, then /ɪ ɪ ɪ ɪ ɪ/ one can feel the difference in the jaw muscles. It will sometimes be easier for the students to produce the lax sounds if they can notice this difference.

Rounding In English the lips are more rounded with the back vowels (*cawed, code, could, cooed*), than with the front vowels. Rounding is not a phonemically significant factor in English, but it can be a factor in helping the students produce the vowels comprehensibly.

Diphthongization There are only three true diphthongs (combinations of two vowel sounds) in English /aɪ/ /au/ and /ɔɪ/. But all

English vowels have a tendency to end with a different tongue position than they begin with—compare French and Spanish /i, a, u/ with English for example. Note also that lax vowels are even more diphthongized than tense ones.

Length Vowels are longer before voiced consonants than before voiceless ones; the vowel in *hit* is not as long as that of *hid, beat* not as long as *bead.* This information may be of use to students in whose languages length is phonemic.

Language Differences in Segmentals
Which Interfere with Pronunciation

1. Lack of the Sound in the Native System

For most learners of English, the /ð/ (*thy*) and /θ/ (*thigh*) pair is difficult because the sounds are absent from their languages. The task for the learner is to add a new phonemic set. Another difficulty occurs when the native language lacks one of the voiced-voiceless members of a set or one of the vowels of English. The problem then is one of perception; students simply do not hear the difference between /s/ and /z/ or /i/ and /ɪ/.

2. Allophone in Native Language Is a Phoneme in the Target Language

In Spanish [ð] is an allophone of /d/ between vowels (*dedo*), but our Spanish students are always surprised when we point it out to them. Because allophones do not affect the meaning, they are not perceived as distinct in the native language.

3. Phonemes with Different Distributions in the Two Languages

In English /ŋ/ occurs only in syllable final position (*sing, singer*). In other languages, it occurs in syllable initial position as well. Native speakers of English can hear the sound without difficulty, but pronouncing /ŋ a/ is difficult for them.

4. Phonemes Occur in Unfamiliar Combinations

English has a large number of consonant clusters, both at the beginning and at the ends of syllables (*st*raight, gli*mpsed*), which will cause problems for students in whose mother tongue these combinations do not occur.

*5. Native and Target Languages Have Similar Phonemes
at Different Points of Articulation*

French and Spanish /d/ and /t/ are dental, i.e., pronounced with the tongue tip against the back of the teeth. English /t/ and /d/ are alveolar and pronounced with the tongue farther back. The difference may not be perceived aurally by the learner, but it is a factor which contributes to the "foreign accent."

Suprasegmentals

Suprasegmental phonemes include stress and rhythm, juncture and intonation. They are called suprasegmentals, as Wardhaugh puts it, because they "must always be 'overlaid' on the segmentals (vowels and consonants) since they can never occur without them."[4] It is these elements of the sound system which give a language its characteristic quality so that a listener can identify a language although he cannot distinguish individual words. The suprasegmental phonemes constitute the major difficulty for students in acquiring a good pronunciation.

Stress and Rhythm

In any language some of the syllables in an utterance will be spoken with more force or intensity than others. In some languages these stressed syllables always come at the same place; the stress is fixed by automatic rules on a particular syllable in the utterance. In French for example, it always falls on the last syllable of an utterance. English is characterized as a "free stress" language;[5] that is, the stress is not dependent upon the place in the utterance, but can occur on any syllable depending upon various factors. For example, the meaning of single words can be changed by shifting the stress: "The man is going to *con·dúct* the orchestra." "The soldier received a good *cón·duct* medal." Words which would not ordinarily be stressed can be for the purpose of emphasis: "I didn't say *the* book, I said *a* book."

---

[4] Ronald Wardhaugh, *Introduction to Linguistics* (New York: McGraw-Hill, Inc., 1972), p. 65.

[5] Bertil Malmberg, *Phonetics* (New York: Dover Publications, Inc., 1963), pp. 81-82.

Linguists usually describe four levels of stress for sentences as in the following example:

ă dûstў briéfcàse

´ primary
^ secondary
` tertiary
˘ unstressed[6]

For teaching purposes, however, we should concentrate on stressed (primary and secondary) and unstressed syllables, especially at the beginning levels. As a rule, only words in the following categories are stressed: nouns, verbs, adjectives, adverbs, demonstratives (*this,* etc.) and interrogatives (*who*, etc.); but words of more than one syllable have different stress on the various syllables, as in the "briefcase" example above.

The timing of syllables gives a language its characteristic rhythm. In many languages, each syllable (stressed or unstressed) receives an equal amount of time as in French and Spanish. In English the stressed syllables tend to occur at regular intervals and the unstressed syllables in between are reduced and given less time. Fries gives the following illustration:

The DOCtor's a SURgeon.
The DOCtor's a good SURgeon.
The DOCtor's a very good SURgeon.
The DOCtor's not a very good SURgeon.

and says that "the actual time between the stresses would be approximately the same in spite of the difference in the number of intervening syllables."[7] One of the characteristics which makes spoken English very difficult for foreign students to comprehend is this tendency to reduce and run together all unstressed syllables.

In informal speech, the unstressed vowels are frequently reduced to a mid-vowel, such as /ə/. In "he wants <u>a</u> c<u>ou</u>ple <u>of</u> bottles <u>of</u> beer" all the underlined syllables will be pronounced /ə/. This phenomenon makes comprehension very difficult because the sound has little relation to the written representation in the students' books. This and other aspects of informal speech will be discussed in the chapter on Listening Comprehension.

---

[6] Wardhaugh, p. 64.

[7] Charles C. Fries, *Teaching and Learning English as a Foreign Language* (Ann Arbor: The University of Michigan Press, 1945), pp. 23-24.

Juncture

The difference between *nitrate, night rate* and *Nye trait* is juncture. It is the combination of sounds into syllables which allows us to distinguish between *a nice man* and *an ice man* or between *keep sticking* and *keeps ticking.* Usually context will be sufficient to clarify the meaning, and exercises on juncture of this type are beyond the level of all but the most advanced learners of ESL, and therefore have not been included here. The teacher should be aware of this feature in order to diagnose student problems in comprehension, but efforts to teach it should be resisted.

Intonation

Intonation is the rising and falling of the voice as we speak. It is sometimes illustrated as notes on a musical scale. The four pitch levels usually described for English are:

4   extra-high (used for emphasis or contrast)
3   high
2   normal (mid)
1   low

We also need to describe the end of the utterance (terminal). There are two main ones: ↑ rising and ↓ falling. In English, intonation is related to sentence stress, since the accented syllable is often spoken on the highest note. We will discuss only the two most common patterns here.[8]

Pattern 1. /2 3 1 ↓ / This pattern is used for most declarative sentences, requests or commands, and for WH questions.

Examples:

```
2        3    1
I'm going downtown.

2                3      1
I'm going downtown tomorrow.
```

---

[8] For a more detailed discussion of intonation patterns see Norman C. Stageberg, *An Introductory English Grammar,* 2nd ed. (New York: Holt, Rinehart & Winston, Inc., 1971); or Clifford H. Prator Jr. and Betty Wallace Robinett, *Manual of American English Pronunciation,* 3rd ed. (New York: Holt, Rinehart & Winston, Inc., 1972).

```
2                    3      1
Please get me some cigarettes.
```

```
2    3  1
Come here.
```

```
2         3   1
Where is he going?
```

```
2                        3   1
When is she going to New York?
```

Pattern 2. / 2 3 3 ↑ / This is the pattern for yes-no questions, or any question with statement word order.

Examples:

```
2       3   3
Are you going?
```

```
2                        3      3
Will they be here in a few minutes?
```

```
2        3   3
You're not ready?
```

```
2           3 3
It's time for class?
```

The preceding discussion is a very general outline of the English sound system. We have included it because, in our experience, teaching pronunciation is more influenced by a technical knowledge of the linguistic features than any other skill. Grammar can of course be said to be an exception, but all teachers have studied some version of grammar while few are familiar with phonology.

GENERAL ELEMENTS OF A PRONUNCIATION LESSON

The basic steps of a pronunciation lesson are the same whether the lesson comprises a class by itself, as it does in our program, or fits into a ten minute segment of an hour during which all skills are taught, as is the procedure in most language classrooms. These basic steps are (1) selection and presentation of the sound feature to be taught, (2) recognition of the new sound and discrimination between similar sounds and (3) production of the sound feature, first in words and phrases and finally (4) in a communicative situation.

In Step 5, our students are also taught the basic rules for the various spellings of the sound in order to keep "reading pronunciation" at a minimum. Such mispronunciations are typical of native speakers as well; so many Americans pronounce *diphtheria* with a /p/ that it has now become an accepted usage. English spelling is a major source of interference in learning a good pronunciation and should be dealt with systematically in the pronunciation lesson.

Teaching the Segmental Phonemes

Step 1. Selection and Presentation

As in teaching any other language skill, pronunciation is best taught by introducing only one thing at a time. Just as the teacher should not introduce more than one segmental phoneme at once, he should also avoid complications of new stress and intonation patterns. Since for native speakers stress and intonation automatically form a part of all segmental sounds, it is very easy to forget that differences which we do not perceive can cause major difficulties for the students who do perceive them.

Most texts will have done a careful sequencing, but occasionally there are slips so the teacher should check (1) that new vowels are presented with previously learned consonants and vice versa, (2) that examples of the sound in all positions are included (initial—"*p*at," medial—"c*u*ps" and final—"shee*p*") and (3) that intonation and stress patterns used for practicing longer utterances are not new ones.

The first step in actual classroom procedure is to introduce the sound, to focus the student's attention on the teaching point. Campbell suggests using the native language at this stage.[9] If native language use is not possible, then the teacher should write on the board a line from a previously learned dialogue or a sentence from a text and underline the feature, e.g., /i/ "What did h*e e*at?" If the same routine is followed lesson after lesson, the students soon learn what to expect and use of the native language should not be necessary. If there is no example to be found in the text, the teacher should make up a simple sentence using vocabulary the students have already learned.

---

[9] Russell N. Campbell, "The Language Laboratory and Pronunciation Teaching," *English Language Teaching* XXII, no. 2 (January 1968): 148-55.

Step 2. Aural Recognition and Discrimination

Aural recognition of a new sound is a very difficult step for students in whose mother tongue the sound is absent or exists as an allophonic variant. It is frequently claimed that a sound "cannot be reproduced except by chance"[10] unless the students can first recognize, that is, hear the sound. This is not absolutely true,[11] and there are exceptions when it is useful to have students produce two sounds in order to be able to discriminate between them. But as a general guideline, it is profitable to enable students to identify and discriminate between the new sounds and familiar, similar sounds, such as /s/ and /z/.

The aural discrimination exercises should not take more than three to five minutes in the actual classroom presentation. As soon as the students can identify and discriminate the sound, the teacher should move on to the next step.

When students are just beginning to learn a new language, they understand very little and are easily confused as to what to listen for. It is important at this step that the students know precisely what they should listen for and that the teacher follow careful procedures in modeling the exercises. One way to do this is always to place the new sound in a fixed position on the board. For example, in one lesson the new sound /ɪ/ is to be contrasted with /i/. The known sound /i/ is in the column at the left:

1	2
beat	bit
heat	hit
meat	mit

When /ɪ/ is later contrasted with /ɛ/, the /ɪ/ words are in Column 1:

1	2
bit	bet
lit	let
wit	wet

---

[10] Pierre Leon, "Teaching Pronunciation," in Valdman, ed., *Trends in Language Teaching* (New York: McGraw-Hill Book Company, 1966), p. 59.

[11] Eugene E. Briere, "An Investigation of Phonological Interference," *Language* 42(1966): 768-96.

In modeling the exercises, each member of the contrasted set should have the same intonation. The normal intonation for words in a list is with falling intonation on the last item (one, two, three). When modeling minimal pairs, one must take care to give each of the words the same intonation or the students will hear two differences in the last item: intonation and phoneme difference, and they will not know which is the significant feature.

Drills for Teaching Aural Identification

Minimal Pair Drills The most common technique for aural discrimination is the use of contrast, either with a similar sound in the native language or of two sounds in the target language. The native language–target language is most successful with the vowels and is especially useful for demonstrating the diphthongization of English vowels in contrast with a vowel system which does not have this characteristic. An example for speakers of French learning English:

French	English
qui	key
si	see
des	day
les	lay
dos	dough

The teacher models the pairs and then asks in French if the students can describe how the vowel sounds differ. The students describe the English vowels as longer (probably) and notice that the voice seems to go down at the end of the English words. The teacher then repeats the pairs in random order:

qui/key
see/si
see/see

and the students are asked to identify in which language the word was spoken: "French/English, English/French, English/English." The exercise can be expanded to include three words /des/des/day) or even four, but beyond this, the students have difficulty remembering and the drill diminishes in effectiveness.

In classes of heterogeneous language backgrounds, aural discrimination will necessarily have to be confined to sounds in English, and care should be taken to contrast new sounds only with those previously learned.

Same-Different Exercise Drills The purpose of these exercises is to ascertain whether or not the students can hear the phonemic contrasts. The teacher pronounces pairs of words (*bit/beat*) (*beat/beat*) and the students are asked to identify whether the sounds are the same or different. They respond "different" or "same." The next step is to give three items and have the students identify which ones are the same.

	1 2 3		
T:	bit/beat/beat	S:	2 and 3
	beat/bit/beat		1 and 3

In order to check the students' perception of the sound in context, Strain has the same kind of exercise using minimal sentences:

1. He bit me. He beat me. (different)
2. Tim beat me. Tim beat me. (same)
3. Did he live? Did he leave? (different)[12]

Just as it is important to have the students practice the phonemes in all positions in a word, it is equally important that the sounds be practiced both in stressed and unstressed positions in a sentence. The tendency in English to reduce unstressed vowels makes sounds in this position much more difficult for the students to hear and they need practice from the beginning stages in exercises like the following where the teaching point is the /i/-/ɪ/ contrast:

T: He's heating the saúce. S: different
He's hitting the saúce.

Sound Identification Drills These exercises require the student to relate the modeled sound to one he has previously learned. The column headings with one example remain on the board as the teacher models the items and the students identify the sounds.

Board:	1	2
	bit	bet

---

[12] Jeris E. Strain, "Teaching a Pronunciation Problem," in Croft, ed., *Readings on English as a Second Language* (Cambridge, Massachusetts: Winthrop Publishers, 1972), p. 76.

T:	lit	S:	1
	yet		2
	met		2

The exercises can be made more difficult by using the same technique as in the same-different drills.

T:	lit/yet/met	S:	1/2/2
	bit/hit/bet		1/1/2

All of the preceding drills are to help the student sort out bits of the code, but no real learning will be accomplished until the students have a chance to practice discrimination in the context of real language; i.e., until they can see how the code combines with the message. In the following exercise, the teaching point is the /i/-/ɪ/ contrast. It is assumed that the students know the vocabulary and comprehend the grammatical structures. The teacher makes statements and the students declare the "message" to be true or false.

1.	If a man bit a dog, it would be news.	1.	True
2.	Students always write with a pin.	2.	False
4.	Students often write with a pen.	4.	True
5.	A sheep can take us to the United States.	5.	False
7.	If a man beat a dog, it would be news.	7.	False
8.	A ship can take us to the United States.	8.	True[13]

Step 3. Production

Once the students have demonstrated that they can distinguish the new sound, they must learn to produce it, first in isolated words and phrases, later in sentences, and finally in communicative utterances. In minimal pair drills, students are frequently asked to practice with words they don't know the meaning of. The reason for this is, of course, that the primary criterion for selecting words for pronunciation practice lies in the sounds of the words rather than in their meaning. *Thy* is not a very useful word for the students to know, but it is useful in the minimal pair *thy/thigh*. We have mixed feelings about asking our students to practice with words they don't know or which are of little use to them, but we feel that the practice with minimal pairs is so useful in teaching pronunciation that we

---

[13] Fe R. Dacanay, *Techniques and Procedures in Second Language Teaching* (Dobbs Ferry, New York: Oceana Publications, Inc., 1963), p. 203.

accept the unavoidable drawbacks. The teacher should, however, take care to make very clear to the students that this is not a lesson in vocabulary, and if the students want to know the meaning of the words, they have to look them up at home. As Leon so correctly points out, "Most adults want to understand what they are asked to imitate,"[14] and our students would gladly digress on the meanings of the words in the minimal pair lists if the teacher let them, but it is not a productive use of class time.

Drilling with words the students don't understand is only acceptable in minimal pair drills. In drills on the phrase and sentence level, students must understand what they are saying as the very teaching point in these exercises is to decode *meaning* through sound.

In the production step of the lesson, the basic procedure is for the teacher to model the utterance and for the students to imitate. The teacher should stand up facing the class and (in a large class) walk around so that everyone gets an equal chance to hear clearly. He should take care to speak at normal speed and not slow down because otherwise his pronunciation becomes distorted. Teachers should pronounce words as they occur in their own dialect of English; unless they can code-switch comfortably, they will only confuse their students. Teachers who are not native speakers of English should use tape recordings of native speakers as much as possible. The students should drill with their books open; the written word reinforces the oral version and alleviates any lack of short term memory.

Drills for Teaching Sound Production

Repetition Drills The first step is a minimal pair drill where the new sound is contrasted with a previously learned sound:

1 (previously learned)	2 (new sound)
pot	putt
lock	luck
rob	rub

The teacher reads across the columns, first word by word, then by pairs. The students repeat chorally and then individually. Rarely do

---

[14] Leon, p. 5.

all students imitate perfectly, and the teacher must then correct them. We will discuss techniques for correction presently.

Next the class proceeds to repetition and imitation of phrases and sentences:

a duck
a dock
The bomb is a dud.
Boom!!! The bomb wasn't a dud.[15]

Once the students have mastered the sound to the teacher's satisfaction, they should proceed to testing drills of which there are various types.

Testing Drills

1. Identification—opposite
In these drills the teacher gives one item, the student identifies which sound (by the column on the board) and gives the other contrast:

Example: Board: 1   2
                  bit   beat

        T: beat   S: 2-bit
            hit   1-heat

Decanay extends the practice to sentence recognition. The students have already learned the sentences in the introductory dialogue. "Listen carefully and tell which sentence it is. Then give the other sentence."

              1   2
           leave   live

T: He's going to leave.   S: Number 1
    What's number 2 then?   He's going to live.[16]

Davison also has a variation using sentences. The students are instructed to read the sentence first with word (a),

---

[15] Walter Davison, *Sound To Speech: A Pronunciation Manual for English as a Foreign Language* (Pittsburgh: University for International Studies, n.d.), p. 10.

[16] Decanay, p. 200-201.

then with word (b), then once more with either word. Another student identifies the word in the third reading.

1. (a. bomb) (b. bum)   A_____can cause a lot of damage.
2. (a. mom) (b. mum)   My _____got lost in the crowd.
9. (a. lock) (b. luck)   She depends on her _____ to avoid burglars.[17]

2. Frame drills

Robert Allen suggests the use of word frames for practicing various phonemic contrasts, especially the vowel contrasts. The frame d____n can be used to cue the students to many vowel sounds: *den/Dan/din/done/dune.* The frame can be made much more complicated (and therefore teach the constraints on syllable structure) by varying the frame /d__nK/ /dr__nK/ /dr__nKs/.[18] Strain uses a sentence frame and asks the students to complete it using charts or pictures as cues:

(b) It's his _____.

ship	lip	chin	meat
sheep	tea	knee	milk
key	cheek	fish	

(d) Did she _____ it?

eat	leave
fill	feel
see	kiss[19]
fix	

This exercise is also a good one for vocabulary expansion.

Step 4. Contextualizing the Practice;
Use of the Sound in a Communicative Situation

The drills which the students do should progress quickly from the sound in isolated words to phrases and sentences. But phrases

---

[17] Davison, p. 7.

[18] Robert L. Allen, "The Use of Rapid Drills in the Teaching of English to Speakers of Other Languages," *TESOL Quarterly* 6, no. 1 (March 1972): 24.

[19] Strain, p. 77.

and sentences are not really communicative either, and if the students are to be able to use the newly learned sounds in everyday situations, their classroom practice must also contain exercises where the focus is on the meaning the sound carries rather than on the sound itself.

One of the easiest ways of having the students practice sentence length utterances in a meaningful context is by asking them questions. With books closed and the board erased, the teacher asks questions which require recapitulation of the introductory material (for beginning classes) or opinion-type questions designed to stimulate discussion (for more proficient students), e.g., "When is bombing justifiable?" Discussion-type questions are excellent for practicing real communication.

Step 5. Sound-Symbol Correspondence

One of the major causes of poor pronunciation is interference from spelling. English spelling is not regular (*enough, though, through, cough, hiccough*) and students frequently make mistakes through false analogy. As Prator points out, the students will have to learn the orthographic system at some time,[20] and following Allen, Allen and Shute, we find it most efficient to teach pronunciation and spelling together.[21]

After the students have learned to produce a new sound, they are given the various spellings of that sound in rules and generalizations, like, "The letter combinations *kn, gn, mn, pn* in initial position have the /n/ sound."[22] They practice production of the /n/ sound by reading after the teacher from lists of words like *knot, gnu, mnemonic* and *pneumonia*. The students are not asked to memorize either rules or vocabulary; they do sufficient practice in class so that they can read such words without interference from the orthography.

The students learn, in this order, the common usual spelling of the sound, less common spellings, sight words and homophones. For

---

[20] Clifford H. Prator, "Phonetics vs. Phonemics in the ESL Classroom: When is Allophonic Accuracy Important?" *TESOL Quarterly* 5, no. 1 (March 1971): 61-72.

[21] Robert L. Allen, Virginia French Allen and Margaret Shute, *English Sounds and Their Spellings* (New York: Thomas Y. Crowell Co., 1966).

[22] Judy Vernick, "Sound-Symbol Correspondence in ESL," mimeographed (University of Pittsburgh, English Language Institute, 1975): p. 4.

the vowels they also learn the rules for the name and base sounds. The teacher should be careful to have the students induce the rules from examples as the result otherwise is likely to be an undue ratio of teacher talk.

Name-Sound Base Sound Vowel sounds are divided into name sounds and base sounds as a device to teach one of the basic spelling rules of English: addition of -e changes the basic sound to the same sound as the name of the letter.

Base sounds	Name sounds	Letter
/ɪ/ bit	/ai/ bite	*i*
/ɛ/ pet	/i/ Pete	*e*
/æ/ bat	/e/ bate	*a*
/a/ not	/o/ note	*o*
/ə/ cut	/u/ cute	*u*

Sight Words These are words which have a pronunciation which is different from other words with a similar spelling. For example, "double o" words are most commonly pronounced /ʊ/ *look, took, book, shook, good, wood*; but there are a number of common words with "double o" which are pronounced /u/ *too, food, mood*. The students are taught the rule "-oo- is pronounced /ʊ/" and learn the others as exceptions when they are learning the spellings which represent /u/.

Example: Target sound /ə/. Students have learned spellings with /u/ (*nut, putt*) which are most common. Here is an exercise from Vernick:

"Listen carefully as the 2 lists of words are pronounced.

A	B
nut	note
hum	home
cup	cope

Where would you put the words *some, come* and *one*? On the basis of spelling, you might put these words in column B. But because they are pronounced more like the words in column A, they belong there. *Some, come* and *one* are SIGHT WORDS because they are pronounced differently from most words which have the spelling oCe. . . . In these SIGHT WORDS, the letter *o* has the #1 or /ə/ sound. The final letter *e* is silent.

SAY: some   come   one
      none   love   done
      above   dove   glove."[23]

Homophones Homophones are words with different spellings which are pronounced the same (*two/too/to, night/knight*). Common homophones should be presented as variant spellings for the sound in question. The following is another example from Vernick:

"LISTEN as these pairs are pronounced.

    1. in   inn
    2. not   knot

In and *inn* are pronounced exactly the same, and so are *not* and *knot*. Words which are pronounced the same but spelled differently are called HOMOPHONES."[24]

Homographs These are words with the same or similar spellings with different pronunciation: cón•duct/con•dúct, pŕe•sent/pre•sént; sím•ply/im•ply; wál•low/al•lów. Some items in this category, such as Kreidler's example of /au/ *brown cow* and /o/ *slow show,*[25] will be accounted for when the sounds themselves are presented. Others (cón•duct/con•dúct) depend on external factors such as function in a sentence and should be taught only in the context of sentences.

At beginning levels the students should be given practice with name and base sounds, sight words and homophones but the practice with more difficult patterns which involve stress changes should be reserved for more advanced levels when the students' proficiency is high enough to discuss the items in terms of sentence and word structure.

Testing Sound-Symbol Correspondences Once the students have mastered the sound-symbol correspondences, quizzes of various types reinforce the learning and assure that the students learn to spell. To test recognition, Vernick has a variety of exercises:

Examples: Circle the letter or letter combinations that signal the /n/ sound.

---

[23] Ibid, p. 17.

[24] Ibid, p. 6.

[25] Charles W. Kreidler, "Teaching English Spelling and Pronunciation," *TESOL Quarterly* 6, no. 1 (March 1972): 5.

Example: (n) u (n)

1. c o l u (m n)   2. (n)u t   3. d e s i(g n)

Write the words from column B that has the same final sound as the word in column A.

	A		B
Example:	sun	*fun*	sum
			fun
1.	column	_____	bomb
			sign

Match the words from column B with their HOMOPHONES in Column A.

	A		B
Example:	in	*inn*	two
			knot
1.	no	_____	*inn*
			gnu
3.	not	_____	know[26]

For production, dictation exercises are the easiest to construct and they are an excellent check on listening comprehension as well as spelling. The construction of dictation exercises is discussed in the chapter on listening comprehension.

Teaching the Suprasegmental Phonemes

Prator points out that the suprasegmental phonemes have not been given sufficient attention in the ESL classroom.[27] The probable reason for this is twofold: (1) suprasegmental phonemes involve linguistically very technical and difficult information, and (2) it is doubtful that students learn no matter how much they are taught. Still, stress, intonation and juncture influence the comprehensibility of our students once they are past the very beginning levels more than any other aspect of their pronunciation, so that we feel that we simply cannot ignore the matter.

The basic sequence of presentation, recognition and production should also be followed with intonation, stress and juncture. It is

---

[26] Vernick, pp. 12-13.

[27] Prator, p. 67.

important that the students understand exactly what the teaching point is and that they have the necessary linguistic information for meaningful practice.

Intonation

Step 1. Presentation

Virginia Allen suggests that a short dialogue be recorded in the native language and the target language. With the volume turned low enough to obscure the words, the student tries to identify his native language just from the intonation.[28] If the class is a heterogeneous one, each student can be asked to speak his native language for two minutes on the first day of class. Then the taped recordings can be used a few days later as a demonstration.

Once the students are aware that there are differences between languages in intonation, they will need some kind of graphic representation of the contour in English. Beginning students will not profit from linguistic lectures, but a graphic symbol such as an arrow ✗ ↘ following the utterance, a contour for the whole utterance ⌒⌒or a gesture of a raised or lowered hand at the end of the model sentences will serve to remind beginning students of the intonation pattern.

The procedures for the presentation of suprasegmental patterns are the same as for the segmentals (see page 94).

Step 2. Aural Discrimination

As soon as the students learn a grammatical pattern which requires an intonation different from previously learned patterns, they should have contrastive exercises in discrimination; for example, when they are learning the *yes-no* questions after having learned *be* in declarative sentences:

T:	He's in class.	S:	Statement
	He's in class?		Question

The cues should differ in intonation only so that the students will learn to listen for this common pattern.

Beyond this, there is very little to be done in teaching

---

[28] Virginia French Allen, "Teaching Intonation: From Theory to Practice," *TESOL Quarterly* 5, uo. 1 (March 1971): 74.

suprasegmentals to beginning students. The exercises described below are most effective with intermediate level students.

Step 3. Production

Following the mimicry of a model, most techniques for production involve some kind of dialogue material.

Allen suggests early practice with short dialogues of single word utterances:

He:	Ready? ↗
She:	No. ↘
He:	Why? ↘
She:	Problems. ↘
He:	Problems? ↗
She:	Yes. ↘
He:	What? ↘
She:	Babysitter. ↘ [29]

This technique focuses on intonation almost exclusively to convey the meanings and the voice must rise and fall within the space of a very few syllables.

Higgins and Lewis describe an exercise in which the students are given an oral cue marked for intonation and a series of responses to be read with the same pattern:

> Cue: I'm going to live in England.
>
> Responses: You must be crazy.
>   You're out of your mind.
>   You'll freeze to death.
>   What about your girlfriend?

In addition to intonation patterns, the cues can be designed for practice on particular segmental phonemes:

> Cue: What time is it?
> Response: Five to one.

or for practice with language styles:

> Cue: I'm terribly sorry.
> Responses: It's quite all right.
>   No damage done.

---

[29] Ibid, p. 76.

ᶦNot to ⸝worry.
ᶦNever ⸝mind.[30]

These kinds of exercises are useful at the intermediate and advanced stages when students sometimes balk at typical "listen and repeat" phonological drills. The teacher reads the cue and the students read the responses from the text individually, using the same intonation as the teacher's.

At advanced levels, when students have discussed the intonation features which indicate anger, humor, astonishment, etc., the students can be given dialogues marked for the emotion to be conveyed and later unmarked dialogues for which they must deduce the intonation patterns from the contrast and context:

X: May I see your license?
Y: Certainly, sir. I have it right here. Oh! Where is it?
       Excuse me. I can never find anything in this purse.
X: I can wait.
Y: Do you have to have it? Can't you just. . . .
X: I must see the license.
Y: Well. . .Oh, I know, George, I gave it to you last night.
       Don't you remember?
Z: You did? Oh, that's right. Yes, I have it right here in
       my wallet. Here you are, sir.
X: Thank you. Yes, this is fine. When is the wedding?

The students silently read the dialogue, which is ambiguous until the last line, and then decide the identity and relationship of the speakers in class discussion. They should be led to see the ambiguity and the function of the last line in clarifying the situation, i.e., at the office of the Justice of the Peace as opposed to a policeman stopping a traffic offender. Then they read the dialogue aloud with proper intonation.

Stress and Rhythm

In actual practice it is not possible to practice stress apart from intonation, since stress usually coincides with the highest pitch of the intonation contour. It is useful to consider them separately, however, for stress sometimes functions independently and the students should be made aware of its importance in English.

---

[30] J. J. Higgins and J. Windsor Lewis, "Teaching Intonation in the Language Laboratory," *English Language Teaching* XXIV, no. 1 (October 1969): 47-48.

Steps 1 and 2. Presentation and Aural Discrimination

As Michael Vodden points out, the very idea of stress must be presented if the student's native language does not use it as a phonemic feature. He suggests whispering as a technique to demonstrate stress in English.[31] By removing voicing and therefore pitch and intonation, the stressed syllables are clearly delineated.

As a beginning exercise, the students underline the stressed syllables in sentences which are read in a whisper. They then mark stress for sentences read in a normal voice. In order for the students to be able to decipher how stress can change meaning, they should have exercises in which they choose appropriate rejoinders. The students have a printed set of possible responses and the teacher reads (or plays a recording) of the dialogue. There are no clues in the written material; the students must rely on the suprasegmentals to get the meaning. The following exercises combine stress and intonation.

The student listens to the cue and responds appropriately to the cue by the teacher. The teaching points are stress and tag question intonation.

> T: You didn't *eat*\that watermelon, did│you?
>
> S: No, (I gave it away).
>
> T: You didn't eat *that*\watermelon, did│ you?
>
> S: No, (I ate the other one.)
>
> T: You didn't eat that *water│melon,* did│you?
>
> S: No, (I ate the banana.)[32]

In the next exercise, the student must choose the appropriate paraphase of *what?*. They hear the dialogue and choose from written answers.

> X: I'm reading Jones' new book.
> Y: What?   A: I didn't hear what you said.
>   B: Oh really, I didn't think it was out yet.
>   C: I didn't think you were capable of such a thing.

---

[31] Michael Vodden, "Rhythm and Intonation," *English Language Teaching* XXII, no. 3 (May 1968): 246-52.

[32] Gary Esarey, "Pronunciation Exercises for Advanced Learners of ESL," mimeographed (University of Pittsburgh, English Language Institute, 1975): p. 20.

Step 3. Production

For beginning students, it is enough if they learn to stress the word or syllable which coincides with the highest point in the intonation contour, and the same kinds of exercises used to practice intonation will suffice. More advanced students will need practice on compound noun stress (a salad bowl/a big bowl), stress as it interprets grammatical meaning (go buy it/go by it), stress in conversations and the affective meanings of various stress and intonation patterns.

Compound Noun Stress Here is a sample lesson by Virginia F. Allen for teaching compound noun stress in contrast to the adjective plus noun (a big bowl) which the students have already practiced.

Situation: It's almost Christmas. People are thinking about what presents they're going to buy to put under their *Chrístmas trees.*

Repeat: (show picture) Chrístmas trees.

In néwspaper ads and magazíne ads you will find many things that you would like to buy for people.

Repeat: néwspaper ads
magazíne ads

Maybe some of the things are really too expensive to buy, but we can always pretend. Here are some things that a woman might like:

Repeat: (show picture) a hándbag
a cóffee pot (a cóffee maker)
some cándle sticks
a sálad bowl

(Call attention of the students to the stress on the first element.)

This is a tree for Christmas. A Chrístmas tree.
This is a bag for carrying in the hand. A hándbag.
This is a pot for coffee. A cóffee pot.
These are sticks for candles. Cándle sticks.
This is a bowl for salad. A sálad bowl. It's a wooden sálad bowl.

(Hold up pictures and have students identify them.)

Men seem to be more difficult to choose presents for, but here is a *wríst watch.*

Repeat: (show picture) a wrist watch

And here is a pocket watch.

Repeat: (show picture) a pocket watch

(Holding these last two pictures up in turn as clues, elicit the following sentences:)

I'd like to look at pocket watches.
We only have wrist watches.

I'd like to look at wrist watches.
We only have pocket watches.

(Ask students to name any other presents they would like to buy for people: a necktie; an ash tray; a record player; a table lamp; a desk lamp; a cream pitcher; a sugar bowl; etc.)[33]

Stress in Conversations Virginia F. Allen points out that there are stress differences in utterances depending on whether they introduce the topic or develop it. The students need to have some guidelines for knowing which words to stress and she gives the following rules:

Rule A: In a sentence which *introduces* a topic (or starts a conversation) the nouns, adjectives and verbs (other than forms of BE and HAVE) are usually pronounced more loudly, and on a higher pitch, than the auxiliaries, articles, conjunctions, pronouns and prepositions.

Rule B: Nouns which are used as *objects* of verbs usually receive more stress than nouns used as *subjects*.

Rule C: In sentences which introduce topics, verbs are not usually stressed unless they are followd by *pronoun* objects.

Did they FINish it?
but We've rented an APARTment.[34]

---

[33] V. F. Allen, Handout from a Course in Methods of Teaching English as a Second Language, Teacher's College, Columbia University.
[34] V. F. Allen, "Teaching Intonation," p. 78.

The students can be given this information (or be led to deduce it from modeled dialogues) and then practice with dialogues like these:

X:	It's WET.	(First utterance)
Y:	It's NOT wet.	
X:	It IS wet.	(Later utterances, developing the
Y:	It's not VERY wet.	topic)
X:	It SEEMS very wet to ME.	

X:	I've lost an umBRELLa.	(First utterance)
Y:	A LAdy's umbrella?	(Later utterances)
X:	Yes, a lady's umbrella with STARS on it. GREEN stars.[35]	

The students read along as the teacher models the dialogues and their visual attention as well as their aural attention is focused on the stressed syllables. Later the students can be given similar unmarked exchanges for which they determine and discuss which syllables to stress and then practice aloud.

The practice could then continue with only topic introducers for which the students provide the developing utterances.

T:	The newspapers went on strike today.
S1:	(Do you think it will be a *long* one?)
S2:	(It *could* be. They haven't had a raise in *three* years.)
S1:	(Well, I hope not. *Mornings* are *awful* without my *paper.*)

Affective Meaning of Stress and Intonation Native speakers of any language learn early to interpret anger, amusement, sarcasm, weariness, etc.—all the emotional states and attitudes that are expressed unconsciously by the *way* things are said, the "tone of voice." By the time we are adults, we perceive these factors at an unconscious level in our native language and few learners of foreign languages are ever taught that these patterns in the target language may be different. Listening to Slavic languages gives us the impression that the speakers are having an argument because the normal pattern is one which in English is associated with anger.

---

[35] Ibid, p. 77.

At the intermediate and advanced levels, where students may be in contact with native speakers, there should be exercises and information and discussion on these topics. The exercise might begin with some comparative dialogues in various foreign languages contrasted with English. The students would know the setting of the dialogue—asking information, being angry, being amused, etc.—and the volume would be turned down so low (see Intonation, Step 1) that only stress and intonation are audible. It is at this point that the students will see that the message and the code are at times inseparable. Listening comprehension exercises and then production of various patterns by controlled dialogues and role play can follow in the sequence outlined above.

Step 4. Contextualizing the Practice

To ensure transfer from the pronunciation class to everyday life, the students practice with situations they are likely to encounter outside the classroom. With intermediate and advanced students we use a series of role play activities and the students also give oral reports to the class. We will discuss oral reports here; role play activities are discussed in the chapter on Speaking.

Oral Reports Oral reports are excellent practice on the intermediate and advanced levels: they put the responsibility for production on the student, they give recognition to the fact that the student has something to contribute, and they give practice in the public use of the language (many of our students will later have to do seminar presentations).

The procedures are as follows: First the student picks a topic and writes up his report. The students may choose any topic they want, with the only constraint that it must lend itself to the organizational rhetorical devices they are presently studying in the writing class. If, for instance, they are studying chronological organization, then the topic must be one which lends itself to a chronological organization. After the student has written up his report, he goes over it with the teacher, who checks it for grammatical errors and organization. The teacher may even ask the student to read a part of the report to forestall any gross errors of pronunciation of key words. Next, the student gives the report in class. He is not allowed to read the report, but can only have notes.

He does of course not have to memorize the report but only to be very familiar with it and to try to use the same patterns. The report cannot be longer than six minutes—it can well be shorter—and is followed by questions or a discussion. The presentation of the report is taped, and at a later session the teacher goes over it with the student, analyzing it for errors of pronunciation and grammar. At this level, students are well able to correct themselves and this should be encouraged as much as possible. The teacher only says "There's a mistake in this last sentence; see if you can find it" and then plays that segment of the tape over again. The emphasis on self-monitoring is one of the most efficient techniques we have found for improving pronunciation. In addition, the individual attention is highly motivational in promoting language learning and our students are surprisingly eager to do oral reports. Individual attention is also the major drawback of an otherwise excellent procedure: it is very time consuming.

Throughout the exercises in pronunciation, the progression is from controlled exercises to less structured ones in which the student is allowed more freedom to express his own ideas. When the students engage in conversational exchanges in the classroom using normal stress and expressing their own ideas, there is every reason to hope they will continue the practice with other native speakers outside the classroom.

Correcting Pronunciation Mistakes

The principles for correction of faulty pronunciation are similar to those for correcting grammar mistakes. At the early single word drilling phase, errors should be corrected immediately by the teacher modeling the correct form and the student imitating. If he cannot imitate, then the teacher must resort to the strategies discussed below.

In conversational exchanges, errors on the particular teaching point should be corrected as well as items which interfere with comprehensibility. Other mistakes should be overlooked. For prepared and recorded speeches and presentations, the same guidelines apply as when correcting free compositions, i.e., judge content and form separately. It is important to find a middle way between correcting so much that the student becomes frustrated and

discouraged and so little that he is at a disadvantage in confronting
native speakers outside the classroom.

Strategies for Correcting

There are three basic ways to get students to achieve a decent
pronunciation if imitation is not sufficient: (1) by giving linguistic
description, (2) by comparing the sound to one in the native
language and (3) by modification of another English sound.

Giving linguistic information should not deteriorate into long
linguistic lectures, but brief explanations (a minute or so) are very
helpful in making students understand what they are doing wrong. It
is especially helpful to contrast or compare the target sound with
sounds in the students' native language. There are three ways of
giving linguistic information: (1) by diagrams of the vocal organs, (2)
by phonetic description and (3) by demonstrating.

Diagrams like this one are fairly easy to learn to draw on the
board:

The tongue may be left out of the drawing, and the teacher instead
uses his hand in side view to demonstrate the position of the tongue.
The difference between a dental /t/ and an alveolar /t/ is quickly
demonstrated in this way. The visual demonstration should be
accompanied by an oral modeling of the two sounds so that the
students can discriminate between the two. Using diagrams should
also be accompanied by a linguistic description which points out the
salient feature of the position of the tongue, in this example the
difference between pronouncing a /t/ with the tongue right behind
the teeth or touching the gum ridge. There is no need to use terms
like *dental* and *alveolar*.

Linguistic descriptions should be very simple. A Spanish
speaker's difficulty with /ð/ in *th*ose can be dealt with either by
pointing out that it is the same sound as /θ/ in *th*in but voiced (all
students should have been taught about voicing very early in the
course) or that it is an allophonic intervocalic variant of /d/ in
Spanish. The teacher simply says "It is the same sound you have in

lado. Say *lado* and see what the sounds feel like. Now try it with *those."* Or with a German speaker who is having trouble with /č/ in *ch*in, all the teacher needs do is to write /t/ + lieb*ch*en on the blackboard and explain that the sound is a combination of /t/ plus the sound the student has in lieb*ch*en to have instant success.

Demonstration works well with some sounds. The teacher can exaggerate initial aspirated stops by blowing forcefully after /t/ in *tin, pin,* etc. He can light a match and blow it out with the aspirated /p/ in contrast to the steady burning when he pronounces an unaspirated /p/. He can (delicately) stick his tongue out with the interdental /ð/ *thin* and insist he also see the students' tongues when they practice. For /æ/ in *ash,* the teacher can say, "Look, first you open your mouth wide and say ahhh. Then you smile with your mouth wide open, /æ æ æ/" while he demonstrates. This is a good place in the lesson for the teacher to ham it up as it reduces tension and makes the students less self-conscious.

In the last corrective exercise, the student was asked to modify a sound in English that he could pronounce correctly. This is often an efficient procedure. One way an English sound can be modified is by holding the point of articulation steady while changing the manner of articulation. A student who has trouble with the /ŋ/ sound in *sing* can be told "Say /k/. Good. Now don't move your tongue at all and try to say /n/." More likely than not he will come up with a passable /ŋ/ sound.

Sometimes the learner's native sound system will lack one member of a minimal set in English. Swedish has /s/ but not /z/, Spanish has /f/ but not /v/ as phonemes. The difference between these in English is one of voicing, so the students can do exercises which emphasize this distinction. The teacher has them say alternately /sssssssss/zzzzzzzzz/sssssssss/ with their hands on their throats to help them feel the difference. In addition, the Spanish speaker needs linguistic information about the difference between /b/ and /v/ as he has one sound for both letters in his mother tongue and frequently confuses them in English. Once, one of our students, a six foot Paraguayan, came into our office to commiserate that he had such trouble with his bowels and that he needed help. It was an awful moment until we realized that he wanted help with his pronunciation of vowels.

One useful practice for students who have difficulty with their vowels is Pike's "bracketing" exercises:

First the front vowel is pronounced, then the back vowel, and then the student attempts to pronounce a variety in between the two. This is especially effective if the student is mimicking the instructor.[36]

The bracketing may of course be one of high-low as well as of front-back vowels. The students practice first with familiar sounds on either "side" of the difficult new sound. Students who have successfully learnt /u/ in *cooed* and /o/ in *code* and now have trouble with /ʊ/ in *could* may be taken through bracketing exercises. First the teacher models and the students repeat /u-o-u-o/ several times. The teacher tells them to try to pronounce a sound in between the two, he continues to model /u-ʊ-o/, and the students to repeat. As soon as the students can do the exercise successfully, they should proceed to exercises on words, phrases and sentences as described above.

Another trouble spot for many students is the consonant clusters in English. Most students will need systematic practice on consonant clusters in all positions—beginning, medial and final. Robinett suggests a procedure for students who have great difficulty with practice on consonant clusters. She gives the example of *washed* /št/ which is difficult for some learners. She suggests practicing first with the sounds spread over two words *wash two cups* and then to proceed to a vowel following the cluster *washed a cup* since the students can then pronounce the second consonant as if it were the beginning of a new syllable *wash-ta-cup*. The exercises then proceed to practice with adjacent consonants: *washed fifteen cups.*[37]

And finally, this chapter closes with a list of possible remedies for particular trouble spots. The list was prepared by Carol Levenson, an instructor in the Institute, for one of our teacher training courses, and it is a very helpful demonstration of how to go about dealing with problems in pronouncing the English language.

Description of Common Problems and Suggested Correction Techniques

1. school   /eskul/
   Problem: /e/ added before /sk..../ [or /s/ + consonant (C)]

---

[36] Kenneth Pike, *Phonemics* (Ann Arbor: The University of Michigan Press, 1947), p. 16.

[37] Betty Wallace Robinett, "Simple Classroom Techniques for Teaching Pronunciation," in Croft, ed., *Readings on English as a Second Language* (Cambridge, Massachusetts: Winthrop Publishers, 1972), p. 85.

Reason: /sC/ occurs word initially in English, but not in Spanish, since when /sC/ is found in Spanish, the /s/ ends a syllable and the following consonant begins the next. The Spanish speaker will tend to make a vowel sound before /s/ to make it a complete syllable.

Solution: Have the student practice words with /sC/ in initial position, telling him to lengthen the /s/.

Example: school
sports
store
sleep

Then have him repeat short sentences containing the words, making sure that the words are not preceded by a vowel sound in the sentence.

Example: Our school has good sports teams.
Smoke filled the burning store.

2. hiccough /hikɔp/

Problems: 1./i/ instead of /ɪ/
2./ɔ/ instead of /ə/

Reason: Student may not have the /ɪ/ and /ə/ sounds in his language or not in the same environments. In problem 2 the student may be transferring the vowel sound from "cough," if he is mispronouncing the word while reading it. Show him a picture of a cup. If he pronounces it /kɔp/, then the first reason is involved.

Solution 1: To help the student produce the /ɪ/, tell him to to relax his mouth, dropping the tongue slightly. As he gradually relaxes, stop him when he has hit upon the sound and have him repeat it in several words (example: hick, bit, pick).

Minimal pairs: Pete Pitt
beat bit
leak lick

Sentences: Give me a little bit.
                         Pitt is a big school.

Solution 2:   Go through the general procedures,
                         having the student make the /ə/ by
                         asking him to pretend he is lifting
                         something heavy and to make the noise
                         that accompanies the action. If another
                         sound comes out, try a physiological
                         description (tongue central, etc.).
                         Have him practice the sound in a list
                         of words (example: cup, but, cut, luck).
                         Minimal pairs: caught   cut
                                                 brought   but
                                                 Maud   mud
                                                 naughty   nutty

Sentences: Don't run in the mud.
                         The duck had fun in the tub.

3. hit   /hi:t/
     Problem: /i:/ instead of /ɪ/
     Reason: /ɪ/ not present in language or not
                         found in this environment.
     Solution: Basically that for /i/ and /ɪ/.Tell the
                         student to try to pronounce "hit" as
                         many times as he can in a second or two
                         (see 2, Solution 1).

4. fried rice   /flaɪd laɪs/
     Problem: /l/ instead of /r/
     Reason: Student's language does not have
                         contrast between /l/ and /r/ or there
                         is no /r/ sound and /l/ is closest.

     Solution: Follow general procedures. Tell or show
                         student that the sides of the tongue
                         should touch the bottom of the upper
                         molars. Have him practice /r/ in various
                         postions in the word (first initially,
                         then intervocally), but before having
                         him attempt combinations such as "fr"
                         and "br" have him make a small vowel
                         sound /ə/ between the consonants

(fəraɪd), then gradually bring the
consonants together by faster repetition
of the word.

Minimal pairs: lay   ray
                 play   pray
                 teller   terror

Sentences: Roger is really very rich.
Are there rats and roaches
in your apartment?

5. Shibboleth   /sibole ð/
   Problems: 1. /s/ instead of /š/
                  2. /i/ instead of /ɪ/
                  3. /ð/ instead of /θ/

Reason 1:   Student may not have /š/, or at least
not in initial position, or may not have
distinction between /s/ and /š/.

Solution 1:   Follow general procedures. Show student
how to make sound by having him say /s/
then raising the tip of his tongue onto
the ridge above and behind the teeth.
Have him practice the /š/ alone
(example: shore, shake, trash, etc.).

Minimal pairs: same   shame
                    sore   shore
                    save   shave

Sentences: Should I shop or go see a
show?
Are you sure she'll come?

Reason 2:   See 2, Solution 1.
Solution 2:   See 2, Solution 1.
Reason 3:   Student's language may have /ð/ without
its voiceless counterpart (Latin-
American Spanish), or /θ/ not found in
final position.

Solution 3:   Follow general procedures. Have student
learn to produce sound by putting his
tongue between his teeth and blowing
out (this should prevent voicing).
Give him practice with words such as

with
math
teeth
tooth
faith

Minimal pairs:
teethe	teeth
either	ether
mouth (v)	mouth (n)

Sentences: The baby is teething.
His teeth bother him.
I don't take math either.

6. running

/r ə nin/

Problem: /n/ instead of /ŋ/

Reason: Student either doesn't have /ŋ/ sound or else /ŋ/ does not appear in final position.

Solution: Follow general procedures. If the student is a Spanish speaker you can try asking him to say *ingles* several times, each time taking a sound off the end. After /s/, /e/ and /l/ have been dropped, he is left with *ing.* Have him repeat the sound, then add an initial sound (*ring, sing*), then add a syllable (*boring, racing*). Practice sound in *-ing* words.

Minimal pairs:
taken	taking
sit-in	sitting
be-in	being

Sentences: Gene's playing ping pong in the canteen.
This building has built-in air conditioning.

7. noise

/n ɔ ɪs/

Problem: /s/ instead of /z/

Reason: Student may not have a /z/ phoneme. /z/ may be an allophone of /s/ but not in final position. His language may have a tendency to unvoice all final consonants.

Solution: Follow general procedures. If student has a /z/ allophone, have him pronounce a

word in his language with the /z/ sound
(e.g., Spanish *mismo*). Have him put
his hands over his ears while he says
it to sense the buzzing caused by the
voicing or have him put his finger to
his throat to feel for the movement of
the vocal cords. Have him repeat English
words similar to his words while he
senses the voicing (words should have
/z/ finally: e.g., *ease, he's, keys*).
Perhaps the same procedure used in 6 can
help (take away /o/, then /m/.

Minimal pairs:

fuss	fuzz
dense	dens
dance	Dan's
ace	A's
pace	pays

Sentences: Sentences with *has* not
followed by *to.*
Sentences with *was* not
followed by *to.*
Sentences with *is* not
followed by *to.*

8. this thing

/dis tiŋ/
/zis siŋ/

Problem:

1. /d/ instead of /ð/
2. /t/ instead of /θ/
3. /z/ instead of /ð/
4. /s/ instead of /θ/

Reason:

Student does not have interdentals in
language, or at least not in word initial
position.

Solution:

Follow general procedures. Have students
put tongues between teeth, voice as they
did for /d/ and /z/ which should give
/ð/, and blow out (unvoice) for /θ/.
Have them practice many words with /ð/
and /θ/.

minimal pairs:

den	then	tin	thin
dough	though	tank	thank
dine	thine	taught	thought

dee	thee	torn	thorn
		tick	thick

zen	then	sing	thing
see	thee	sink	think
sign	thine	sin	thin
		sank	thank
		sick	thick
		some	thumb

Sentences: This is something new.
I think I should thank that man.
Then we thought of another thing to do.

9. vanish   /bænɪš/
   Problem: /b/ instead of /v/
   Reason: Student doesn't have /v/ sound, or at least not in initial position (when he sees v in initial position he pronounces it /b/ like Spanish)
   Solution: Follow general procedures. Have student place his upper teeth on lower lip and voice.

Minimal pairs:

ban	van
beer	veer
berry	very
buy	vie
bet	vet
best	vest
boat	vote

Sentences: Vince is a Vietnam veteran.
Vote for the very best one.

10. honest   /hanɪst/
    Problem: /h/ instead of no sound. This may be a problem of generalizing that the *h* is pronounced at the beginning in all cases. The problem is one of sound-spelling correspondence.

11. hot   /hɔt/
    Problem: /ɔ/ instead of /a/
    Reason: Student may have /a/ phoneme, but it is not represented by o (if reading) or there may not be a phonemic difference between the sounds in his language.
    Solution: Follow general procedures. Have student pronounce list of words in which o is pronounced /a/ (cop, lot, socks, etc.).

Minimal pairs:

caught	cot
taught	tot
naughty	knotty

Sentences: There are a lot of cops in the mob.
I bought lots of pots and pans.

12. hat   /hat/
    Problem: /a/ instead of /æ/
    Reason: Student may not have /æ/ in his language, and /a/ is the closest. If reading, may make a correspondence between written a and /a/, since that is the correspondence in his language.
    Solution: Follow general procedures. Have a student aim for the sound between /a/ and /ɛ/, gradually moving his tongue and mouth muscles. When he hits on the sound, give him lots of words to practice, (cat, fat, back, lab, etc.).

Minimal pairs:

cot	cat
rot	rat
rock	rack
mod	mad

13. coat   /kɔt/
    Problem: /ɔ/ instead of /o/
    Reason: Student may not have /o/ phoneme, or there may be no contrast in his language between /ɔ/ and /o/.

Solution: Follow general procedures. Tell student
              to move gradually from the /ɔ/ position
              to /ʊ/, rounding his lips, and stop him
              when he gets the /o/. Give practice
              on the sound (home, phone, cope, note,
              etc.).

Minimal pairs: laud   load
                 caught   coat
                 bought   boat
                 naught   note

Sentences: My home phone number is
              HO 4-5600.
              She bought a coat for cold
              weather.

14. gate   /get/
    Problem: /e/ instead of /eⁱ/
    Reason: Student may not have /eⁱ/ in his language.
    Solution: Follow general procedures. If student
                 has /i/ in his language you can get him to
                 pronounce /e/ + /i/ very quickly together
                 to make the sound in *gate*. (Practice—
                 take, late, paid, make, etc.)

    Minimal pairs: met   mate
                     pen   pain
                     led   laid
                     let   late

    Sentences: I made a cake today.
                  He paid a late fee.

4

Listening
Comprehension

Introduction

Comprehending the spoken form of the target language is one of the most difficult tasks for the language learner, yet it is probably the most neglected skill in second language teaching. This neglect stems of course from the objectives of much language teaching in situations where the students are not likely to be exposed to native speakers, but the neglect is probably most of all due to our ignorance about the nature of the process of listening comprehension. The lack of knowledge on a theoretical level influences our knowledge of what and how to teach our students to comprehend the spoken language. The field of reading instruction, for instance, has profited greatly from recent work in psycholinguistics; there is no corresponding body of knowledge for listening comprehension. A literature on the subject does exist, and Rivers summarizes some of it;[1] but the

---

[1] Wilga Rivers, "Linguistic and Psychological Factors in Speech Perception and Their Implications for Teaching Materials," in Pimsleur & Quinn, eds.,

practical implications for language teaching are far from clear to us, and in this chapter we have preferred to approach the teaching of listening comprehension solely in terms of our own trial and error experience in dealing with our students' difficulties.

In language teaching, listening comprehension used to be thought of as a passive skill. Discussions prior to 1970 rarely consider listening comprehension as a skill to be taught in its own right, separate from pronunciation and grammar, and textbooks typically ignored the subject. Like reading, listening comprehension is no longer regarded as a passive skill:

> "the process of speech recognition is an active interplay of guessing, approximation, expectation, and idealization that normally makes extensive use of all the redundancies found in a typical speech situation, phonological, morphological, syntactic, semantic, as well as many varieties of nonlinguistic redundancies."[2]

If "the goal of listening comprehension is to be able to understand native speech at normal speed in unstructured situations,"[3] then one needs to identify such a range of speech situations as the students are likely to encounter, from formal lectures to casual chats, from face to face encounters to telephone messages and radio and TV presentations, and then systematically present the students with exercises which teach them how to listen and what to listen for in such situations. At the beginning levels, it is enough to expect the students to be able to understand the code of formal classroom style; at later stages they will need information and practice with less formal varieties of the spoken language so that they will understand people outside of the classroom. Advanced students who are going to study in an English speaking environment will need to learn how to listen to lectures and take notes, to comprehend native speakers in all kinds of speech situations, and to understand radio and TV broadcasts.

The Psychology of Second Language Learning (Cambridge: Cambridge University Press, 1971).

[2] William S-Y Wang, "The Basis of Speech," in Carroll E. Reed, *The Learning of Language* (New York: Appleton-Century Crofts, 1971), p. 296.

[3] Kenneth Chastain, *The Development of Modern Language Skills: Theory to Practice* (Philadelphia: CCD, 1971).

GENERAL PRINCIPLES IN TEACHING
LISTENING COMPREHENSION

We have found Morley's guidelines, based on her work in speech perception and on her experience in the classroom, to be eminently sensible for the construction of listening comprehension material. They provide a general set of principles for teaching listening comprehension (LC).

1. Listening comprehension lessons must have *definite goals,* carefully stated. These goals should fit into the overall curriculum, and both teacher and students should be clearly cognizant of what they are.
2. Listening comprehension lessons should be constructed with *careful step by step* planning. This implies, according to Morley, that the listening tasks progress from simple to more complex as the student gains in language proficiency; that the student know exactly what the task is and is given directions as to "*what* to listen for, *where* to listen, *when* to listen, and *how* to listen."
3. LC lesson structure should demand *active overt student participation.* She states that the "most overt student participation involves his written response to the LC material," and that immediate feedback on performance helps keep interest and motivation at high levels.
4. LC lessons should provide a *communicative urgency for remembering* in order to develop *concentration.* This urgency, which along with concentration is a key factor in remembering, should come not from the teacher, but from the lesson itself. This is done by giving the students the writing assignment before they listen to the material. (It serves the same function as the "before" questions in the reading class.)
5. Listening comprehension lessons should stress *conscious memory work.* One of the goals of listening is to strengthen the students' immediate recall in order to increase their memory spans. In Morley's terms "listening is *re*ceiving, receiving requires thinking, and thinking requires memory; there is no way to separate listening, thinking, remembering."

6. Listening comprehension lessons should "teach," not "test." By this, Morley means that the purpose of checking the students' answers should be viewed only as feedback, as a way of letting the students find out how they did and how they are progressing. There should be no pass/fail attitude associated with the correction of the exercises.[4]

PRACTICE IN LISTENING COMPREHENSION

Virtually everything students do in the foreign language classroom involves listening comprehension to some extent, and it seems difficult to know just where to incorporate listening comprehension exercises into the curriculum. The guideline should be the specific teaching point of the activity: exercises on the phonological code (e.g., distinguishing voiced-voiceless pairs as *eyes-ice*) should be done in conjunction with the pronunciation segment of the lesson, as should practice on cognate words which students recognize in their written form but not in their spoken version. Exercises on the grammatical code, such as distinguishing between *he's eaten* and *he's eating,* should be done in conjunction with the grammar segment. We also practice recognizing varieties of speech (the formal-informal distinction) in the grammar class as it is primarily the grammatical patterns which trouble the students, but such practice can equally well be done anywhere in the curriculum.

Many listening comprehension exercises lend themselves particularly well to work in the language laboratory. The students are set a specific task such as answering questions or solving a problem. When they complete their task, they check their own work from an answer key so that they get immediate feedback on how well they have done. As with all work, it is important that the students have some tangible record of how they are performing, and the immediate correction of these exercises gives them an evaluation and record of their performance as well as responsibility for their own progress. If a laboratory is not available, a tape or cassette recorder in a quiet corner of the classroom is excellent for group work, and teachers who are not native speakers of English should especially try to use as

---

[4] H. Joan Morley and Mary S. Lawrence, "The Use of Films in Teaching English as a Second Language," *Language Learning* 22, no. 1 (June 1971): 101-3.

many exercises as possible which have been recorded by native speakers.

Format and Presentation of the Exercise

Typically the format of a listening comprehension exercise consists of a passage of oral language of various types—narration, description, directions, etc.—and a set task for the students to complete as an indicator of the degree of their comprehension. Common tasks are answering questions, solving problems, taking dictation, and even drawing pictures to correspond to the information given.

The steps of a listening comprehension exercise are similar to those of a pronunciation lesson:

1. Selection of the teaching point
2. Focusing of students' attention
3. Listening and completion of set task
4. Feedback on performance

Step 1: Selection of the teaching point

The subsequent list of techniques for specific teaching points will suggest the range of items students need to practice on. The important point to be aware of is that structures and vocabulary be controlled so that exercises are not beyond the students' level of proficiency.

Step 2: Focusing of students' attention

The students must be aware of the purpose of the exercise in general and the nature of the specific task in particular before they listen to the passage. An easy way to alert them to what they are going to do is simply to say: "Today you're going to listen to an exercise which will help you understand native speakers outside the classroom," or "Today you are going to listen to an exercise which will help you to be able to follow a classroom lecture." The students should be given whatever written material is necessary for them to complete their task before they listen to the passage; they should know before they listen whether they are going to answer comprehension questions (and if so what those questions are) or to draw a picture. There should always be an example at the beginning of the exercise to help those who may not have understood the verbal directions.

Step 3: Listening and completion of exercise

If teachers read the material to the class, they must take great care to read with normal speed and intonation. Students always ask teachers to speak or read slower, but such requests must be resisted. Slowing down tends to distort stress and intonation, but most of all it gives the students no practice in understanding normal speech, which after all is the purpose of the exercise.

Rather than slowing down, teachers can play or read the exercise over again. The number of times students need to listen to an exercise depends on the length and difficulty of the exercise, on the nature of the set task, and always on the students' proficiency. If the task can be completed during the listening, and the listening is relatively easy, once is enough. If the students must recall facts in order to answer questions after having listened, they may need to hear the passage more than once. The students themselves are the best judge of how many times they should listen to an exercise. If they have difficulty with a passage, they will want to listen more than once; if they find a passage easy, listening more than once will be very boring, and they should be encouraged to give their opinion freely about the number of times they want to hear a specific exercise.

Step 4: Feedback on performance

The easiest way for students to receive feedback on their performance is to supply them with an answer key and have them correct their own answers. The teacher should regularly check on their progress so that recognition can be given to those who do well and help given to those who are having difficulty.

TECHNIQUES FOR SPECIFIC TEACHING POINTS

Techniques for listening comprehension can be classified according to the various teaching points: (1) exercises on the phonological code, (2) on the grammatical code, (3) on the message at the sentence level, (4) on variations of language style, or (5) on the total meaning of a passage or communication situation. Each point needs to be taught in increasing complexity as the students progress in their learning, i.e., advanced students will still need work with the grammatical and phonological codes, but the structures will be more complex, and beginning students should also be given an introduction to other than formal spoken style. Some exercises, however, such as taking notes from lectures and listening to radio programs, are not feasible with beginning students because they are not proficient enough in English. The following activities have been organized according to teaching points, and the order coincides roughly with increased proficiency.

Decoding Sounds, Stress and Intonation, and Sound-Symbol Correspondence

The aural discrimination exercises discussed in the chapter on pronunciation should be used as models for practicing the segmental phonemes. Our students need further practice with the supraseg-mentals, stress, and intonation, because of their effect on the spoken language as opposed to the written language, which the students may already comprehend.

An important aspect in work on listening comprehension is to teach the students the relationship between the spoken and written forms of the language. Students frequently fail to understand the spoken form of an utterance which they recognize perfectly well in its written form. Morley suggests two exercises, one on vowel reduction and the other on word stress. The students are given a printed set of sentences and are instructed to circle the word containing the reduced vowel or to mark the stressed word as the teacher reads the sentences. The number of items to be marked is in parentheses at the end of each sentence.

Vowel reduction

Example: (Can)(you) come (to)(the) party? (4)
   1. Do you want bacon or eggs? (3)
   2. I would like a sandwich and some French Fries. (4)[5]

Stress

   Example: Someone had closed the door. (3)

   1. It was after midnight when I stopped working. (4)
   2. I started to get ready for bed. (3)[6]

---

[5] Joan Morley, "On Developing Listening Comprehension Lessons and Complementary Activities: Some Practical Methods and Materials for the Classroom" (Paper delivered at Materials Development Conference, University of Toronto, June 1971).

[6] Ibid.

The sentences in these exercises can be based on the structural patterns in the grammar component of the curriculum that the students are learning for production. At more advanced levels, the exercises can be used with dialogue material to teach the students the stress variations in developing conversations (see pages 112-13).

Another kind of listening exercise, which we use in the reading class for vocabulary development, helps the students recognize the sounds of the words they are learning as well as giving them practice in rapid listening. The students have a printed list of a dozen or so new words. The teacher reads the words in random order and the students mark the words 1, 2, 3, etc. in the order they are read.

"Number the following words in the order in which you hear them:

features	intervals	purposes
practice	set	pattern
numerous	impossible	certain[7]

A more difficult exercise requires the students to listen to a whole passage and mark the member of a pair of printed items which they hear. Here is an example from Barnard:

Listen to the passage again. In the following pairs, cross out
the word which is incorrect (following the order of the passage).

(a) country-countries
(c) lighter-light
(g) label-level
(h) Nigeria-a given area
(k) situation-situated[8]

Exercises like this can be used for practice with grammatical structures as well as for different sounds that the students have trouble with.

Decoding Structures

Listening comprehension exercises commonly form part of the grammar class to give students practice in recognition of grammatical elements. (See the examples of discrimination drills in Chapter 1.) At

---

[7] Helen Barnard, *Advanced English Vocabulary, Workbook One* (Rowley, Massachusetts: Newbury House Publishers, 1971), p. 117.

[8] Ibid, p. 133.

the beginning levels, the students listen to same-different drills and to drills which require them to identify grammatical categories of patterns. The following are some other exercises which help direct the students' attention to the grammatical features of the language they hear.

Dictation

Old-fashioned dictation exercises are excellent practice for listening comprehension. Dictation can take two forms, either spot dictation or the dictation of a complete passage. In either case the procedures are essentially the same. First the passage is read (either by the teacher or on tape) at normal speed as the students listen. Then the passage is repeated in "meaningful mouthfuls" with pauses for the students to write. (The meaningful mouthfuls are rather short for beginning students and increase in length as the students' auditory memory increases. The length of the pause is geared to the slower students, so everyone has time to write.) Finally the passage is reread at normal speed so the students can check and if necessary correct their work.

Spot dictations require the students only to fill in the blank spaces of the written passage they have before them and therefore need not be as controlled as complete passage dictation. That is to say, the written passage may contain structures which the students can recognize, but not necessarily produce. Complete dictations should only contain material which the students have previously studied for productive use for which they are excellent review exercises. Here is a sample spot dictation which reviews present continuous and present perfect:

> The local football team is in first place. They (*have beaten*) every other team in their league and now they (*are leading*) in the race for the trophy. The team star (*has given*) a warning to the opposing team: "We (*'re giving*) you one chance to score, but after that we (*'re eating*) you alive." The opponents do not seem afraid, however, and (*are continuing*) their practice sessions.

Morley adds a repetition phase to her listening and dictation exercises so that the sequence is (1) listening, (2) repeating, and (3) writing. The students hear a sentence, repeat it, hear it again, and then write it. They then are instructed to check their answers as they listen for the third time. Each blank that the students fill in has the number of words in parentheses at the end of the blank. For example:

1. _____ (9 words)
The students hear: Did you buy this car or the other car?
2. _____ (6 words)
The students hear: The teachers gave us the directions.[9]

Our students do these exercises as part of their language laboratory program. The teacher puts the answers on the board, and the students check and record their own scores. At the beginning level, each lesson should also be checked by the teacher because students often overlook mistakes, especially when their native language does not use the Latin alphabet.

Barnard uses dictation in another type of exercise which helps the student comprehend grammatical relationships and focus on particular features such as article usage, verb morphology, prepositions, etc. The students listen to a passage and attempt to complete the exercises as follows:

The passage 'The Scarcity of Diamonds' will now be read to you. When you hear the following adjectives, write the articles (if any) which precede them and the nouns which follow them. (a)

(a) _____ any natural _____
(b) _____ special _____
(c) Listen to the passage 'The Scarcity of Diamonds' once more, and write the *uncountable* nouns that you hear.[10]

The students' attention is thus focused on various grammatical aspects of the passage and, as a final step, all the features are recombined in a complete dictation of the same passage.

Exercises for Recoding

The phonological and grammatical exercises presented above are necessary to focus the students' attention on the forms, but they will never become fluent listeners unless they have practice in decoding meaning as well. To help the students to be able to recode what they hear for retention, they are given practice with structures which have similar meanings.

---

[9] Joan Morely, *Listening/Writing: Understanding English Sentence Structure* (Ann Arbor, Michigan: English Language Institute, 1974), p. 13.
[10] Barnard, p. 133.

Exercises like the following are commonly found in grammar tests:

"Circle the sentence which has the same meaning as the one you hear."

T: The man is going to work tomorrow for the first time in months.

Answers:
1. The man hasn't worked for a long time.
2. The man doesn't like to work.
3. The man is going to work for a few months.

Unless the students understand "for the first time in months" they are not likely to choose the correct answer. Such exercises should be done in preparation for taking notes. The next step is to read a passage and have the students write a one sentence summary.

A similar but more difficult exercise requires the students to listen to a passage and then check all the appropriate answers. The specific teaching point of the following exercise is the subordinators (*in spite of, unless, because*). We do not teach all of these for production, but the students must comprehend them when they read or hear them. The teacher reads a short description of a situation and the students check the appropriate answers:

T: Bill is not doing very well in biology, a course he has to pass in order to graduate. His friends want him to go to the movies tonight. He doesn't know if the professor has scheduled an exam for tomorrow. He's going to call a classmate and if there is a test, he can't go—he'll have to stay in and study.

Answers:
1. Bill can go unless he has a test.
2. Bill will go because he doesn't have a test.
3. Bill won't go if he has a test.
4. Bill can go if he doesn't have a test.
5. Bill won't go unless he has a test.

Listening for the Message

In addition to exercises which concentrate on specific aspects of form, students need practice in listening to entire passages where the main purpose is to extract the message rather than to concentrate on specific words or phrases. This is not to say that the exercises do not have discrete teaching points; many of them do, such as the use of prepositions in the first exercise below. The student's attention, however, is focused not on the code, but on the problem to be solved or the questions to be answered by using the information provided by the passage. These exercises are designed to help the students reach the stage of the fluent listener who remembers what has been heard and can use the information to solve problems.

Exercises in listening for the message can be categorized in terms of how much and how long the students must remember the material heard. In the *problem solving* exercises, they work out the problem step by step as they listen and it is completed at the end of the reading. In *answering questions,* the students may take notes or fill in blanks as they listen, but they must also remember some details of what they hear in order to answer questions after the reading. The problem solving activities are often regarded as games by the students, and the others as work. In terms of developing listening skills, the problem solving exercises are excellent for motivating the students, but for overall development of memory, they will need the others as well.

Problem Solving

The grammar teaching point of this exercise from *Listen and Guess* is prepositions. The students listen to the conversation and draw a picture.

A: Good morning, Joe.
J: Good morning, Anna. Anna, today I want you to draw another picture. . . .
A: How many items are there in the picture?
J: There are six items in this picture. . . .
      . . .
A: Is the table in the middle of the picture?
J: Yes, it is. . .
A: And is the chair near the table?
J: Yes, it's very near the table—but it's not in front of the table, and it isn't beside the table. But it's near the table, yes.
A: Is it under the table?
J: No, it isn't under the table.
A: Well, is it *on* the table?
J: Yes, it is. . .[11]

[11]Robert L. Allen and Virginia F. Allen, *Listen and Guess* (Teacher's Manual) (New York: McGraw-Hill, 1965), p. 46-47.

When the students finish, they compare their drawing with the one provided in the teacher's manual.

At more advanced levels, these exercises can be made much more challenging. Here is one from Morley: The students listen to descriptions and fill in the information on the chart.

> Now look at the diagram. Notice that on the left side of the diagram you find *country, field, city* and *hobby.* Notice that across the top of the diagram you find *red house, blue house.* . . . .Listen to each statement. Find the correct square, write the correct word from the list below.
>
> 1. The student from Turkey lives in the middle house. Write *Turkey* in the correct square.
> 2. The student in the field of Engineering lives on the far right. Write *Engineering* in the correct square.
> 13. The student on the far right is going to Boston.[12]

13

	Red House	Blue House	Green House	White House	Purple House
Country			*Turkey*		
Field					*Engineering*
City					*Boston*
Hobby					

As a final step in the exercise, the students are tested on their information by answering questions:

1. Who plays the guitar?
2. Who is going to study in San Francisco?[14]

---

[12]Joan Morley, *Improving Aural Comprehension* — Teacher's Book of Readings. (Ann Arbor: The University of Michigan Press, 1972), p. 76-7.

[13]Joan Morley, *Improving Aural Comprehension* — Student's Workbook. (Ann Arbor: The University of Michigan Press, 1972), p. 137.

[14]Morley, *Improving Aural Comprehension* — Teacher's Book, p. 77.

Answering Questions

As we said above, these exercises require the students to remember some of the information they hear in order to respond correctly to questions following the listening. In all cases, they have read the questions before they listen; the main difference between these exercises is that some require the students to "take notes" by filling in information as they go along, whereas the others require the students just to listen.

Here is one for beginning students. The teaching point is the cardinal and ordinal numbers. The students fill in the blanks as they listen and the comprehension question is based on the information they have filled in.

Tape: *Cardinal Numbers*   *Ordinal Numbers*

Example: She is _16_ years old.   Example: It is the _25th_ of May.

1. The coat cost _____ dollars.   1. California is the _____ largest state.

2. John bought _____ new ties.   2. Alaska was the _____ state.[15]

Then the students turn the page, listen to a comprehension question such as "How much did the coat cost?", return to their answers if necessary and write the short answer (*50* dollars or whatever was said on the tape.)

In the following less controlled exercise, the student listens to an extended passage, takes notes by filling in the set of questions and then answers a cumulative question (number 11). In order to answer the questions, the student must remember two or more sentences in some cases and synthesize the information heard.

(1) *Introduction*

"You will hear a short reading titled "U.S. Geography: Some Contrasts Past and Present." Answer the questions as you listen. Some are very simple questions; some are more complicated questions. Notice the way adjectives are used in giving the contrastive information. Also notice the use of the chronological signals: "original," "recent," "used to be," "but now."

(2) *Your Task*

Listen: Answer the questions. Also make a list of the adjective-noun phrases used in giving the information (question #11 below).

---

[15]Morley, *Improving Aural Comprehension* — Student's Workbook, p. 3

QUESTIONS

1. How many states are there in the United States? _____
2. How many were original states? _____
3. Why are they called "the original" states? _____
6. Alaska is bigger than Texas. Give the size comparison.
   "Alaska is _____ _____ _____ _____Texas."
9. What are the highest and lowest altitudes to be found in the
   United States and in which state is each located?

   highest _____ _____ ____

                 number of feet   name of place   state

   lowest _____ _____ ____

                 number of feet   name of place   state
   below sea level
11. List as many of the adjective noun phrases as you can remember.
   Example: "oldest state"

[16]

In the spoken passage, the order of information for question 9 is from right to left, i.e., the state is given first, then the height and then the name of the place, adding to the difficulty of answering the question.

In the second type of question answering exercise, the students listen to short passages and then answer comprehension questions on the whole passage. At beginning levels, simple conversations work very well. The students listen and then answer questions as the teacher poses them:

Inspector Robert Jones is a detective.
He lives near a library.
Inspector Jones is in the library now.
He is talking to Miss Green.
Miss Green is the librarian.

Inspector Jones:	Good morning, Miss Green.
Miss Green:	Good morning, Inspector.
	Can I help you?
Inspector Jones:	Yes, you can.
	I'm looking for a good book.
Miss Green:	This is a good book, Inspector.
Inspector Jones:	What is it?
Miss Green:	It's a detective story.

---

[16]Morley, "On Developing Listening Comprehension Lessons."

Inspector Jones:	Good! I like detective stories.
	What's the murderer's name?
Miss Green:	I can't tell you that, Inspector.
	I'm a librarian.
	I'm not a detective.[17]

The questions provided with this passage are all information questions which can be answered directly from the passage, such as "Is Robert Jones a detective?" "Can Miss Green tell him the name of the detective?" etc.

Students above the beginning levels need experience with exercises on a variety of topics. We use exercises with passages selected from local papers, magazines, radio editorials, i.e., materials written for native speakers. The students listen to the passage and then answer multiple choice or true-false questions. Here is an exercise by Francis:

FROM: The *Pittsburgh Press,* May 27, 1973
Innocent Bystanders

In 1964 a young lady named Kitty Genovese was assaulted and murdered outside her apartment in Queens, a borough of New York City. What differentiated her murder from most others was that several of her neighbors saw or heard the crime. They did nothing about it because they didn't want to get involved.

As a result of the Genovese murder, psychologists began studying what they call the "bystander effect." This is a form of social behavior which holds that individual bystanders are more reluctant to help in dangerous situations if they are surrounded by other non-responsive onlookers. There is safety in numbers when the numbers are inclined to do nothing.

Individuals are more inclined to help out in dangerous situations when they are alone.

Peter Levy associates at the University of Illinois, writing in a recent issue of the "Journal of Personality and Social Psychology," reveal, as a result of their controlled experiments, that the more one is surrounded by passive bystanders, the less likely he is to get involved in any situation, safe or dangerous. In short, to avoid involvement, the best tactic is to disappear into the faceless crowd. It provides maximum social and psychological protection.

---

[17]L. G. Alexander, *Question and Answer: Graded Oral Comprehension Exercises* (London: Longmans, 1967), p. 10.

Instructions:
You will hear the passage once. Then turn to your answer sheet. You will see a series of statements referring to the passage. Decide whether each statement is true or false. Indicate your answer by encircling the correct response.

1. Kitty Genovese's murder was different from others because several people witnessed it without doing anything.

   A. True
   B. False

2. Her neighbors did nothing about it because they didn't want any complications.

   A. True
   B. False

3. What psychologists call the "bystander effect" means that individuals are never willing to help out.

   A. True
   B. False

4. People are less inclined to help out when they are alone.

   A. True
   B. False

5. Individuals may avoid involvement in a situation by disappearing into a crowd.

   A. True
   B. False[18]

Teaching Variations of Style

Students are normally taught the fairly formal English of the classroom and textbooks, which makes it difficult for them to understand the informal English they run into in the street. Students who live in an English speaking environment need practice with understanding informal English although they should not be taught it for production. Only very advanced students (who have no trouble

---

[18]Gladys Francis, "Listening Comprehension Materials," (Pittsburgh: University of Pittsburgh, English Language Institute, 1973). The reading passage is taken from the *Pittsburgh Press,* May 27, 1973.

with listening comprehension) are proficient enough to keep the styles separate in their production. But our students always complain that they have trouble understanding people outside of the classroom, and they need help in sorting out the characteristics of informal style which contribute to their difficulty.

We use dialogues to this purpose. The teacher introduces the dialogues by asking the students if they speak—in their own language—in the same way to their teachers, parents, and friends. They don't, of course, as they are well aware, and the class briefly discusses the variables (speakers, situation, content, mood, channel, etc.) which affect the choice of speech style. Then the teacher reads the dialogues at natural speed with all the ellisions and contractions:

A. Variations on a Theme #1.

Last weekend, Bill went to see a very popular movie, starring one of his favorite actors and a beautiful young actress. He's discussing it with Nancy.

Nancy: Hey, Bill. What did you do over the weekend?
Bill: Saw the new flick with Peck and Welch.
Nancy: Oh, yeah? How was it?
Bill: Peck was great as usual, and well, you don't go to see great acting from Raquel.
Nancy: Know what you mean. All the guys go to watch Raquel. For me Peck is the drawing card. Gotta go to class— see you later.
Bill: So long.

On the way home on the bus, Bill sits next to a lady who lives down the street. She is a good friend of Bill's parents.

Mrs. Cassetti: Did you have a pleasant weekend, Bill?
Bill: Yes, thank you. I studied quite a bit, but Saturday I took the evening off and went to the new movie with Gregory Peck and Raquel Welch.
Mrs. Cassetti: Oh, did you? Did you enjoy it?
Bill: Gregory Peck was very good—he always is. Raquel isn't expected to be a great actress, I guess.
Mrs. Cassetti: Yes, I suppose you're right. All of the young men certainly seem to enjoy her movies. From my point of view Gregory Peck would be the reason for going. I have to get off here. It was nice to see you, Bill.
Bill: It was nice talking to you. Goodbye, Mrs. Cassetti. [19]

---

[19] Mary Newton Bruder, *MMC — Developing Communicative Competence in English as a Second Language* (Pittsburgh: University of Pittsburgh, Center for International Studies, 1973), p. 173-4.

The students do not look at the dialogue as the teacher reads the first time, contrary to the procedures for using dialogues to introduce grammatical structures when they do follow the reading in their text. What we are after is the shock value of not comprehending the first dialogue at all and the second version almost completely. The students then receive copies of the dialogue and read silently as the teacher repeats the reading.

The teacher then writes *sound, grammar,* and *vocabulary* on the board, elicits from the students how the dialogues differ in these categories and writes the differing items under each heading. Such discussions serve to make the students sensitive to style differences and facilitate their comprehension of informal English. The students later listen to the same dialogues in the language laboratory.

Total Meaning of a Passage: Listening to Lectures and Taking Notes

Students like ours, who plan on attending universities where English is spoken, need specialized listening skills. They must be able to understand long lectures and to take notes and make summaries from such lectures.

Stage I. Our students follow a series of lectures which are arranged so that the students are given a steadily decreasing amount of information about the lecture as their note-taking skills increase. At Stage I the students are introduced to basic considerations of note-taking and given a list of common symbols (& = *and*; ∴ = *therefore*; → = *becomes*) and abbreviations (e.g.; i.e.). They are also given lists of the common rhetorical devices and expressions which speakers use in organizing their lectures.

NOTE-TAKING CUES

Besides having to write rapidly, you must know how to determine what is important and should be written down in your notes, and what is not important or redundant and can be left out. Certain words and phrases can signal you that the lecturer is introducing ideas or emphasizing a specific point. For example, to let you know that there are several important points, the lecturer may say, "First, ... Second, ... ," and so on.

Here is a list of words and phrases that signal different ideas. Study them so that when you hear them you can recognize their importance and function.

Introduction of an Idea

Numerical Statements

$$\text{There} \begin{cases} \text{are} \\ \text{were} \end{cases} \begin{cases} \text{two} \\ \text{several} \\ \text{many} \\ \text{numerous} \end{cases} \begin{cases} \text{causes} \\ \text{results} \\ \text{reasons} \\ \text{consequences} \dots \end{cases}$$

Introductory Statements

$$\text{First, I want to} \begin{cases} \text{explain} \\ \text{talk} \\ \text{describe} \dots \end{cases}$$

$$\text{The} \begin{cases} \text{idea} \\ \text{topic} \\ \text{subject that I intend to} \\ \text{theory} \end{cases} \begin{cases} \text{discuss} \\ \text{define} \\ \text{describe} \\ \text{talk about} \end{cases} \text{is} \begin{cases} \text{important} \\ \text{of interest} \\ \text{useful} \\ \text{significant} \end{cases}$$

Rhetorical Questions

(Rhetorical questions are merely statements in the form of a question. No answer is expected to the question; instead, it is used often as a way of introducing a topic to be discussed.)

Why is a demand curve downward sloping?

What caused the fall of the Roman Empire?

Development of an Idea

$$\text{In the} \begin{cases} \text{first} \\ \text{second} \\ \text{third} \end{cases} \text{place} \dots \quad \text{A further} \begin{cases} \text{cause} \\ \text{reason} \\ \text{explanation} \end{cases} \text{is} \dots . \quad \text{Another}$$

Contrast of Several Ideas

Although. .... Even if. .... However. .... Unless ... Whenever ....

Purpose or Result

In order that. . . .
As a result of. . . .
Therefore. . . .

Transition of Ideas

Let us
$\left\{\begin{array}{l}\text{look at}\\ \text{consider}\\ \text{think about}\\ \text{turn to. . . .}\end{array}\right.$

If
$\left\{\begin{array}{l}\text{these facts}\\ \text{what we have discussed}\\ \text{these ideas}\\ \text{our hypothesis}\end{array}\right.$
is
are
$\left\{\begin{array}{l}\text{true}\\ \text{plausible}\\ \text{correct}\\ \text{verifiable}\end{array}\right.$
then. . . .

Transition words

Consequently. . . . For this reason. . . . Nevertheless. . . .

Chronology of Ideas

First. . .	Afterward. . .	Prior to. . .
Another. . .	Finally. . .	Again. . .
In the beginning. . .	Subsequently. . .	The next. . .
Before. . .	At last. . .	Following. . .

Emphasis of Ideas

Let me say again. . . .
This is important because. . . .
was

Summary of Ideas

To conclude. . .
In summary, let me say. . .
Let us review what we have discussed.
The reasons stated before are. . .
As we have seen. . .[20]

---

[20]Megan Trow-Madigan, "Developing Listening Comprehension: Model Exercises to Develop Note-taking Skills," (Pittsburgh: University of Pittsburgh: English Language Institute, 1974, ms.)

The teacher then introduces the topic of the lecture and hands out a list of important vocabulary items, some with their glosses and others without:

VOCABULARY WORDS FOR "HOUSING AND THE ELDERLY
IN PITTSBURGH"

The following words are given and defined by the lecturer in the context of the lecture:

> generation gap
> ancillary
> mates
> digress
> status
> pioneer program
> liaison
> Food Stamp Program
> hair technicians

The following words are used by the lecturer but are not defined:

> *Urban Redevelopment Authority* —a government agency that is in charge of building new roads, houses, and public facilities, especially in areas that are old or poor in a city
> *to tear down a home* —to destroy or demolish a house in order to build something else in its place
> *components*—parts, as in "there are three components to the program for aiding the elderly"
> *janitorial services* —the work performed by a person who cleans or maintains a public building
> *arthritis* –a painful condition of the joints in the body; it often occurs in the fingers or elbows when a person becomes older
> *fall foliage* —the leaves on the trees during autumn are brightly colored yellow, red, and brown, and are no longer green
> *bingo* –a popular game played by groups of people in which cards containing letters and numbers are completed horizontally, vertically, or diagonally when the numbers are called out by a person in charge of the game

The students are also given a detailed outline of the lecture they are about to hear. These handouts are best given a day before the lecture so the students can study the vocabulary and outlines at home without wasting valuable class time.

HOUSING AND THE ELDERLY IN PITTSBURGH

I. Problems of old people in Pittsburgh
  A. Not enough public housing
    1. 5000 on waiting list
    2. Some sleep in parks
  B. Loneliness
  C. Generation Gap
    1. Everyone over 62 years of age is put into the same category
    2. People who are 62 have different problems than people who are 92
  D. Losses suffered by old people
    1. Physical health
    2. Income
    3. Mates: husband or wife
    4. Homes, due to urban redevelopment
    5. Status
    6. Interest in life around them

II. Three part ancillary (supportive) program to aid old people
  A. Social Services
    1. Help elderly with governmental agencies
      a. Food Stamp Program
      b. Social Security Administration
    2. Help elderly with transportation and appointments at medical clinics
  B. Homemaker Services
    1. Help elderly who are unable to care for themselves or their apartments
      a. Scrub floors, wash windows
      b. Personal care: bathing, washing hair
    2. Try to keep the aged physically, psychologically, and socially independent as long as possible and out of public institutions
  C. Volunteer component
    1. The "fun" part of the ancillary program

2. Tries to entertain the aged by trips, tours
   a. Flower show
   b. Aviary to see the birds
   c. Fall foliage
3. Movies
4. Bingo
5. Beauty academies send students to style hair
6. Immunizations against influenza ("flu" shots)[21]

The next step is the lecture itself. Following the lecture, the students discuss any questions with the speaker. Once the students have gained some expertise in listening to lectures and taking notes, we try to bring guest speakers into the classroom, partially for variety, but primarily to accustom the students to various manners of speaking.

Stage II is done in the laboratory, where the students listen to a second lecture on the same topic. The students have before them a vocabulary list, a less detailed outline, and a set of comprehension questions to be answered after listening to the tape. They are instructed to read the questions before the lecture so as to focus their listening on specific points of information.

Stage II. The students are given an outline with the basic points and blanks which they fill in as they listen to the lecture. They then answer comprehension questions on the basis of the notes they have taken:

PURE AND APPLIED SCIENCE

I. Science
   A. General definition of science _____
          _____
          _____
   B. Shortcomings of the definition—Doesn't distinguish between pure (theoretical) science and applied science (technology).
II. Pure science
   A. Definition—development of theories or models which explain relationships among different phenomena.
   B. Examples
      1. _____
         _____

---

[21]Ibid.

2. _____

_____

III. Applied science
  A. Definition—the application of the working laws or principles of pure science to the practical affairs of life and to the increase of people's control over their environment.
  B. Examples
    1. _____
    2. _____
    3. _____
IV. Relationship between pure and applied science
  A. Applied science is practical extension of pure science such as in:
    1. Theoretical investigation of radioactivity applied to cancer treatment.
    2. _____
    3. _____
    4. _____
  B. Applied science stimulates pure research such as when the applied scientist discovers _____

_____

_____

_____

Answer each of the following questions in complete sentences.
1. What is the definition of *science* contained in this selection?
2. According to the author of this lecture, what is the difference between pure and applied science?
3. Give at least one example of pure scientific research contained in this lecture.
4. Give at least one example of applied science or technology contained in the lecture.
5. Briefly explain the relationship between pure and applied science as it is described in this selection.
6. Give an example of how pure scientific research is applied to practical problems in your own field of study.[22]

---

[22]Gary Esarey, Patricia Furey, John Hoover, Judy Kettering, Howard Selekman, "Exercises for the Intermediate ESL Curriculum" (Pittsburgh: University of Pittsburgh, English Language Institute, 1974 ms.)

Stage III. The students have a "bare" outline and a set of comprehension questions to focus their listening. They fill in the outline with notes and then answer the questions.

NOTE-TAKING EXERCISE

  I. Middle Class
      A. Nineteenth Century
      B. Present Day
  II. Working Class
 III. Upper Class

NOTE-TAKING EXERCISE QUIZ

1. What is the main idea of the passage? Where is it expressed?
2. What economic unit now dominates the economy?
3. What fraction (½, ¾, etc.) of the present day labor force is the "new middle class?"
4. What has happened to unskilled labor?
5. What per cent of the labor force belongs to the upper class group?
6. *Briefly* explain what changes have occurred in the middle class over the past 100 years.[23]

Stage IV. The students have the major headings of the outline but must take their own complete set of notes and then answer questions.

NOTE-TAKING EXERCISE

Hurricanes—Vocabulary

1. *latitudes*—regions defined by their distance north or south of the equator
2. *disaster*—any happening that causes great harm or damage
3. *evaporate*—to change from a liquid or solid into vapor
4. *condense*—to make more dense or compact; reduce the volume
5. *clockwise*—in the direction in which the hands of a clock rotate
6. *counterclockwise*—in a direction opposite to that in which the hands of a clock move.

Outline of Basic Points

Do not write on this paper. This outline is just to give you an idea of what to listen for. Write down as much as you possibly can during the passage.

---

[23]Ibid.

I. Location where hurricanes are born
II. Types of weather conditions formed in the area
III. Description of a hurricane
   A. Definition
   B. Eye
   C. Facts

Questions

1. In what three months are most of the hurricanes formed?
2. Describe briefly how a hurricane is formed.
3. What is the "eye" of the hurricane?
4. Give two reasons why the area in the North Atlantic latitudes just above the equator used to be a disaster area.
5. Can hurricanes last for more than a few hours? If so, how long? [24]

Stage V. The students have only the comprehension questions which they answer after listening and taking notes at their own discretion.

Stage VI. The lectures up to this stage have been relatively short, around 10 minutes in length. Stage VI lectures are from 50 minutes to an hour and should be in the student's academic field. We have a series of lectures for the laboratory with study guides and comprehension questions, but listening for that long to a disembodied voice is difficult. We use such lectures only with students who are unable to attend an academic class in their own field.

Most of our students at the advanced intermediate levels do attend academic classes, and their class notes are checked periodically by the English teachers. By the time the students have successfully completed stage VI, they are sufficiently prepared in listening comprehension to follow academic classes.

SOURCES AND USES OF NATURAL MATERIALS FOR LISTENING

Listening materials for students learning to cope in an English speaking environment should consist of samples of natural language from as many different sources as possible, so the students will have experience with many varieties of topics, situations, and speakers.

---

[24]Ibid.

Radio and TV are excellent sources, but the teacher can also collect samples of conversations with a cassette or portable tape recorder.

Snatches of conversation can be put to good use in training the students for standardized listening comprehension tests.

Woman: I wonder if Eleanor Lee is still working in the shoe factory.
Man: I thought I'd told you. She's a cashier in that new coffee shop, the one across from the bus station, her brother says. I was talking with him in the post office yesterday. He works there you know.

Third Voice: Where is Eleanor Lee working now? Circle the right answer.
Student's Answer Sheet:
        A: In a bus station
        B: In a coffee shop
        C: In a post office
        D: In a factory. [25]

The following exercise requires certain cultural information:

Woman: Dear, I'm hungry. Aren't you?
Man: Yes, come to think of it I am. (Lifting of telephone and dialing) Room service? Please send a menu to 320 right away.
Question: Where is the couple?

The exercises are contrived ones, but this kind of problem can be worked out for the conversations captured on the tape recorder.

Live demonstrations of various types can be recorded, especially if they are the type which have "audience participation." Morley's exercise on "How to Run a Film Projector" is a five minute demonstration with one person doing the explanation and listeners who interrupt to ask questions and get clarification on certain points. The student listens and writes down the steps in the presentation and is asked questions about the number of voices, the domination by one or more questioners, etc. [26]

The teacher should check with local radio and TV networks regarding the policy for use of broadcast materials in classes.

---

[25]Virginia F. Allen, "Listening and Reading" (Paper read at the 1966 NAFSA Conference), p. 5.
[26]Morley, "On Developing Listening Comprehension Lessons."

Permission is usually given on a limited basis for certain types of material, such as editorials, and in this way many listening-speaking activities can be designed.

If there is a continuing news story, the students can be assigned to listen to the broadcasts of various stations, to take notes, and then to discuss variations in coverage in class. If there are talk shows on the local stations, the students can be assigned to record opinions on a specified topic to be discussed in class the next day.

The students can be asked to watch a TV documentary which will then be discussed in class. It is best, however, if they have a specific question in mind before they watch. Listening to the radio or watching TV in a foreign language is extremely difficult because of all the cultural information which the students do not yet have. If we want them to be able to use radio and TV as sources of learning, they will need specific guidance. An assignment such as "watch Walter Cronkite tonight and we'll talk about the news tomorrow" will do little to teach them how to listen. Instead, they should be told "Watch the news tonight on (channel) and be prepared to report three items from the story on (current topic)."

For students outside an English speaking environment, there are many commercial recordings on phonograph records or tapes of readings (poetry, plays, and short stories), of old radio programs, and, of course, popular music. Our students listen to popular music in the laboratory to reinforce the grammatical patterns which they are studying. The music should be an integral part of the program, with specific goals and purposes (even if only in the teacher's lesson plan), or it will be treated as a mere diversion.

CONCLUSION

Fluent listening results only from wide exposure to the target language and much practice in seeking specific points of information from spoken sources. Fluent listening can and should be taught from the very beginning stages of language learning. The teacher's task is to provide an opportunity for the students to listen to the speech of native speakers and to sequence and coordinate such activities with the rest of the curriculum. In this chapter we have attempted, by outlining general principles, procedures, and types of listening comprehension activities, to suggest how teachers can go about providing their students with practice in listening to the target language.

5
Reading

READING AND VOCABULARY STUDY*

Introduction

In spite of the fact that reading is the most important skill of all for most students of English throughout the world, it is a skill that has been much neglected in the audio-lingual tradition of language teaching. Reading was considered decoding speech written down, a skill which would naturally transfer from a command of the oral skills which were the major focus of audio-lingual programs. We now believe that the spoken and written forms of a language differ qualitatively, both in syntax and in vocabulary, and that if we want our students to be able to read, we must teach them to do so.

---

*We have previously acknowledged our debt to all the instructors in the English Language Institute, but this chapter constitutes a special debt. It is permeated with Lois Wilson's thinking about and experience in teaching reading, and this is an appropriate place to acknowledge her significant contribution, not only to this chapter, but to our entire reading program.

This chapter will deal with procedures and techniques for teaching students to decode meaning—lexical, structural, and cultural—from graphic symbols. It is not concerned with decoding graphic symbols into sound, and teachers who are faced with teaching initial reading in English as a second language are referred to the discussions of that process in other texts.[1]

With Goodman, we look on reading as information processing:

> The reader, a user of language, interacts with the graphic input as he seeks to reconstruct a message encoded by the writer. He concentrates his total prior experience and learning on the task, drawing on his experiences and concepts he has attained as well as the language competence he has achieved.[2]

The basic assumption of this chapter and the rationale for many of the procedures to be outlined is Goodman's thesis that good readers decode directly from the graphic stimulus (decoding is the process of going from code to message in information theory) and only then encode the meaning as oral output.[3] In other words, oral language forms no necessary part of reading for meaning. The proficient reader draws on three kinds of information, according to Goodman.[4] The first is graphophonic information, the sound-symbol relationship, which we assume our students already know but teach for encoding in pronunciation. The second is syntactic information, the information implicit in the grammatical structures of the language. Native speakers already know the grammar of their language and they draw on this knowledge in their reading. The foreign student needs to be taught how to do this. And finally there is semantic information: readers draw on their experiential conceptual back-

---

[1] See, for example, Faye Bumpass, *Teaching Young Students English as a Second Language* (New York: American Book Company, 1963); Fe R. Dacanay, *Techniques and Procedures in Second Language Teaching* (Dobbs Ferry, New York: Oceana Publications, Inc., 1963); Mary Finocchiaro, *Teaching Children Foreign Languages* (New York: McGraw-Hill, 1964); Francis C. Johnson, *English as a Second Language: An Individualized Approach* (Melbourne: Jacaranda Press, 1971).

[2] Kenneth Goodman, "Analysis of Oral Reading Miscues," in Frank Smith, ed., *Psycholinguistics and Reading* (New York: Holt, Rinehart and Winston, 1973), p. 162.

[3] Kenneth Goodman, "Reading: A Psycholinguistic Guessing Game," in D. V. Gunderson, *Language and Reading* (Washington, D. C.: Center for Applied Linguistics, 1970), p. 113.

[4] Goodman, "Analysis of Oral Reading Miscues," p. 164.

ground in order to supply a semantic component to the message. In order to do this, the reader needs access to both lexical and cultural meaning, in Fries' terms,[5] and this aspect as well has to be taught to the foreign student. Ultimately we believe with Smith that reading is learned rather than taught,[6] and that one learns reading by reading, in the mother tongue as well as in a foreign language, and this belief also influences our procedures.

The objectives of teaching reading are self-evident; we read for information and for pleasure. On the very elementary level, however, reading serves primarily (1) to introduce basic grammar patterns and vocabulary items in context and (2) to reinforce this basic knowledge.

SOME PRIMARY CONSIDERATIONS

One of the most important aspects of teaching reading is the selection of the reading text. There are some fairly obvious considerations. The reading selections should not contain marked dialect or slang features (many pocket books are unsuitable in this aspect) or old-fashioned language use (which rules out many classics in their original versions). The selections should have high interest value to the students and the simplest way of establishing this is by asking the students their opinions of the readings and then eliminating low interest selections from future curricula. The content should not contrast with the students' own cultural values. It seems that it is easier to read what is interesting and ideologically compatible, at least at the earlier stages.[7]

Michael West argues against using readings with a local setting as it results in a vocabulary of low frequency: *bullock* being much less frequent than *horse* is the example he gives.[8] We would argue the

[5] Charles Fries, *Teaching and Learning English as a Foreign Language* (Ann Arbor: University of Michigan Press, 1945).

[6] Frank Smith, "Twelve Easy Ways to Make Learning to Read Difficult," in Frank Smith, ed., *Psycholinguistics and Reading* (New York: Holt, Rinehart and Winston, 1972), p. 184.

[7] Jonathan Anderson, "The Development of a Reading Laboratory for Second Language Learners," *RELC Journal* 3, nos. 1 and 2 (June-December 1972): 50-59.

[8] Michael West, *Learning to Read a Foreign Language* (London: Longmans, Green, 1955).

opposite; students need the vocabulary of what is relevant to their world. It is also easier to learn to read when the cultural background is familiar and students can draw on cultural information in the decoding process. Actually we have had very good results with Asimov's science fiction *Nine Tomorrows*, which tends to be culturally neutral.[9] On the intermediate and advanced levels, the students also need to be exposed to types of writing other than narratives and dialogues, which are the basic staple of elementary level texts. They need practice with critical reading (decoding and evaluation) of such diverse types of writing as descriptions and directions, explanations and analyses, arguments and persuasions, summaries, and nonfictional narration such as news reporting, history, and biographies.

But by far the most important consideration in selecting texts is the level of reading difficulty, which must be matched to the overall proficiency of the students. In the past, there was great emphasis on using texts which had been simplified in vocabulary and syntax, and at the very beginning levels this practice still remains a necessity. Today there is a strong trend away from simplified or edited material toward texts which exhibit the complexity typical of unsimplified written English. Even so, there is a great range in reading difficulty levels, and these must be ascertained. A number of reading formulas exist,[10] none of which has proved to be very accurate. The most successful procedure for determining the level of reading difficulty is the cloze test.

There are several variations in constructing and scoring a cloze test, and we are here following the recommendations of Haskell.[11] In order to construct a cloze test, you select a reading passage of about 250 words for each reading selection being considered as a text. Leave the first and last sentence intact. Beginning with the second sentence, delete every fifth word throughout the reading

---

[9] Isaac Asimov, *Nine Tomorrows* (Greenwich, Connecticut: Fawcett Publications, 1959).

[10] See for example Dale E. and J. S. Chall, "A Formula for Predicting Readability," *Educational Research Bulletin* 77 (1948): 11-20.

[11] John Haskell, "Refining the Cloze Procedure for English as a Second Language," *English Record*, Winter 1974). See also John Oller, "Scoring Methods and Difficulty Levels for Cloze Tests of Proficiency in English as a Second Language," *Modern Language Journal* LVI (March 1972): 151-158.

passage, leaving an underlined blank in its stead. If a word to be deleted is a number, skip to the following word and delete that instead. You will end up with a passage like this:

The test should not be timed. Students should have the _____
to do a practice _____ before they ·begin the _____
proper, and they should _____ advised that even native
_____ cannot guess correctly at _____ the words.

The test should not be timed. Students should have the opportunity to do a practice passage before they begin the test proper, and they should be advised that even native speakers cannot guess correctly at all the words.

There are two methods of scoring the cloze test. The first method consists of accepting as a correct answer only the exact word which appeared in the text. The second method allows any word acceptable in meaning and structure to be counted as correct. Thus in *He came* _____ *down the hill* (*running* deleted), *walking* would be acceptable while *walked* would not. Students are not penalized for misspelling as long as it does not involve a grammatical error, such as *came* for *come*. Haskell recommends that when testing a reading selection for an entire group the exact word method of scoring be used; there is no significant difference in results between the two methods of scoring, and the exact word method is much more expedient for correction purposes, especially for teachers who are not native speakers of English. However, when testing the reading level of difficulty for an individual, it makes more sense to use the appropriate word method. (Cloze tests can also be used as proficiency tests, and then the appropriate word method should definitely be used.)

Anderson reports on a study which calculated the cloze scores corresponding to the traditional levels of reading, the independent level, the instructional level and the frustration level.[12] At the independent level, students read on their own without difficulty; at the instructional level, students can read but need assistance and instruction from the teacher; and at the frustration level students become hopelessly bogged down even with the teacher's help.

---

[12] Jonathan Anderson, "Selecting a Suitable 'Reader': Procedures for Teachers to Assess Language Difficulty," *RELS Journal* 2, no. 2 (December 1971): 35-42.

Anderson does not state for which method of scoring the calculation was performed but it seems likely these figures are for exact word scoring:

Levels of reading	*Cloze test percentage scores*
Independent level	Above 53 percent
Instructional level	Between 44 and 53 percent
Frustration level	Below 44 percent

For appropriate word scoring these figures would have to be raised, but there is no adequate research to allow for exact specification.

Another aspect which merits consideration is when to begin reading. Some programs, which follow the audio-lingual approach, have advocated the delay of reading or indeed of any exposure to the printed word until the students have mastered the phonological system of the target language and are somewhat fluent, although fluency may be within a very limited repertoire. This procedure was based on the belief that oral mastery was a necessary requisite to reading. This may still be true for first grade children in bilingual education programs, who are also simultaneously learning to decode graphic symbols, but adults who know how to read in the mother tongue should begin reading from the first day. Studies by both Marty[13] and Lado support this notion, and Lado concludes: "although it is possible to learn to speak without reading, it seems a more effective strategy to learn to read simultaneously with learning to speak."[14]

The distinction between intensive and extensive reading is basic to teaching reading.[15] In intensive reading, the student's attention is focused through instruction on the linguistic features which enable him to decode the message; in extensive reading, the approach is similar to that of reading in the native tongue; the student reads, at his own level and pace, directly for meaning.

---

[13] Fernand Marty, *Language Laboratory Learning* (Middlebury, Vermont: Middlebury College, 1960.)

[14] Robert Lado, "Evidence for an Expanded Role for Reading in Foreign Language Learning," *Foreign Language Annals* V, no. 4 (May 1972): 451-454.

[15] According to L. G. Kelly, *25 Centuries of Language Teaching* (Rowley, Massachusetts: Newbury House, 1969), p. 131, Harold E. Palmer was the first to make this distinction.

INTENSIVE READING

We will discuss the procedures for teaching intensive and extensive reading separately and will begin with intensive reading because this is where the teacher's efforts are primarily concentrated. Intensive reading deals with the study of those features of language, syntactical and lexical, which the reader draws on in order to decode the message. Intensive reading is also concerned with related skills, such as developing strategies of expectation and guessing meaning from context, as well as with using dictionaries. The major objective of intensive reading is developing the ability to decode messages by drawing on syntactic and lexical clues, and the emphasis as in all reading is on skills for recognition rather than for production of language features.

In teaching reading, pace and variety of exercises are especially important, and that has been an important consideration in designing the curriculum which we use in the Institute. The following basic lesson organization is designed for a 50 minute lesson—on all levels—and a teacher with a 50 minute class in which to teach all skills will have to modify the lesson plan. Steps 1 and 2 should always be included in a reading lesson; steps 3 and 4 need not be included in every lesson but should appear somewhere in the curriculum.

Lesson Organization for a Class in Reading

1. Checking through comprehension questions
   handed out previously on reading
   assigned for the day's lesson.   (5-10 minutes)
2. Introducing the next reading assignment:
   a. Giving meaning and pronunciation
      of new words in the next reading
      assignment.   (5 minutes)
   b. Giving comprehension questions
      on the next assignment.   (5 minutes)
3. Beginning level: Intensive study of
   grammar patterns for recognition only.
   Intermediate-advanced level: As above
   plus intensive study of rhetorical
   devices for paragraph construction.   (15 minutes)
4. Activity: from day to day a different
   activity such as word study, dictionary
   exercises, read and look up, etc.   (15 minutes)

It should readily be seen that virtually all actual reading takes place outside of class. Reading is the individual activity par excellence, and unless there are contextual constraints on the teaching situation, such as lack of electricity in the homes, there is no sense in wasting class time on actual reading. There are some exceptions to this. Occasional reading in class can help the teacher spot students with poor habits, such as constant lip movement, head movement, poor concentration, and excessive backtracking. Another exception is large classes which are conducted with a great deal of group work, for which reading is eminently suitable. Yet another exception is teacher survival; no one can teach effectively for six hours and more a day, yet such teaching assignments are more common than not. In such situations, teachers must coast through part of the lesson, and a reading period is a restful activity. These are valid reasons why students may spend class time in reading, but most of the time it is an inefficient use of class time.

It should also be noted that there is no class time spent in reading aloud by the students. Reading aloud, as both Goodman and Smith point out,[16] is recoding rather than decoding, and in teaching reading the emphasis should be on reading to decode the message. It wastes time and gives the wrong focus to the lesson to have the students read aloud. Furthermore, it is perfectly possible to read a passage aloud and not understand a word. Typically, even native speakers who are asked to read, say, a poem aloud in class will concentrate on the delivery, with little attention to the content. It is cruel to ask students to read an unknown passage aloud and then to ask them comprehension questions, yet it is often done. We do teach our advanced students to read reports aloud, a skill they will need in university seminars, but it is done in the pronunciation lesson.

One final matter before we get to the details of the actual lesson. Students need to work with both a dictionary and a reference grammar. One frequently runs across admonitions in the literature for students to abandon the bilingual dictionary as soon as possible. To read with a dictionary is a frustrating experience at best, and to read with a dictionary where one must look up the words in the explanation as well becomes simply counterproductive. We advise our beginning students to use bilingual dictionaries and do not encourage the switch to monolingual dictionaries until the inter-

---

[16] Frank Smith, *Understanding Reading* (New York: Holt, Rinehart and Winston, 1971).

mediate level and then only after the students have been taught how to use them. For most general reading, a good pocket dictionary will suffice and is much easier to use than a desk dictionary, although university-bound students should own one and learn to use it.

Much the same holds for reference grammars. A reference grammar of English written in the mother tongue is more efficient at the elementary level than an all-English grammar. With our beginning students, we use their regular grammar text as a reference grammar; for our intermediate and advanced students we use Crowell or Quirk and Greenbaum,[17]

Checking Comprehension Questions

Comprehension questions are in West's terms either *after*-questions or *before*-questions.[18] After-questions are just that, questions which are asked or read after the actual reading and whose purpose is to check that the students did the reading assignment and that they understood it. More importantly, before-questions serve to focus the student's attention on the important points of the passage during the reading and are a teaching rather than testing device. They are asked or read, and occasionally discussed, before the students do the reading. Both after- and before-questions can be any of the five types of questions Norris outlines:

> Five types of questions for comprehension can be described and graded according to (a) the linguistic form of the required response, and (b) the relation between the information that is needed to answer correctly and the information provided in the reading selection. I list the five types here in order of increasing difficulty for the student.
>
> *Type 1*: Information from the reading sufficient for the answer is contained in the question itself.
>
> > a. Answerable simply Yes/No or True/False
> >
> > Before Frank left for town, did his wife hand him an umbrella? (Yes or No)?
> >
> > Before Frank left for town, his wife handed him an umbrella. (True or False)

[17] Thomas Lee Crowell, *Index to Modern English* (New York: McGraw-Hill, 1964); R. Quirk and S. Greenbaum, *A Concise Grammar of Contemporary English* (New York: Harcourt, Brace, Jovanovich, 1973).
[18] Kelly, p. 136.

b. Multiple choice of answers is given with the question.

What did Frank's wife hand him before he left?

_____ an umbrella, _____ a piece of cloth, _____ a letter

Type 2: Answerable with information quoted directly from the reading selection. (WH questions—*who, when, where, what*—usually not *why* or *how* questions.)

What did Frank's wife hand him before he left for town?

Answer: (She handed him) a piece of cloth (before he left for town).

Type 3: Answerable with information acquired from the reading selection, but not by direct quotation from a single sentence (Usually *why* or *how* questions).

How did Frank explain his difficulties to his wife?

Answer: First, Frank told her. . . Then he said. . .

Type 4: Answerable from inference or implication from the reading; the information is not stated explicitly in the selection.

How do you suppose Frank's wife felt about his explanation?

Answer: Well, since she looked cross, I suppose that she. . .

Type 5: The answer requires evaluation or judgment relating the reading selection to additional information or experience of the reader.

What would you have done in Frank's place?[19]

Type 4 and 5 questions are rarely included in textbooks and do not lend themselves easily to written answers. It is important that the teacher remember to add such questions to the oral discussion of the reading. Students can also be assigned to prepare some type 4 and 5 questions for their classmates. They can be very simple: "Was Snow White's stepmother a nice person?" "Why didn't you like her?" and should be included in the curriculum as early as possible.

As little time as possible should be spent on going through the answers to the written comprehension questions. There is no sense at all to have each student first read the entire question aloud and then add true, false or whatever is the correct answer. The students have all read the questions, they have them in front of them, and it is quite sufficient for the teacher to say: "What is the answer to

---

[19] William Norris, "Teaching Second Language Reading at the Advanced Level: Goals, Techniques, and Procedures," *TESOL Quarterly* 4, no. 1 (March 1970): 28-29.

Question 1, Mary?" and for Mary to answer simply "False." Only where there is divergent opinion should the question be discussed. Class time is much better spent on inference and opinion questions, interspersed by the teacher among the factual questions. Teachers tend to waste a lot of time on comprehension exercises, and it is unproductive: the students have already achieved what they stood to profit from the exercise and all they need is a rapid verification of their work. This is not to say that questions the students had difficulty with should not be discussed, but rather not to spend time on what the students already know.

The teacher should check that each student really does prepare comprehension questions before coming to class. Simply walking through the classroom while checking the exercises and glancing at each student's paper will usually achieve this. The students should be told to correct their papers in a different color pencil or ink and to tally up their number of correct answers. The exercises should be collected and checked, if not each time at least occasionally, so the teacher can see how each student is doing. Depending on the situation, the exercises may be graded.

The reasons for these procedures are obvious. First of all, it ensures that the students do the reading, a serious worry for most teachers of reading. Second, it gives the students an indication of how they are doing. Third, it gives teachers an indication of how both they and the students are doing. Fourth, and most importantly, it provides a mechanism for the teacher to react to individual student's behavior. There is nothing more discouraging to students, even with teachers they dislike, than the teacher's ignoring or ignorance of the individual's efforts and performance. Especially with reading, where achievements are rather intangible, as many records as possible should be kept.

For a very beginning class, the teacher may want to add a lot of *after*-questions of the WH kind (*who, what, where, when, how* kind of questions): "Whom did he meet?" "What did he say to the girl?" This gives the class opportunity to talk in a controlled situation where the answers are simply lifted from the reading—they must speak the answers rather than just read them—but it is an exercise in improving short-term memory rather than in reading. On intermediate and advanced levels there need not be a close discussion of the text unless the teacher wants to use the reading as a springboard for class discussion, a perfectly valuable activity but it is not teaching reading.

Introduction of
the Next Reading Assignment

Meaning and Pronunciation of New Words

The study of vocabulary is the most neglected area of all in language teaching, yet there is increasing evidence both from first and second language acquisition studies that the semantic relationship is more important than the syntactic for receiving messages. The one thing that most interferes with our students' reading is poor vocabulary and we have recently come to accept the fact that our students have been right all these years when they have complained about not knowing and not being taught enough words.

Vocabulary study is just that, the learning of words, item by item. We distinguish between vocabulary taught for productive and receptive use. In the grammar class all words are taught for productive use, for the ability to recall and use these words for communicative purposes. We teach the more common content words, those words which have semantic rather than grammatical meaning, like *dog* and *run* and *fast*. But in grammar the primary emphasis is on the functors or function words, those words which primarily carry grammatical meaning, like the auxiliaries, articles, conjunctions and the like. The students must learn most of the functors for productive use if they are to speak grammatically.

In reading the emphasis conversely is on content words, but for receptive use, for the ability to recognize the meaning of a word in context, which is after all what reading is all about. But it is not possible to make any absolute statements about teaching vocabulary for productive or receptive use in reading because some students will *use* words they have learned through reading while others will not. Reading does lend itself to the enrichment of productive vocabulary, and the teacher can indicate to the students the words they should learn for their own usage.

The two major concerns in teaching vocabulary are what to teach and how to teach it. The criteria for selection of vocabulary differ depending on whether the vocabulary is taught for productive or receptive use. For productive use the two most cited criteria are frequency of occurence and degree of difficulty.

Frequency of occurrence can be established by reference to

word lists such as Thorndike and Lorge's[20] and West's[21] Although there are many problems with word lists,[22] they can serve as a guide line for the selection of vocabulary if used with some common sense. The word lists are also useful as check lists; at the intermediate level, students should be familiar with most of the words in the West list.

The other criterion which is often discussed is degree of difficulty[23] (difficulty is defined as the time it takes to learn an item), usually with the recommendation that one should proceed from easy to difficult. There are, however, serious problems with "difficulty" as a criterion for selecting vocabulary. There is no "absolute" difficulty, and although one may identify causes of difficulty as due to phonology, morphology, codability, distribution, etc., that identification still does not allow any accurate ranking of words by difficulty. With heterogeneous classes, the task becomes hopeless since mother tongue interference is an important factor of difficulty. But more important, many words which are difficult (we can observe the difficulty by the errors made on them) are of extremely high frequency and must be taught in the very beginning lessons. *Do* and *make* are a good example of a very difficult pair, especially for speakers who have one word for the two of them. Degree of difficulty, therefore, should not be considered as a criterion for the selection of vocabulary, but rather it should be taken into account for methods of teaching vocabulary.

In our view, the most important criterion for selecting vocabulary should be semantic saliency, the marked need for a word in order to make or understand a statement that is of importance to the speaker. The higher the semantic saliency of a word, the easier it is learned. Taboo words are a good example; our students learn them with no teaching at all. The needs and interests of the students then

[20] E. L. Thorndike and I. Lorge, *The Teacher's Word Book of 30,000 Words* (New York: Teachers College, Columbia University, 1944).

[21] Michael West, *A General Service List of English Words* (New York: Longmans, Green, and Company, 1953).

[22] Charles Fries and A. A. Traver, *English Word Lists: A Study of Their Adaptability for Instruction* (Ann Arbor, Michigan: Wahr, 1965).

[23] See for example M. Higa "The Psycholinguistic Concept of Difficulty and the Teaching of Foreign Language Vocabulary," and R. Lado, "Patterns of Difficulty in Vocabulary," in K. Croft, ed., *Readings on English as a Second Language* (Cambridge, Massachusetts: Winthrop Publishers, 1972).

should be the major guideline in selecting vocabulary to be taught for active production.

The criteria for selecting productive vocabulary should also be kept in mind when choosing a reading text. But once the selection of a reading passage is made, it becomes in fact the criterion for selecting vocabulary items for recognition in order to facilitate the reading. The main consideration simply should be to select the key words necessary to grasp the main plot or main theme, whatever the frequency of the words in English. It should be admitted that this is an intuitive and nonobjective process, but we know of no other. At advanced levels it is difficult to know with a given class which are new vocabulary items. The teacher can simply ask a good student to read the passage ahead of time and to underline the words he doesn't know. We have found this to be a very helpful guide.

Once the selection of vocabulary is made, the words will have to be taught. It is probably more true of vocabulary than any other aspect of language learning that words are learned rather than taught. So it would be more accurate to say that the words will have to be presented to the students so that they can learn them. On the very beginning level the teacher reads the whole passage aloud while the students follow silently in their books. At this level so many of the words are new that we don't attempt any written glosses, and the teacher explains the meaning of the new words. Furey has listed a number of different ways of giving explanations:

1. If the word is one which the teacher feels is known by the other students and could be clearly explained by them, he might refer the individual's question regarding meaning to another member of the class. This method is particularly useful for fairly common, concrete items which can be easily explained in simple terms.

   Ex: S1: What are *trousers?*
        S2: A kind of clothing. Pants. (S2 points to the pants of one of the male students in the class.)

2. Especially at the beginning level, gesture and pointing out of referents in the real world is a succinct and efficient way of illustrating meaning.

       What does *put on* mean in the sentence, *I put on a sweater if it is a cold day.*
       T: Making the appropriate "putting on" or dressing gestures, the teacher says "I put on my hat," "I put on my sweater."

3. The listing of synonyms (or antonyms), as long as they are terms the student already knows, can be an effective way of illustrating meaning.

This technique seems to be particularly useful in explaining common adjectives.

Ex: S: What is a kind person?

T: A person who is nice, pleasant, helpful, good.

4. When a questioned item refers to a class or group of items or activities, the citing of specific examples of these objects or activities may be an appropriate way of directing the student toward comprehension.

Ex: S: What does the word *continent* mean?

T: Asia, Africa and Europe are all continents.

5. Sometimes an abstract term may be best explained by means of illustrative sentences. The teacher must be certain to use examples which clearly delimit the meaning of the item under consideration.

Ex: S: What does the word *respect* mean in the sentence, *I respect that man more than anyone I've ever met.*

T: We respect a person who is very brave. We admire and respect someone who does good things for other people. We don't like and respect people who are mean and selfish.

6. In many cases, it is possible to give a fairly lucid dictionary-type definition of a word.

Ex: S: What does *lightning* mean?

T: Lightning is the very bright light we see during a rainstorm.

7. If the student has been exposed to the appropriate wordstudy materials, the teacher might direct him toward inferring the meaning from both structural clues and context.

Ex: S: What does the word *governor* mean in the sentence, *The governor of Pennsylvania met with the president last week to try and get more money.*

T: What kind of word is *governor*? Tell me what kind of word it is by looking at its position in the sentence and its suffix. What does the *-or* ending on words mean? etc.[24]

To this should be added the use of translation. If the teacher knows the students' native language, the glossing of individual words in the mother tongue is by far the most efficient way of explaining a word at this level. We realize that such a procedure sounds like heresy to many, but there is considerable psycholinguistic evidence to support

---

[24] Patricia Furey, "Some Notes on the Teaching of Vocabulary," manuscript (Department of General Linguistics, University of Pittsburgh, 1974).

such a viewpoint,[25] and our own experience both in teaching and learning foreign languages bears this out. We are firmly in favor of translation of individual words as a technique for teaching vocabulary at the beginning level. But this technique only works when the student knows the lexical equivalent in his mother tongue. At more advanced levels, the students learn words for new concepts for which they have no equivalent in their mother tongue, and these words have to be taught in English, in context. Translation of an isolated word should not lead to a general discussion in the native language; the translation is simply intended to forestall any discussion of words.

Beyond the very beginning level, the teacher does not read the entire reading selection aloud but only pronounces the new words, with the class repeating them. In many texts, the new words are identified and glossed by the textbook writer; if not, the teacher will have to identify and gloss them. Words to be mastered for productive use may be identified by an asterisk.

Here are some vocabulary items and glosses which we have had to prepare for Asimov's *Nine Tomorrows*, which we use with the advanced beginners. They are on dittoes and handed out in class. The words are to be learned for recognition.

1. *warrant*—justify; defend by giving a good reason for

    The good quality of the cloth warrants the high price of the dress.

2. *fee*—a sum of money paid for a service

    Doctors and lawyers get fees for their services.

3. *drive* (n)—energy; a force that makes one work harder

    That young man with drive will rise fast in the company and may become president some day.

In writing glosses, one attempts to use simple and familiar words in the explanations, but with languages closely related to English, words we feel to be esoteric and difficult in English are often cognates and as such easily recognized by the students. They find the inclusion of such cognates in the explanations to be very helpful. With homogeneous classes, a gloss in the mother tongue is also helpful. There is no need to spend class time on the explanations and glosses; they can safely be left to the students' perusal at home. An exception to this

---

[25] Jack Adams, *Human Memory* (New York: McGraw-Hill, 1967).

are some of the "difficult" words to which the teacher should alert the students' attention. These words include:

1. deceptive cognates (English *assist*—Spanish *asistir* "attend")

2. words with different connotations (English *liar*—Spanish *mentira*) or values (*ambitious* has negative connotations in many languages)

3. words which are the exact equivalents but have a different meaning. (American *second floor* is many people's *first floor*)

4. words for new concepts; either the referent does not occur in the mother tongue (*jaywalking*) or the student does not know the word in his mother tongue either (*morphophonemics*). Learned words do not necessarily fit here; *nomothetic* is easily glossed in English and the concept is familiar even if the word is not.

5. words with different distribution (*take* and *bring*)

6. words for uniquely American phenomena (*pep rally*)

But on the whole, any temptation to talk about words should be resisted.

A key question concerns the number of words per lesson a student can be expected to learn for recognition. In an experiment with our Spanish speaking students at the intermediate level, Levenson showed that they could easily handle 25 words and probably more.[26] These students' major deterrent to facile reading lies in poor vocabulary, and we are putting increasing emphasis on lexical acquisition. These students are highly motivated, but it seems likely that any adult student should be able to handle 20-30 new words for each lesson. Whether he would want to is another question.

Comprehension Questions on the Next Assignment

As we said above, as far as possible the comprehension questions given before the reading should serve to focus the students' attention on the important points of the reading rather than being

---

[26] Carol Levenson, "Presentation of Vocabulary of a Foreign Language: Optimum Number of New Items per Lesson and Effect of Context," manuscript (Department of General Linguistics, University of Pittsburgh, 1973).

just trivial polite questions. They lend themselves very well to dealing with cultural information, such as American attitudes toward competition, winning and home towns, topics which are likely to be unfamiliar to the students and which might conceivably interfere with their interpretation of the reading. Only those questions which are meant to focus on cultural phenomena need to be discussed in class; the rest can be left for the students to decipher at home.

The format of the questions one chooses will depend partially on the kind of testing situation the students will eventually face. Our students will have to take objective standardized tests, such as the Michigan or TOEFL, and they do many true-false and multiple choice type questions, such as these on a selection from the *Nine Tomorrows:*

2. Before the competition started, what were George's feelings about Trev?
   a. He hoped that Trev would win, and he felt no resentment against Trev.
   b. He did not want Trev to win.
   c. He hoped Trev would win, but he also felt resentment against Trev.

4. The gray-haired man said he was cheering for Trevelyan because

   a. he was from the same hometown.
   b. there was no one from the man's town competing, so he cheered for the town George was from.
   c. he was George's friend and would cheer for anyone George cheered for.

Write true or false

_____ 7. Trevelyan always wanted to work on Novia.

_____ 8. Most people want to stay on Earth rather than go to Novia.

In addition to such objective questions, the teacher might add some inference or opinion questions for the students to reflect on as they read the passage. An opinion question on the reading serves very well as the topic of brief essays for the writing class.

On the intermediate and advanced levels, when the students are beyond simple narrative, they may also be asked to do outlines, summaries, paraphrase, précis writing or brief analyses of the main points. The discussion of this work would fall under Step 4 of the lesson plan above, and should be as closely correlated as possible with the writing part of the curriculum.

Preparing for the next reading assignment demands much of the teacher's time outside of class, but in class ten minutes is ample time for this activity. But it is a crucial activity and should not be overlooked.

Intensive Study of Grammar Patterns for Recognition

The proficient reader draws on syntactic information as well as lexical in order to decode the message of the passage. Native speakers already know the grammar of their language, and they use this knowledge for clues in their reading. Foreign students must be taught to do so. As Wilson points out, structural clues are especially important for foreign students because they have a limited vocabulary and can therefore not afford to ignore structural cues as native speakers often do.[27] Another reason, she points out, for stressing the importance of structural clues is that they can help the student increase his content vocabulary.

On the elementary level we teach recognition, i.e., *decoding only* of (1) those structural patterns which occur late in the curriculum for production but are needed early in reading (such as relative clauses) and (2) those patterns which occur mainly only in writing (such as certain types of nominalizations). The teacher "briefly presents the pattern to the class and helps them understand the significance of the word order and important function words,"[28] in other words a linguistic explanation of the grammatical rule. Our assumption is clearly that reading is a problem-solving activity where an explanation of general principles helps students in their reading. This exercise from Wilson will clarify the procedures:[29]

Teaching point: One Type of Relative Clause

Step 1. Review of familiar patterns
The teacher writes the following sentences on the blackboard, he reads them aloud and the students repeat.

Food at Webster Hall Hotel is expensive.
Some students have a lot of money.
These students eat lunch at Webster Hall Hotel.

---

[27] Lois Irene Wilson, "Reading in the ESOL Classroom," *TESOL Quarterly* 7, no. 3 (September 1973): 259-267.
[28] Ibid, p. 261.
[29] Ibid, pp. 264-265.

He then asks simple comprehension questions such as "Who has a lot of money?" and "Where do these students eat?"

Step 2. Presentation of new pattern
The teacher combines the second and third sentences.

Students (students have a lot of money) eat lunch at Webster Hall Hotel.

He then replaces the word "students" inside the parentheses with "who" and erases the parentheses. Finally, he repeats the comprehension questions.

Step 3. Generalization
The teacher asks the class what "who" means in this sentence. He also asks them what the two sentences are in this sentence.

Since this pattern is a difficult one the teacher should present one or two additional examples using "which" and "that." At least one of these examples should have the relative clause at the end of the sentence. Possible sentences are:

The only apartments which are vacant are too expensive.
There are several organizations that help people with emotional problems.

After these examples the teacher can tell the students that the included sentence beginning with "who" or "which" or "that" is called a relative clause and relative clauses always follow nouns.

The students are then given a set of sentences with questions to complete for homework:

1. The cafeteria which is in the Student Union serves lunch and dinner.

   Where is the cafeteria?

2. The men who were appointed by the chairman will go to Washington.

   Who will go to Washington?

It is important to remember that at this stage the students are never asked to produce the pattern, only to recognize the structural cues for accurate decoding.

Allen points out that the recognition of synonymous sentences has often been left to chance, and that students need practice in recognizing which two sentences in a set of three have approximately the same meaning in exercises like this:

a. Ed had to stop running long enough to catch his breath.

b. Although Ed longed to stop and catch his breath, he had to keep running.

c. Ed longed to stop and catch his breath, but he had to keep running.[30]

She also points out the value of writing as training for reading. Here is another exercise called sentence synthesis, formerly popular in British textbooks, which can be used for recognition of synonymous sentences. The class is divided into groups, and each group handed a set of sentences like this:

1. Someone asked Larry Smith a question.
2. The question was about his reading habits.
3. He answered.
4. The answer was that he read detective stories.
5. Detective stories take the mind off pressing concerns.

They are told to rewrite them in one sentence.[31] When finished, each group writes their sentence on the blackboard. The sentences are invariably different and usually synonymous. The class then decides with the teacher's guidance which is the more elegant version. This exercise can be done in five or ten minutes; the competitive aspect (the class makes it competitive whether the teacher wants it or not) gives it the quality of a game and is a pleasant change of classroom activity, but above all it provides intensive practice in examining synonymous sentences and their syntactical devices. The easiest way to construct such exercises is to begin with the long embedded sentence and then to rewrite it in shorter sentences, leaving out as many of the syntactical devices as possible. Teachers can either write the sentence themselves or else select a suitable sentence from the reading passage.

---

[30] Virginia French Allen, "Trends in the Teaching of Reading," *TESL Reporter* 6, no. 4 (Summer 1973): 17.

[31] The sentence will be something like: *Asked about his reading habits, Larry Smith answered that he read detective stories in order to take his mind off pressing concerns* or *When someone asked Larry Smith about his reading habits, he answered that detective stories take the mind off pressing concerns and that is what he read* or *Someone asked Larry Smith a question about his reading habits and he answered that he read detective stories because they took his mind off pressing concerns.* The first version was the original sentence, adapted from *Time Magazine.*

A major problem lies in identifying those grammatical patterns which should be taught for passive recognition in reading and later for active use in writing. A list of such patterns needs to be carefully correlated with levels of proficiency, as some patterns will cause difficulty to beginning students but not to intermediate and some to intermediate but not to advanced. Truly advanced students should ideally be beyond sentence level work on recognition of syntactic clues. We know of no such systematically established list and the following is a very tentative outline, based primarily on Allen[32] and our own experience. It is intuitively ordered on the bases of students' needs (really frequency of occurence), but we have no data to justify the order and the list should be regarded simply as a guideline.

LIST OF GRAMMATICAL PATTERNS TO BE TAUGHT FOR RECOGNITION IN READING

1. postponed subject after *it* and after *there is/there are* (it is invariably a wise man who. . .; there are more than twenty buildings on the campus)
2. conjunctions
3. substitution words (nor *did* he, she said *so*)
4. sentence connectives (*finally, moreover,* etc.) and conventions of punctuation
5. passives, statives, and irregular past participles
   with agent (The committee *was appointed by* the president.) without specific agent (The health service *is located* in the main building.)
6. relative clauses
   with subject focus (The man *who went to Washington* is my cousin.)
   with object focus (The man *whom my cousin saw* went to Washington.)
   possessive relative clause (The man, *whose cousin you know,* went to Washington.)
   in prepositional phrase (The man $\left\{ \begin{array}{l} to\ whom\ I\ sent \\ the\ letter \\ from\ whom\ I \\ received\ a\ letter \end{array} \right\}$

---

[32] Allen, pp. 1-2; 15-19. Some of the examples are hers, as well. See also Kyle Perkins and Carlos A. Yorio, "Grammatical Complexity and the Teaching of Reading in an ESL Program", manuscript; and Mary Eleanor Pierce, "Sentence Level Expectancy as an Aid to Advanced Reading," *TESOL Quarterly* 7, no. 3 (September 1973): 269-277.

went to Washington.)
with ellipsis (The man my cousin saw went to Washington.)

7. nominalizations

John's late arrival
That John arrived late
For John to arrive late   } was surprising.
John's arriving late
What John said
I like *to see John arrive late.*

8. infinitives
with *it* transposition (*It* is fun *to travel*)
with noun preceding as subject of infinitive (He wanted *John to go.*)
with noun preceding as object of infinitive (Students should have *books to read.*)
in order to (He came *to* get his book.)

9. participial constructions
with subject omitted
present participial phrase (*Traveling to Washington,* he met my cousin.)
past participial phrase (*Asked about his health,* he only smiled.)
with subject expressed
present participial phrase (He saw *horses running* across the plain.)
past participial phrase (*His work finished,* he went home. *With expletives deleted,* the document is still shocking. *Having eaten the apple,* Adam repented.)

10. transposed elements
adverbial clause in initial position (*Although most people deplore it,* graffiti are widespread.)
initial prepositional phrase with subject-verb inversion (*Of special interest to teachers* is the Language Methodology Center.)
initial adverb with *do* in statement form (*Rarely did* he fail to do his lessons.)
topicalization (*Intuition* as discovery procedure he found rather doubtful.)

11. negation:
scope (I don't think I can come [I can't come].)
double negatives (No one has nothing to offer to society [Everyone has something].)

Chomsky doesn't not pay taxes for nothing.
[There's a reason he doesn't pay taxes.])

Note that categories like conjunctions and sentence connectives should not be taught in one unit but should be sequenced a few at a time throughout the course.

On the intermediate and advanced levels the students should primarily be working on the paragraph level and above. In our program, this work is coordinated with their writing classes and so taught for actual production as well, with the reading and writing skills reinforcing each other.

Students should be taught to become familiar with different types of writing. Lafene has classified these as follows:

I.   Major types of writing
    1. Explanation and analysis
        a. a process
        b. an opinion or point of view
        c. event(s) and phenomena
        d. instructions and directions
    2. Argument
        a. persuasion
        b. refutation
        c. examining both sides of a point
    3. Description and summary
        a. a thing
        b. a person
        c. a place
        d. an event
        e. concepts
    4. Narration
        a. a series of events; a report
        b. biography or autobiography
        c. historical events
        d. fiction or nonfiction
II. Methods of development for major types of writing
    1. Illustration and/or exemplification
    2. Comparisons and contrasts
    3. Partition—dividing something into parts and explaining or describing each
    4. Classification—putting things into categories
    5. Definition—formal, descriptive or operational

6. Cause and effect
7. Reasoning—if. . , therefore. . .[33]

In order to be able to understand such writing and to reproduce it, students must learn (1) to identify main ideas, subpoints and supporting details, (2) to recognize the rhetorical devices that typically go with different types and methods of development of ideas in writing and (3) to recognize those structural patterns which are typical of specific types of writing.

The before-questions which students on the intermediate level are given concentrate on the basic points of the reading in order to accustom them to critical reading where they routinely identify main ideas and supporting details. Here are some such questions on a reading where the author argues for guaranteed income, from *Plain English Rhetoric and Reader.* [34]

1. What is the main idea sentence for this reading passage?
   a. What are the two opinion words in this sentence?
2. List all the reasons which the author uses to support the main idea sentence.
3. List the opposition arguments that the author refutes.
4. The reason in Paragraph 5 is weakly supported. What could the author do to support this reason more strongly?
5. In your country, is there a system of paying money to people who cannot earn enough to take care of themselves? Would you agree with the author's proposal in your country? Briefly support your answer.

The students answer these questions in writing as homework and the questions then are discussed in class the following day. Care should be taken in constructing the questions that the students cannot answer simply by copying sentences from the reading but have to summarize and synthesize. The students correct their wrong answers themselves but with a different color pen so that the teacher, when checking their homework, can tell both how well they did with the reading and how well they followed the class discussion. A large number of uncorrected wrong answers signals serious problems.

---

[33]Julia Lafene, "Prospectus for Suggested Project for Materials Development," manuscript (Department of General Linguistics, University of Pittsburgh, 1974).

[34] G. Cowan and E. McPherson, *Plain English Rhetoric and Reader* (New York: Random House, 1970). The questions are written by Lois Wilson.

The students need to learn for this particular reading passage the rhetorical devices which typically go with persuasive writing, such as conjunctions which show condition, concession or contrast (*in case that, in as much as, whether or not,* etc.), and sentence connectives which show consequence (*accordingly, consequently,* etc.), or which contrast or limit related ideas (*conversely, still less,* etc.). These rhetorical devices lend themselves very well to written exercises of types which will be discussed in the chapter on writing.

Persuasive writing typically uses many conditional patterns, and the students need to work on these. They frequently have difficulties with conditionals which have the *if* clause deleted, as in this passage:

> If he wins the election, he will carry out a thorough reform of city practices. He will restore the parks to their original beauty.

The second sentence has the *if* clause *If he wins the election* deleted although the sentence still presupposes that he has to win the election if there is going to be any restoring of parks. Students frequently misread such sentences and take as a statement of fact that he is going to restore the parks. Another pattern which gives them difficulty is *Suppose that he won the election,* which they take at face value and think that he did win the election. The students need to work with such patterns in class prior to the reading, using exercises similar to the one on page 175-6.

All types of writing have their own characteristics, and we have only chosen the exercises needed for one type—persuasion—in order to demonstrate the three major teaching points for each reading passage: identifying (1) the main idea and supporting details, (2) rhetorical devices, and (3) structural patterns typical of certain types of writing. Students need to work through exercises on these three teaching points for all types of writing and their development.

Activities

A good reading program should contain a variety of activities, and to this purpose the last fifteen minutes of the reading class differ from day to day in the Institute. All of these activities, however, are important to a reading program and should be incorporated from time to time in any reading program, be it on a daily or occasional basis. The order they are listed in is not significant.

Word Study

Word study differs from the study of vocabulary. The study of vocabulary concentrates on learning lexical equivalences of mother tongue vocabulary and, after the beginning level, on lexical items for new concepts. The emphasis is squarely on the semantics. Word study concentrates on the morphology and syntax of words in order to help the student guess intelligently at the meaning of words. We know very little about the efficient teaching of word study, and there is a tendency to have word study become a catch-all category. One thing, however, should be kept clearly in mind. We are teaching decoding of words for efficient reading, and this means that the students should not necessarily be asked to produce words through the processes of word formation they are studying. Given *excite, excitement* students invariably come up with **combinement, *disturbment* and so on, and this is an unnecessary confusion. For reading purposes, the teaching point is the recognition of a noun form of *combine* but not necessarily the ability to produce *combination.* If that is desired, *combination* is better taught directly as a vocabulary item. The emphasis on word study should generally be on decoding, and this objective should be reflected in the type of exercises the students are given.

There are three major areas for word study. The order they are listed and discussed in here is purely arbitrary, but somewhere in the program these points need to be covered, and we have found it most efficient to teach them for decoding purposes only in combination with the reading activities.

a. Function words which are not taught as grammar should form part of the word study program. These are likely to be synonymous with more common expressions, which the students already know, so all they learn is to recognize that *his talking notwithstanding* and *for all his talking* are roughly similar in meaning to *in spite of his talking, lest* to *unless,* etc. These expressions are typical of formal style and are not likely to occur in beginning level reading selections.

b. Closed list content words which do not form part of the grammar course need to be studied. They consist of such things as irregular plurals like *brethren, sheaves, plaice* and the like, which countless children around the world can chant, but it really makes little sense to teach such words for productive use. On the other hand the rules for the formation of such plurals are simple and easily taught for recognition. Irregular verb forms also belong here, many of which are more frequent in the irregular form than in the infinitive, like *cleft, flung, forsaken,* and *slain,* none of which we really would want our students to use in their everyday speech, but which they still need to know for their reading. They need to learn substitute verb forms like *I did so, so will I, I have too,* etc. They need to learn words with negative distribution, like *hardly, scarcely, barely.* This is by no means meant as a complete list, but it probably represents the more important types of closed list content word items that should be taught. Obvious omissions, like irregular adjectives and adverbs, are presumably taught in the grammar course for productive use.

c. Word formation is traditionally the very heart of word study. It is the study of roots, stems, prefixes and suffixes and their combination into words, as in the relationship between *amaze, amazing,* and *amazement.*

In word formation, there are two separate teaching points: (1) the lexical meaning of roots and prefixes and (2) the syntactic signals for parts of speech. In teaching roots and prefixes, the teaching point is the lexical meaning of the forms, often in lists like this:

Words	*Prefix*	*Root*
1. Precept	pre- (before)	capere (take, seize)
2. Detain	de- (away, from)	tenere (hold, have)
3. Intermittent	inter- (between)	mittere (send)
4. Offer	ob- (against)	ferre (bear, carry)
5. Insist	in- (into)	stare (stand)
6. Monograph	mono- (alone, one)	graphein (write)
7. Epilogue	epi- (upon)	legein (say, study)
8. Aspect	ad- (to, towards)	spicere (see)
9. Uncomplicated	un- (not) com- (together with)	plicare (fold)
10. Nonextended	non- (not) ex- (out of)	tendere (stretch)
11. Reproduction	re- (back, again) pro- (forward)	ducere (lead)
12. Indisposed	in- (not) dis- (apart from)	ponere (put, place)
13. Oversufficient	over- (above) sub- (under)	facere (make, do)

14. Mistranscribe mis- (wrong)   scribere (write)[35]
                  trans- (across, beyond)

Exercises typically look like this:

> Fill in the blank with the proper negative prefix:
> 1. He always_____ connects the wires.
> 2. He always_____ pronounces the words.
> 3. His work is completely_____satisfactory.[36]

One needs to be very cautious with this kind of work. Put through such exercises, our students tend to become very confused, and worse, discouraged. They become confused for two major reasons. One, even if they learn that *cata-* is a Greek prefix meaning *down* or *against,* there is no way that is going to help them, or us for that matter, to figure out the meaning of *catalogue* and *catastrophe;* the semantic load of many of the prefixes and roots have long since disappeared. Words like *catastrophe, energy, paralysis* should be taught individually as entire words, not as *cata* plus *strophe.* Although the reader trained in Latin may be able to puzzle out the derivation of words like *ambidextrous,* it is of little help to the foreign student who knows neither English nor Latin, except possibly as a mnemonic device.

Second, they learn the negative impact of *dis-* and then they run across *discern, distribute, discuss,* none of which has any negative element. It is doubtful that rules (the prefix X means Y) which cannot be generated freely, and that holds for many, if not most, of the Latin and Greek prefixes, should be taught as rules. An alternative with *dis-* is to limit the rule so that *dis-* is negative only if the students know the stem as a free verb form with positive meaning, as *approve* in *disapprove, like* in *dislike. Cern* and *tribute* will mean nothing.

We have found it a useful criterion to teach by rule those prefixes that can combine with words the students are likely to know. *Ante-* (before) in *antedate; inter-* (between) in *international, post-* (after) in *postwar,* etc. This leaves out some of the most common prefixes as *ad-, admit; com-, complete;* etc., which are simply taught as an indivisible part of the word.

---

[35] Edward Fry, *Teaching Faster Reading* (Cambridge: Cambridge University Press, 1965), p. 126.

[36] Norris, citing a popular text.

There is another difficulty with the exercise on page 185. There is no logical reason why it is *unpleasant* but *displeased,* and the negative prefixes have to be learned word for word rather than by rule for correct production. It is confusing as a teaching device to mix together *dis-, mis-, un-,* etc. And if readers doubt that, let them quickly explain the difference between *disinterested* and *uninterested.* If the teaching point is recognition of negative prefixes, exercises should not ask for production of prefixes. The exercise can be rewritten as:

Fill in the slot:
If he doesn't disconnect the wire before mending the stove, he will
_____ (get a shock)
If he mispronounces the words, the teacher _____

or

True or False:
He always mispronounces the words. He gets an A.   T or F
His work is completely unsatisfactory. His boss will fire him.   T or F

where the exercises test the accurate decoding of meaning only. If the teaching point is to learn the words *disconnect, mispronounce* and *unsatisfactory,* they should be taught separately and as entire vocabulary items.

The second teaching point of word formation is the derivational suffixes, those suffixes which mark words as nouns, verbs, and adjectives. The adverb suffix *-ly* belongs in the grammar component to be learned for productive use, as do the inflectional suffixes of plurals, tense endings and comparatives. The derivational suffixes are the most important aspect of word formation study since recognition of word class is crucial in figuring out syntactic relationships, and ability to identify words for their part of speech is the major benefit from studying the derivational suffixes.

Typically, exercises call for productive use with predictable confusion, and most of what we have said about the prefixes also holds for teaching suffixes, with the exception that most suffixes do not carry any semantic meaning. The difference in meaning between *nation, nationality,* and *nationalism* cannot be puzzled out from their suffixes: they have in common that they have something to do with nationhood and that they are nouns and hence can serve as subjects and objects in a sentence; their lexical meaning must be taught separately and as whole words. However, a student who knows the meaning of *nation*, that *-ality* is a noun suffix and that *-ize* is a verb suffix, is more than likely to puzzle out the meaning of *nationality* and *nationalize* if they are encountered in sentences like:

> He was of American nationality.
>
> The Latin American government nationalized the American copper industry.

and therein lies the value of this type of word study. Exercises like those quoted by Norris, such as this one:

> Fill in the blanks with a noun (plural form) related to the underlined noun in the sentence:
> 1. Our interest was in *art* and (artists).
> 2. Our interest was in *crime* and _____.
> 3. Our interest was in *music* and _____.[37]

ignore the relationship between word class and syntactic meaning. They are confusing in that they bring together several forms with similar meaning for productive use where no rule exists and the items have to be learned one by one. Here are some exercises which attempt to focus on the syntactic meaning carried by the word class, expressed by suffixes:

> Who had more than one job, Singer A or Singer B?
> A. The concert singer, directed by her husband, feared failure.
> B. The concert singer, director of Victoria Opera Hall, feared failure.
> Whose identity is known, Streaker A or Streaker B?
> A. The streaker, reporter of the Pittsburgh Press, was seen in Glenshaw.
> B. The streaker, reported to the Pittsburgh Press, was seen in Glenshaw.

It may seem that such exercises draw the students' attention away from the main point of the sentence, but very often such information contributes significantly to the development of the reading. Surely any reader can imagine very different causes for fear of failure of the poor singer in A and B above. Many experts have pointed out the importance of predictions and expectancy in

---

[37] Norris, citing a popular text.

reading, and such exercises intend to increase the accuracy of the predictions.

Pierce stresses the need to develop expectancy for the type of predication a subject might take. Consider this exercise:

> Underline the complete sentence.
> 1. Many nations contribute to UNESCO
>   Many contributors to UNESCO
> 2. Many investigators of the causes of cancer
>   Many investigate the causes of cancer

which trains the students to ascertain whether they have identified the main predication of a sentence, a crucial necessity in reading.

Here is another exercise (in abbreviated form) by Lois Wilson, which we use in the Institute on the advanced beginners' level.

> There are three common suffixes which identify verbs. They usually carry a meaning of causation. The most common suffix is *ize*.

Example:

> *publicize* The results of the committee's investigations have been widely *publicized* by the newspapers, radio and television.
> *Definition*: to bring to the attention of the people.

The second common suffix identifying verbs is *-ify*.

Example:

> *simplify* The short income tax form *simplifies* the paper work for many tax payers.
> *Definition:* make something simple.

> *Note:* A verb with the *suffix -ize* or *-ify* often has a close, related noun and/or adjective.

The third suffix, which is less common, is *-en*.

Example:

> *widen* The city plans to *widen* the main streets next year.
> *Definition:* to cause something to become wider.

> *Note:* A verb with the suffix *-en* usually has a closely related adjective.

Exercise:

Read each sentence. Circle the identifying suffix of the underlined word. Then write the part of speech and a definition of the underlined word. Use the dictionary to help you.

1. The electric guitar requires special equipment to *amplify* the weak sounds made by the strings.

   Part of Speech:
   Definition:

2. People on the street were *deafened* by the warehouse explosion.

   Part of Speech:
   Definition:

3. There is little chance that the government of Pennsylvania will *legalize* the sale and use of marijuana.

   Part of Speech:
   Definition:

To sum up the discussion on word study, we have made a distinction between teaching vocabulary and word study and argue that word study as we have defined it should be taught in combination with reading for the *decoding* of words. Consequently, exercises for word study should not require active production of stems and affixes.

Read and Look Up

Read and Look Up is a technique developed by Michael West,[39] initially to give maximum individual practice in meaningful reading for large classes. As is occasionally pointed out, the technique is reminiscent of that which some actors use to memorize scripts.

The basic technique of Read and Look Up/is to divide the reading text/into syntactic word groups,/in Nida's "meaningful mouthfuls,"/(as this sentence is)/and then to speak them/rather than to read them aloud./ On beginning levels, the teacher will first model the reading passage, indicating by pauses or by saying "slash" where the students are to mark word group intervals with slashes. The students then read, either individually or chorally, the first word group silently, then look up and speak it aloud from memory. They continue with the second word group, and so on. The major teaching

---

[38] Lois Irene Wilson, "Word Study Exercise—Word Formation Exercise 3," mimeographed (English Language Institute, University of Pittsburgh).

[39] Michael West, *Teaching English in Difficult Circumstances* (London: Longmans, Green, and Company, 1960), pp. 12-13.

point is to train the students to read by syntactic units, but Read and Look Up is also remarkably efficient in improving short-term memory. Students who have trouble with mechanical drills when the utterance length increases profit dramatically in their drill performance after just a few sessions of Read and Look Up. Read and Look Up can also be used for intonation practice, but on the beginning level the teacher needs to model each word group immediately before the students speak it rather than to read the whole passage at once.

With more advanced students the teacher does not model the passage, and students do their own "slashing." Here practice must be individual. Students should be encouraged to increase the length of the word groups. At this level, Read and Look Up becomes teaching by testing. If the teacher does not follow in the book but merely listens, the students' performance in pronunciation and intonation will test their general comprehensibility. At this level, the major benefit of Read and Look Up lies in practice for the future delivery of academic papers and seminar presentations. But it also tests the students' comprehension of grammatical patterns as indicated by their "slashing."

We should point out that training students' short-term memory and pronunciation is not teaching reading, but rather than have three separate discussions of Read and Look Up we have gathered all these points together in one section. Depending on the teaching point, Read and Look Up also belongs in the pronunciation and grammar lessons.

Dictionary Exercises

As students use the dictionary a great deal in their reading, it is a good idea to show them how to find the information they seek. In a dictionary they will find information about the pronunciation, spelling, syllable division, meaning, parts of speech, usage, and derivation of a word. In reading, it is clearly the meaning of a word that is most important to them. And therein lies the problem: most words have more than one meaning and the problem for the students is to isolate the meaning intended by the writer. To that purpose we give students exercises like this one:

Word Study Sheet—Using a Dictionary

Introduction:
The majority of words in English may be used as more than one part of speech (verb, noun, adjective, adverb, preposition, etc.) It is the

position of the word in the sentence which determines the part of speech. For example the word *head* can be a noun or a verb. Which is it in these sentences?

1. *Heads* of companies are usually very busy. _____
2. The soccer player was hit on the *head* by the ball. _____
3. When the repairmen finish their last job, they will *head* for home. _____
4. Dr. Cole *heads* the cancer research team. _____

Sometimes there is a close relationship in the meaning of a word used as a noun and the same word used as a verb. Do you see a relationship between *head* as it is used in sentence (1) and *head* as it is used in sentence (4)? Sometimes the meanings seem only distantly related as in sentences (2) and (3).

Since most English words have many meanings (*head* has 39 meanings listed in *Webster's Third International Dictionary*) dictionaries list the meanings according to part of speech. If you look up the word *head* in a dictionary, you will see first all the meanings for *head* as a noun, then as an adjective and finally as a verb.

Everyone agrees that using a large English-English dictionary is not easy. How do you know which meaning of a word to choose? The following example will show you one way to go about solving this problem. The underlined word in this sentence may be unknown to you.

The snake made threatening noises with his *rattle*.

Webster's Third International Dictionary lists a total of thirteen meanings for *rattle*. However because you can see that *rattle* is a noun in this sentence, you can eliminate the meanings of *rattle* as a verb. This leaves the six meanings of *rattle* as a noun. Using other clues in the sentence (i.e., It has to do with a snake) you can probably choose the correct meaning fairly quickly—"the sound-producing organ in a rattlesnake's tail."

Exercise:

Following is a list of four words with some of their meanings. These words are then used in sentences. First decide the part of speech for the word as it is used in the sentence. Then decide the correct meaning of the word.

Word List:

(Definitions are adapted from *Webster's Third International Dictionary*)

paper

noun	—	(1)	a sheet of vegetable fibers 6/1000 inch or thinner
		(2)	document—usually used in the plural
		(3)	newspaper

verb	–	(1)	to affix paper to something such as a wall
adjective	–	(1)	made completely or almost completely of paper
		(2)	authorized or planned but not carried out

smell

verb	–	(1)	to get the odor of something through the nose
		(2)	to give off an odor or scent
		(3)	to have a bad odor
		(4)	to appear evil, dishonest, or ugly
noun	–	(1)	the property of something that affects the nose
		(2)	the general quality of something

Sentences:

example: It was only a *paper* war.
Part of Speech: ___adjective___ Meaning: __2__

1. The official government *paper* concerning recent economic agreements will be published next month.
Part of Speech: _____ Meaning: _____
2. The whole atmosphere of this court *smells*. No one can get a fair trial here.
Part of Speech: _____ Meaning: _____
3. *Paper* decorations for a party can be dangerous if they aren't fireproof.
Part of Speech: _____ Meaning: _____
4. It was a crisp autumn morning and the air *smelled* especially fresh and clean.
Part of Speech: _____ Meaning: _____
5. The Prime Minister flatly denied the stories in the *papers* which said he would soon resign.
Part of Speech: _____ Meaning: _____
6. Many of the new cosmetics have the *smell* of lemon or other fruits.
Part of Speech: _____ Meaning: _____ [40]

As soon as students have demonstrated that they can use a dictionary in a sensible fashion, they should not have to spend time on written

---

[40] Lois Irene Wilson, "Word Study Exercises—Using a Dictionary," mimeographed (English Language Institute, University of Pittsburgh).

dictionary exercises, which then merely become busy work. However, if thirty or forty restless youngsters need to be occupied without necessarily learning much, dictionary exercises are efficient and sufficiently time consuming. Otherwise, as soon as the students can find their way around in a dictionary (some students even need to learn the principle of alphabetic listing), dictionary work should be tied to the individual's needs in reading and writing.

Speed Reading

A common complaint about the reading of foreign students is the slow rate of their reading, and most reading programs incorporate activities to improve students' speed of reading. This is not speed reading in the Evelyn Wood sense of the term of reading at a rate of four hundred or more words a minute (it requires near native fluency in English to profit from such programs), but simply an attempt to get students to read a little faster. As Wilson points out, students who read too slowly miss both grammar and vocabulary clues because their short-term memory is too short. It is very easy, she adds, to teach students to guide their eyes with their finger or a card on the page. We spend ten minutes three times a week on speed reading in class, and our students eventually do read faster, but it should be honestly stated that whether that increase in speed is due to the speed reading exercises or merely to increased proficiency in English, we don't know. We do know that speed reading exercises increase the students' confidence in their ability to read if the materials are easy enough.

We use commercially available texts for the speed reading exercises, but teachers could easily prepare their own. The format consists of a reading passage and a set of comprehension questions. The students' reading is strictly timed, and after the allotted time is up, they answer the comprehension questions, which are then checked in class. Basically, all speed reading exercises simply cause students to attempt to read faster by putting external pressure on them.

Here is an example of a speed reading exercise:

> Some of the notebooks that George Washington kept as a young man are still in existence, and they show that he learned a little Latin, that he acquired some of the basic elements of good conduct, and that he read a little English literature. At school he seems to have cared only for mathematics. His was a brief and most incomplete education for a

gentleman, and it was all the formal education he was to have, since, unlike some of the other young Virginia gentlemen of his time, he did not go on to the College of William and Mary in the Virginia capital of Williamsburg. In terms of intellectual preparation and power, then, Washington is in sharp contrast with some other early American presidents, such as John Adams, Thomas Jefferson, and James Madison. In later years, Washington probably regretted his lack of intellectual training. He never felt comfortable in formal debate, or in discussions that were not concerned with everyday, practical matters. And inasmuch as he never learned to speak French, he refused to visit France because he felt he would be embarrassed at not being able to speak directly to the statesmen of that country. Thus, unlike Jefferson and Adams, he never reached Europe.

The central idea of paragraph two is:

_____(a) Washington's education showed unusual variety, including as it did, study in fields as varied as mathematics and literature.

_____(b) Washington's education was probably equal to that obtained by other Virginia gentlemen of his age.

_____(c) Washington's education may seem limited by modern standards, but it appears to have been entirely adequate for the duties of his later years.

_____(d) Washington's education was extremely limited and probably put him at a disadvantage in later life.[41]

Guessing Meaning from Context

A major problem in reading, both intensive and extensive, is the sheer number of words the students don't know. Looking each word up in the dictionary becomes prohibitive, and so students are always told to guess at the meaning and they invariably counter that they don't know how. Somewhere in the curriculum, probably at the advanced beginner's level when students begin extensive reading, some exercises should be included which will help them develop strategies for intelligent guessing.

In reading, when we come to a word we don't know, and this is true of reading in the native tongue as well, we first form an

---

[41] David P. Harris, *Reading Improvement Exercises for Students of English as a Second Language* (Englewood Cliffs, New Jersey: Prentice Hall, 1966), p. 59-60.

hypothesis of possible meaning(s), based on the form and context of the word in question. The suffixes of words will usually tell us what part of speech the word is. If that fails, the word order (students know the basic function words by now) should give us enough clues to identify what class of word we are dealing with. Having considered the grammatical context of the word, we next look at the lexical and/or situational context. Lexical context refers to the meaning of surrounding words as they form a lexical cluster[42] which will strongly influence the probability of meaning of our unknown word. *Mark,* for instance, as Fries has pointed out, has many meanings in English, so how does the reader decide on the intended meaning? Look at these sentences:

> He shot but missed the shrdlu completely.
> His boots made shrdlus on the polished floor.
> This lighthouse is an important shrdlu for pilots.
> His shrdlus were always high in school.[43]

The original sentences all have *mark* for *shrdlu* but the process of decoding is exactly the same; we guess from the meaning of the surrounding words. There is just so much that boots can make on a polished floor or that a lighthouse can be to a pilot. The lexical context will limit or fix the probable meaning of a word.

If we are still uncertain, the situational context will help decide the direction of our guess. For foreign students, unfamiliar with culture-specific situations, lack of access to situational context is a frequent cause of difficulty in their reading.

Just making an hypothesis does not of course insure that it is correct. We probably would have guessed at *spots* in the second sentence above. Once readers have made a guess at the new word, there are several options open to them:

1. Stop reading and check the dictionary.
2. Blithely read on not caring whether he understands or not.
3. Reread the sentence several times.

---

[42] In the terminology of Edward M. Anthony, "Toward a Theory of Lexical Meaning," manuscript (Department of General Linguistics, University of Pittsburgh, 1973).

[43] Fries, p. 40.

4. Read the word or even the sentence aloud to himself.
5. Make a mental note of the word and read on, looking for further contexts to verify his guess.

Let's try the process of guessing at the meaning of words from their context. Here is a passage from *Clockwork Orange* by Anthony Burgess.[44]

Read the following selection and then consider the questions below.

'What's it going to be then, eh?'

There was me, that is Alex, and my three droogs, that is Pete, Georgie, and Dim, Dim being really dim, and we sat in the Korova Milkbar making up our rassoodocks what to do with the evening, a flip dark chill winter bastard though dry. The Korova Milkbar was a milk-plus mesto, and you may, O my brothers, have forgotten what these mestos were like, things changing so skorry these days and everybody very quick to forget, newspapers not being read much neither. Well, what they sold there was milk plus something else. They had no license for selling liquor, but there was no law yet against prodding some of the new veshches which they used to put into the old moloko, so you would peet it with vellocet or synthemesc of drencrom or one or two other veshches which could give you a nice quiet horrorshow fifteen minutes admiring Bog and All His Holy Angels and Saints in your left shoe with lights bursting all over your mozg. Or you could peet milk with knives in it, as we used to say, and this would sharpen you up and make you ready for a bit of dirty twenty-to-one, and that was what we were peeting this evening I'm starting off the story with.

Fill in the Parts of Speech and the English Gloss.

Lexical Item	Part of Speech	English Gloss
droogs		
rassoodocks		
flip		
mesto		
skorry		
prodding		

---

[44]Anthony Burgess, *A Clockwork Orange* (New York: Ballantine Books, 1962) p. 9. The English glosses are listed in the "Glossary of Nadsat Language" pp. 185-190 as follows:

droog = friend; rassoodock = mind; flip = wild? [sic]; mesto = place; skorry = quick, quickly; prod = to produce; veshch = thing; peet = to drink; vellocet, synthemesc, drencrom = drugs; horrorshow = good, well; Bog = God; mozg = grain; moloko = milk].

Lexical Item	Part of Speech	English Gloss
veshches		
moloko		
peet		
vellocet		
synthemesc		
drencrom		
horrorshow		
Bog		
mozg		

Droogs probably is *friends* which the grammatical context of *my three* sets up, but it could also be *colleagues* or *brothers*. Later the situational context settles the matter of *friends;* normally you would not bring your colleagues or brothers along for such an evening. *Rassoodock* is clearly *mind* and we guess that primarily from the structural patter of *making up our X* but someone not familiar with the idiom of *making up one's mind* would not be able to use that clue. However, *we were X what to do with the evening* would give us something like *planning, talking about, deciding,* etc. which would be close enough not to interfere with the story. We can't tell whether *flip* is an adverb or adjective. If an adverb it would be an intensifying adverb, like *very;* we can guess that from *bastard.* If an adjective, it denotes some negative quality, and we guess that from *dark* and *chill* and the absence of commas. In either case, *flip* adds a minimum of information. *Skorry* is of course *fast;* the lexical context of *forgotten* and *changing* gives us that. *Peet* is interesting; the first time we run across it, it seems to have the meaning of *spike* or *mix* in *peet it with vellocet,* which we guess from all three contexts: grammatical, lexical and situational. But when we come to *peet milk with knives in it,* we feel uneasy. The lexical context still fits our hypothesis of *spike* but the grammatical context is strange; *in it* doesn't fit that pattern. Finally when we come to *that was what we were peeting this evening* we have an intransitive verb which rules out *spike.* We now reformulate our hypothesis which is to say that we guess again, this time at *drink,* drawing again on the grammatical, lexical and situational context; they are in a milk bar for recreational purposes, it is something you can do with milk, and it can be intransitive. Most readers will probably check back to *peet* in the sentences above to see if their new hypothesis works, which indeed it does.

Now let us examine the various options listed above which are available to readers once they have initially guessed at the meaning of a word. The whole purpose of this activity is to get students going on their reading and not constantly interrupting themselves to look up words. Therefore they should be firmly discouraged from Option 1 of immediately turning to their dictionary. If it is a word important to the passage, and the student still can't make a reasonable guess by the third time he runs across that word, then it is probably a good idea for him to look it up in the dictionary, but the point is that he doesn't stop dead the first time he runs into an unfamiliar word.

Before accepting Option 2 of just reading on, the student will have to make a decision whether the word is important for the story or not. With *flip* above we can safely ignore it, and students need to be assured that it is all right to ignore some words and phrases. They also need to be shown criteria for making such a decision, such as one in a series of negative adjectives, rhetorical devices indicating repetitive statements or rephrasings, etc.

As for Option 3 of rereading a sentence, every teacher we know will tell his students it's a terrible habit for a multitude of reasons. Still, it would be interesting to know how many readers reread *give you a nice quiet horrorshow fifteen minutes admiring Bog* in the exercise above. The fact is that we do reread, but not so much because we don't understand a word as because we have scrambled the syntactic clues. *Horrorshow* is an adjective here, and that confused most of us the first time we read it so that we could not decode the sentence—even though it really makes little difference what the exact meaning of that adjective is. We doubt that anyone can or should stop students from reading a sentence over again *if it is important to the reading passage,* but they need to be taught in rereading to concentrate on syntactic meaning rather than on the semantic which they processed during the first reading.

Students will read strange words aloud to themselves, and we don't know why. It may be with cognate languages that saying the word aloud obscures the spelling and makes the relationship clearer, but that is mere speculation. If it helps, there seems no sense in stopping it.

Finally we come to Option 5, the strategy we want the students to develop: noticing the word, guessing at the meaning, and reading on to confirm or reject the hypothesis. It is hopeless as well as wrong to insist that this be the only strategy that the students use, but it certainly should be presented to them as a viable alternative and the one they should resort to first. They need exercises like the one above—but with English words of course—where they can draw on all the other work they do for reading, grammar pattern recognition, vocabulary, word study, and dictionary exercises. They need to have the process and separate steps of hypothesis formulation and testing made clear to them so that they attack new words in a systematic way rather than through aimless guessing.

Testing

There should be frequent testing of vocabulary in combination with the reading program. We see little sense in giving formal tests on the reading itself; every assignment with its comprehension questions is a test of reading comprehension. But the learning of vocabulary is effectively reinforced by frequent testing; tests should be frequent (once a week) and short (10 minutes) with, if convenient, a longer midterm and final exam. The format of the test depends on the teaching point of the vocabulary items—whether the words were taught for recognition or production. Recognition words are best tested by multiple choice questions; the time spent on preparing the test is more than made up for in correcting it. Or the students may be asked to write a definition for each word. Production words can of course also be tested in such a way; they can also be tested by a cloze test, by supplying the word to a written definition or by using the word in a sentence. But the single-most important point is to test frequently.

EXTENSIVE READING

Extensive reading simply refers to the outside reading students do on their own with no help or guidance from the teacher. Smith and many before him point out that you learn to read by reading, and the objective of extensive reading is exactly that: to learn reading by reading.

The two major problems of extensive reading are (1) selecting reading material and (2) getting the students to do the reading.

Students should begin to read extensively as soon as they can possibly manage; usually this will be at the advanced beginning stage. Ideally they should be reading books that test out at the independent level.[45] In a large class this will vary from individual to individual, and since all work is done outside of class, students may very well read different books. At the beginning levels, where the major emphasis is on getting students used to reading in the target language, they will need to read books that have been adapted for second language teaching since their language skills are still not proficient enough for unexpurgated prose. At this level, bilingual dictionaries are likely to be more efficient, and no one is a more accurate judge of that than the students themselves. If they prefer to use bilingual dictionaries, let them.

At the intermediate level, the students need to begin to tackle unsimplified English prose. This is where the difficulty in text selection enters in. One frequently sees suggestions to use magazines like *Time* and *Newsweek,* but the fact is that their writing is exceedingly difficult and idiosyncratic, and even our advanced students have difficulty with such readings. Short stories, novels, and plays are usually the best bet. What works very well is to have the students read a book they have already read in their mother tongue. Adventure and mystery stories tend to have lively and natural dialogues, nonspecialized vocabulary, and not too complicated grammar. They are excellent except for the sad fact that some students don't like them, and then there is no sense in using them. The students *must* be interested in what they read extensively. Some authors, like Hemingway, may seem to write in very simple straightforward language and so appear easy, but the complexity of the argument and the cultural references render the reading quite difficult.

Our intermediate level students in the Institute, who are going on to do academic work in their own fields, read a text on their own subject matter for extensive reading. At times it is difficult for them to settle on a final selection and they make several false starts, becoming more and more discouraged. In order to expedite their selection of a text for extensive reading, they are given the following exercise:

Some Questions to Ask When Surveying a Book or Article

I. Questions that can be answered without reading the text of the book or article.

---

[45] This is easily tested by a cloze test passage taken from the intended text.

1. What is the title?
2. Who is the author?
3. What are his credentials?
4. Is the book or article up-to-date?
5. Are there pictures, graphs, charts, or exercises?

II. Questions that can be answered after reading a small part of the text. (The first few lines of several paragraphs, the introduction and the conclusion.)

1. Is the reading level too easy, too difficult, or about right?
2. What is the topic of the book or article? (This may not be clear from the title.)
3. Who is the book or article written for?
4. Will the book or article be useful for me?

We then train them in the techniques of SQ3R and hope that it is not a waste of time. SQ3R, which stands for Survey, Question, Read, Recite and Review, are the five steps to be followed in technical reading.

1. *Survey*: When you are assigned a section of a textbook to study, first survey the pages to get a general idea of the material. Skim quickly over the topic headings; look at pictures, graphs, charts, or diagrams; see if there are questions or a summary at the end.

2. *Question*: After a rapid survey, ask yourself questions based on the material you have surveyed. This helps you to read with a purpose, looking for specific answers and anticipating essential points of information.

3. *Read:* Next read as rapidly as possible. Because you know what you are looking for and where you are going, your reading speed should be faster than if you had not first surveyed the pages and formulated questions for which you are seeking answers.

4. *Recite:* At the end of each section, summarize the material by reciting to yourself the important points. This helps you consolidate the information you have read, relate it to previous information, and prepare yourself for what is to follow.

5. *Review*: Finally, when you have finished the assignment, immediately review the material so that it will form a unified whole. Also, when you have the next assignment in the text, review the preceding material,

> surveying it rapidly to refresh your memory. Each
> section, though read separately and at different times,
> will fit together into the total organization of the
> material that the author intended.[46]

The teacher should be braced for a veritable jeremiad from the students after their first extensive reading assignment of unexpurgated English. They should be told firmly that it will get much easier as they read along and that they should not worry about all the words they don't understand as long as they get the major outline of the reading. The important thing is to keep them reading. We begin with ten pages a week for the first two weeks with a gradual increase over fifteen weeks to at least fifty pages a week.

Periodic and systematic feedback on the extensive reading is crucial in order to keep students reading. Such feedback is not only a police action (although it is certainly partly that), but our students like to discuss their readings, and they like the teacher to take a personal interest in their individual work. Without such interest on the part of the teacher, the students' motivation to read drops off noticeably. The feedback most easily takes the form of a written report. If this is done in conjunction with the writing part of the curriculum a proper albeit short report may be expected; if not, a few sentences on a five by eight inch card summarizing the main ideas are sufficient. Alternatively, students may give an oral report to the teacher while the class is otherwise occupied, or they may give the report to the class. If the whole class is reading the same selection for extensive reading, the feedback may take the part of class discussion or role play. It is important that the major focus is on main ideas, and that the students don't get harassed by picky questions or asked about individual vocabulary items. Not only do the students need to learn to ignore some of the words they don't understand, but they also need to learn to enjoy their reading. For many students of English, extensive reading is the one skill which will stay with them long after they have finished their formal studies and is a skill which in itself holds a major reward for the study of English.

---

[46] Richard Yorkey, *Study Skills for Students of English as a Second Language* (New York: McGraw-Hill, 1970), citing Francis P. Robinson, p. 130.

6
Writing

WRITING*

The last of the four skills of listening, speaking, reading, and writing has been much neglected in the audio-lingual approach and less than efficiently dealt with in other approaches to language teaching. This chapter examines the role of writing in language teaching and proceeds to discuss writing as a skill in its own right: the techniques and procedures of teaching composition.

Motives and Objectives

Writing is one way of providing variety in classroom procedures, and it also makes possible individualized work in large classes. Writing tends to increase retention and makes available a source for later

---

*Part of this chapter was based on an article by C. B. Paulston, "Teaching Writing in the ESOL Classroom: Techniques of Controlled Composition," which appeared in the *TESOL Quarterly* (March 1972); we are grateful for permission to quote.

reference. Very importantly, it provides a student with physical evidence of his achievements and becomes a source whereby he can measure his improvement. As teachers of intensive oral courses know, an accurate evaluation of increased oral proficiency by the students themselves is rare. They frequently voice the feeling that they are not progressing; a record of the students' written work may alleviate this problem.

We do know that "materials presented visually are more easily learned than comparable materials presented aurally"[1] and certainly writing contributes to the visual presentation. Another fact in verbal learning is the following: "The more numerous kinds of association that are made to an item, the better are learning and retention. Again this principle seems to dictate against the use of systems of language teaching that employ mainly one sensory modality, namely, hearing."[2]

Another exceedingly important consideration is that of language ability and different styles of learning. Pimsleur has called one component of language learning ability "auditory ability" and he considers this "the main factor differentiating normal achievers from underachievers in foreign language learning. It is hypothesized to be the factor which accounts for differences in people's language learning ability which are not explainable by intelligence or interest."[3] People with low "auditory ability" need to use compensatory skills such as writing in learning languages.[4] Exercises for writing as a service activity which serve to reinforce and consolidate the other language skills have been discussed in the chapters on grammar, pronunciation, listening comprehension, and reading, and will not be mentioned any further in this chapter.

In this chapter we are primarily concerned with writing as a skill in its own right. Skill in writing is a basic necessity in the academic environment, and even the nonacademic student, who has no need to

[1] John B. Carroll, "The Contributions of Psychological Theory and Educational Research to the Teaching of Foreign Languages," in *Trends in Language Teaching* A. Valdman, ed. (New York: McGraw-Hill, 1966), p. 105.

[2] Ibid, p. 105.

[3] Paul Pimsleur, "Testing Foreign Language Learning," in *Trends in Language Teaching*, A. Valdman, ed. (New York: McGraw-Hill, 1966), p. 182.

[4] Wilga Rivers, *The Psychologist and the Foreign-Language Teacher*, (Chicago: University of Chicago Press, 1964), p. 112.

write reports and term papers, will occasionally need to write letters, messages, memos, invitations, and the like. Practice in this type of writing is customarily referred to as composition—writing beyond the sentence level, putting together words in a grammatically acceptable form and ordering the resultant sentences in an appropriate way. At the beginning level, we have three major teaching points in the writing of compositions: (1) correct form of the language on the sentence level, (2) mechanics of punctuation, and (3) content organization.

On the intermediate and advanced levels, the purpose of teaching writing is mainly to teach the writing of research papers, reports, essay, and the like—objectives no different from the teaching of writing to native speakers. But writing also serves as a reinforcement for reading, and this purpose is reflected in the specific teaching points. At this level the teaching points of composition include some work on syntax and vocabulary, but the major emphasis is on rhetorical organization on the paragraph level as well as on the overall composition level. This work includes rhetorical devices like transition words and parallelism, and outlining, note-taking, the writing of footnotes and bibliographical entries.

Techniques and Procedures

The following discussion is organized according to the three major teaching points of composition: (1) correct language form, (2) mechanics of punctuation, and (3) organization of content. These topics will be included on all levels of proficiency (with the possible exception of punctuation); it is primarily the emphasis which differs rather than the techniques and procedures. On the beginning level we concentrate on the correct language form of sentences and their punctuation, but students also learn rudimentary principles of organization. On the intermediate and advanced levels we concentrate on the organization and development of ideas, but the students still need to work on sentence level language skills.

COMPOSITION: CORRECT LANGUAGE FORMS

There are basically two methods for teaching correct language form in writing. One is free composition, where the student writes whatever comes into his head. The other is controlled composition, where by certain controls similar to those in pattern drills the student is helped to produce a correct composition. Controlled composition has several advantages and we use it on all levels. Controlled composition makes it possible to teach one thing at a time while focusing the student's conscious attention on the critical features of the language pattern. Controlled composition makes sequencing and grading of patterns possible, and it gives the student maximum practice in writing correct forms of the language; consequently, correcting is easy.

However, as we will discuss later, it is important to remember that on all levels the students should have a chance to occasionally write free compositions, and that this practice should become increasingly frequent on the intermediate and advanced levels.

Controlled Composition

Typically a controlled composition consists of a written model of some type with directions for conversions or specific language manipulations in rewriting the model. The degree of control lies both within the model and within the type of manipulation the student is asked to execute on the model. In a substitution table composition like the following, where all fillers for each slot are interchangeable, there is complete control, and all the student need do is copy correctly:

> A (1) man (2) walked (3) down the street. A (4) girl (5) was waiting for him outside a (6) shop. As he approached her, she smiled (7) and said, "Hello. How are you?"
>
> (1) tall, young, well-dressed
> (2) with a beard, in a black hat, with sunglasses
> (3) rapidly, hurriedly, impatiently
> (4) pretty, fair-haired, dark-skinned
> (5) in high-heeled shoes, with an umbrella, in a pink hat
> (6) chemist's, grocer's bicycle
> (7) pleasantly, attractively, in a friendly manner[5]

However, if *with a beard* had appeared as a possible selection in (5) it would not have been an appropriate selection, and the student must understand that in order to write an acceptable paragraph. Finally, the student might be asked to provide a suitable

---

[5] D. H. Spencer, "Two Types of Guided Composition Exercise," *English Language Teaching* XIX, no. 4 (July 1965): 158. See also D. H. Spencer, *Guided Composition Exercises* (London: Longmans, 1968).

expression of his own for indicated slots. The degree of control depends on the degree of choice the student has in writing his composition.

The same sequencing from mechanical to communicative exercise which was employed for the structural pattern drills is possible with some types of controlled composition exercises. In the following examples by Moody, which are similar in kind if not in format to Spencer's above, the first frame is a mechanical exercise:

Two of our old students		England	last year.
Mr. Oladipo		Lagos	last week.
Mrs. Ademola	went to	Nsukka	two days ago.
My uncle		Zaria	three months ago.[6]
David's eldest brother		Badagry	

There is complete control since all alternatives are fully interchangeable; students will write correct compositions as long as they can copy carefully the correct answers supplied by the teacher. It is important to realize that the students can produce a correct composition from such a frame and still not understand what they have written. For any learning to take place the teacher must make sure that the students do understand, or the writing practice will become mere busy work. Such mechanical exercises should only be used at the very beginning level.

The following frame is meaningful:

He		sea		she	did not have a car.
		train			could not afford an air ticket.
She	travelled by	air	because	they	could not go there by train.
		car			knew the ships were all full.
They		lorry		he	wanted to get there quickly.
		bus			did not want to pay too much money.[7]

---

[6] K. W. Moody, "Controlled Composition Frames," *English Language Teaching* XIX, no. 4 (July 1965): 150. See also K. W. Moody, *Written English Under Control* (Ibadan: Oxford University Press, 1966).
[7] p.150.

Students cannot write a correct composition if they do not understand what they are doing, structurally as well as lexically. The control is diminished; thus, the correct response directly depends on the students' knowledge of English. The information for responding is still supplied by the teacher, but there is now a right and a wrong choice for the students to make. The final step is to have students write compositions of their own, using the same patterns as in the model but making up their own stories. In the drills this step was named communicative, since the students talk about their own world and opinions, but it may well be that in writing it is not so much communicative as imaginative. In any case, there is no control of lexical items and much less of structural patterns; the students now supply the information for responding, and the problem-solving type of learning process is very different from the habit formation of the mechanical exercises. This type of control, then, employs several composition exercises to cover one grammatical feature, the first rigidly controlled while the last may at times come close to free composition.

There is another type of control, such as that found in Paulston and Dykstra's *Controlled Composition*[8] and in Sandberg's "Drills for Writing Laboratories,"[9] where the controls are gradually relaxed throughout the program and once relaxed do not go back to a closer control again. There is no evidence that one type of control is better than another, but for the beginning levels we believe the zigzag control from mechanical or meaningful to communicative is necessary. No amount of mechanical writing is going to teach a productive generating of sentences, and the students need to work with the relaxed controls, albeit within very simple patterns. For the more advanced levels, we prefer the diminishing controls where the students gain confidence by their steadily increasing liberty.

TYPOLOGY OF EXERCISES

In the following list of techniques of controlling writing, there is no attempt to classify these techniques according to control, but rather they are listed according to type. The reason for this is that many types of controlled composition techniques can serve with

---

[8] Christina Bratt Paulston and Gerald Dykstra, *Controlled Composition in English as a Second Language* (New York: Regents, 1973).

[9] Karl C. Sandberg, "Drills for Writing Laboratories" in *NAFSA Studies and Papers, English Language Series*, D. Wigglesworth, ed. (1967).

varying degrees of control. Moody makes the same "Controlled Composition Frame" shown above serve as the model for mechanical, meaningful and communicative writing. The teacher should be aware of the importance of the degree of control and suit the activities to the needs of the students.

This typology of techniques has been culled from existing texts and from articles on producing materials for teaching composition. It is intended both as a guide for teachers to prepare their own exercises and as a source of reference to more exercises of these types.

There seem to be basically four kinds of controlled composition where the writing exercises derive from (1) substitution tables or frames, (2) models with directions for rewriting the model, (3) pictorial control, or a combination of pictorial control and a written or oral model, and (4) exercises with semicontrol where content and ideas are suggested but with a minimum suggestion for structural patterns. This discussion is limited to techniques of controlled composition where the control is generated by written stimuli.

Substitution Tables

Substitution tables go by many names but primarily they are referred to as tables or frames. They differ from the substitution conversions written from model passages in that all necessary substitutions are indicated to the student either by slot or by number. In the substitution exercises of rewriting models the student has to find all necessary correlative substitutions himself. There are (1) single, (2) correlative and (3) multiple substitution exercises. This is a single substitution exercise from Costinett based on a previous reading:

I feel	tired	today.[10]
	sick	
	exhausted	
	horrible	

A correlative substitution exercise may be quite simple as this one from Moody[11] on page 210 or as complicated as the one form Arapoff[12] on page 211:

---

[10]Sandra Costinett, *Structure Graded Readings in English*, Book Two (Philadelphia: Center for Curriculum Development, 1970), p. 78.

[11]Moody, p. 150.

[12]Nancy Arapoff, "Controlled Rhetoric Frames," *English Language Teaching* XXIII, no 1 (October 1968): 31.

Two of our old students Mr. Oladipo Mrs. Ademola My uncle David's eldest brother	went to	England Lagos Nsukka Zaria Badagry	last year. last week. two days ago. three months ago.

He She They	went there	to inspect a new factory, to study at the university, to see Mr. _____		
		to meet to visit	her their his	friend _____ , sister-in-law,

who which	works	in the Ministry of Foreign Affairs. in the office of a big company.	
	teaches takes	students	from many different countries. of many nationalities.
	makes produces	many kinds of	tires. cloth. electrical equipment. batteries.

He She They	travelled by	sea train air car lorry bus	because	she they he	did not have a car. could not afford an air ticket. could not go there by train. knew the ships were all full. wanted to get there quickly. did not want to pay too much money.

His Their Her	friends brother sister	met	them him her	at the	airport, docks, bus station, railway station, motor park, hotel,
The A An	manager bus taxi old friend				

and took	her them him	to	the his her their a	house. factory. hotel. office.

(1)
Hawaii's climate
Hawaii's weather
The weather in Hawaii
The climate in Hawaii
In Hawaii the weather

(2)
is said to be
is
can be considered

(3)
just as
more
not as
less

(4)
stimulating
interesting
comfortable
monotonous
enjoyable
changeable

(5)
as
than

(6)
(name of your country)'s weather.
the weather in _____'s climate.
the climate in _____ .

(7)
Hawaii
Hawaii's weather
The climate in Hawaii
In Hawaii the weather
Hawaii's climate

(8) There are no seasons in Hawaii,

(9)
is said to have
is
can be shown to be
has
doesn't have

(10)
no variety,
unchangeable,
monotonous,
no seasonal changes,
no seasons,
n't any seasons,
changes,
seasons,

(11)
while
but
and
however
although
and similarly

(12)
_____'s weather
the climate in _____
in _____ the climate

(13) there are

(14)
has
is said to have
can be shown to have
is said to be

(15)
four
two
no

(16) seasons in _____

(17)
no variety
no changes
no seasonal changes
n't any seasons
monotonous

(18)
four
two

(19)
changeable
a lot of variety.

(20)
either.
too.

(21)
seasons,
seasonal changes.

(22) In Hawaii

(23)
The weather in Hawaii
The climate in Hawaii
Hawaii's weather
Hawaii's climate
Hawaii

(24)
the weather
the climate

(25)
is,
can be shown to be,
seems to be,

What they have in common is that the students are asked to choose one filler from each slot and that their initial choice will necessitate later choices. If *Mrs. Ademola* is chosen in the first sentence of Moody's frame, then the pronoun must be *she* in the second. In the same way, in Arapoff's "rhetoric frames" the choice in box (5) is a grammatical one, but "if a student chooses 'Hawaii's weather' in box (1) "he will then select the parallel to this, '. . . .'s weather' in box (6) for he will have learned that grammatical parallelism is a rhetorical device used to promote coherence between ideas in an essay.[13] The latter is a rhetorical choice and involves language manipulations much more sophisticated than in the Moody frame.

Multiple substitution exercises may also be very simple:

> The children   stole   the   apples.
> student/borrow/book;   woman/choose/cake;   porter/lift/suitcase[14]

with the model rewritten as: The students borrowed the books, etc. They may be made meaningful by adding choices which are not appropriate as I pointed out above (a *girl* would not go well *with a beard*). Finally, a paraphrase of a model maintaining structural patterns may be considered the ultimate in multiple substitution exercises:

> Mary was a foolish girl who thought only about beautiful clothes. One morning, she was walking along a road, carrying a basketful of eggs. She was going to the city to sell them and to buy clothes with the money. She was walking in the middle of the road, thinking of the clothes she was going to buy. Suddenly a big car came around the corner. Mary jumped out of the way, dropped the basket, and all the eggs were broken.

The student is asked to rewrite it beginning with "John was a young man":

> John was a young man who cared mainly about lively parties. One night he was drinking at a party, enjoying an evening full of fun. He was singing to the guests to amuse them and to impress Joan with his cleverness. He was standing on the chair in the corner, singing of the girl he was going to marry. Suddenly the host came into the room. John jumped off the chair, sprained his ankle, and all the fun was spoiled.[15]

---

[13]Ibid, p. 28.

[14]Spencer, p. 157.

[15]Anita Pincas, "Teaching Different Styles of Written English" *English Language Teaching* XVII, no. 2 (January 1964): 78.

The teacher needs to take care that the exercise does not become one of ingenuity even for a native speaker, but that the model merely serves as a guide of patterns and organization.

Models with Directions for Rewriting

By far the most common among extant texts is the type of controlled composition which employs a written paragraph or two with directions for rewriting it, employing specific language manipulations. The written paragraph serves as a model, which guides the student to write a correct composition.

Slager[16] lists the characteristics of models for use in controlled composition: they should be short, contemporary, and rather simple in style with a careful and obvious organization. On the more advanced level they should include a variety of those syntactic features which are characteristic of mature prose and they should represent a variety of writing: narrative, descriptive, reflective, factual, analytical, critical, instructional, and hortatory. The model, which serves to guide the student to a correct composition, should be in excellent English, and so should the resultant composition. A paragraph with ten verbs in the past perfect tense is just un-English, and it is not worth sacrificing a decent composition for the maximum practice.

Janet Ross[17] and Paulston[18] have offered suggestions for preparing models: the teacher can write his own, he can adapt existing materials or he can use passages from the readings.

In looking for model passages to convert to specific patterns, one is at first likely to be discouraged since it seems at times difficult to find what one is looking for. Parallelism, for instance, is not very frequent in modern English but it can be found in essays, editorials, sermons, political speeches, in writing which attempts to convince readers. Passives are much rarer than one might think; newspaper accounts are a good place to look

---

[16]William R. Slager, "Controlling Composition: Some Practical Classroom Techniques," *NAFSA Studies and Papers, English Language Series, No. 12,* R. B. Kaplan, ed. p. 84.

[17]Janet Ross, "Controlled Composition," *NAFSA Studies and Papers English Language Series*, D. Wigglesworth, (1967), pp. 47-49. Los Altos, Calif.: Language Research Associates.

[18]Christina Bratt Paulston, "The Use of Model Passages in a Program of Guided Composition," *On Teaching English to Speakers of Other Languages*, Series III, B. W. Robinett, ed. (1966), p. 152. Washington, DC: TESOL.

for them, as are grammars. You can read many pages of fiction without coming across any sentence connectives—the place to look for them is in writing which deals with involved abstract facts, especially in comparison. I remember looking for them in B. A. G. Fuller's *History of Philosophy*, and there in two short paragraphs were nine sentence connectives. Imperatives are surprisingly scarce . . . they can be found in cookbooks and how-to books. Modifications are most easily used with fiction, i.e., the adding of adjectives and adverbs, of relative clauses and the like.[19]

For lower levels one should limit the vocabulary, but the sentence structures (which must of course be known by the students) control themselves, as it were. The control lies in the conversion: either you can convert a structure or you can't; and the difficulty lies in finding or writing convertible structures. Once this is achieved, the other structures in the passage are merely rewritten, and, in fact, all structures are controlled. Of course, if a structure causes semantic difficulty, that is another matter; the one necessity is that the model passage be understandable to the student.

Conversions

Model passages lend themselves to two kinds of writing activity: conversions and what might be called semicontrolled composition, where the model passage serves to suggest content and ideas but with little structural control. The latter is an important step in going from controlled to free composition. We will discuss various types of conversion exercises here. The techniques of semicontrolled composition will be dealt with later.

There are three types of conversions: substitutions, transformations, and modifications. In a substitution conversion the structural patterns of the sentence remain the same as in the model while slots are filled by a specific class of fillers. In a transformation conversion the structural patterns differ from the model although the output remains controlled by the original sentence structures. Modification exercises involve primarily expanding the patterns in the model and are the result of the student's choice.

Substitution Conversions As with substitution tables, there are single, correlative, and multiple substitution conversions. They lend themselves primarily to exercises in the grammatical categories of

---

[19]Ibid, p. 152.

gender, number, and tense, and in replacing synonyms and transition words. Here's a correlative substitution conversion on gender changes:

Model: from Clarence Day, *Life with Father*

Father had the same character as a boy, I suppose, that he had as a man, and he was too independent to care if people thought his name fancy. He paid no attention to the prejudices of others, except to disapprove of them. He had plenty of prejudices himself, of course, but they were his own. He was humorous and confident and level-headed, and I imagine that if any boy had tried to make fun of him for being named Clarence, Father would simply have laughed and told him he didn't know what he was talking about.

Assignment:

Rewrite the entire passage, changing the word *Father* to *Mother* each time it appears. Remember to change the pronouns, nouns and names wherever it becomes necessary.

Student's Composition:

Mother had the same character as a girl, I suppose, that *she* had as a *woman,* and *she* was too independent to care if people thought *her* name fancy. *She* paid no attention to the prejudices of others, except to disapprove of them. *She* had plenty of prejudices *herself,* of course, but they were *her* own. *She* was humorous and confident and level-headed, and I imagine that if any boy had tried to make fun of *her* for being named Clarissa, *Mother* would simply have laughed and told him *she* didn't know what he was talking about.[20]

If the student is asked to underline his changes from the model, the teacher can correct the composition at a glance.

The following exercise is a multiple substitution conversion. As is obvious from this example, substitution exercises need not be as easy as those cited above.

Model: from Gerald Dykstra, "A New Dimension in Laboratories"

"The National Interest and Teaching of English as a Foreign Language," a

---

[20]Paulston and Dykstra, p. 59.

document prepared by the National Council of Teachers of English, quotes a conservative estimate that 400 million people now speak English. Since a very large part of this number speaks English as a second language, the continuing need for teachers of English as a foreign or second language is immediately apparent. In addition, there are millions who are now in English classrooms who will not make extensive use of English as a spoken language but who will use textbooks, reference books and scholarly work in English to complete their own education in almost all professional fields. All of these need qualified teachers. Finally, of course, there are the vast numbers studying English who will never advance far enough to make practical use of English, spoken or written, but who might do so if they had qualified teachers now.

Assignment:

Rewrite the entire passage, changing ... *400 million people now speak English* to ... *400 million men are now learning to cook.* Follow the general structure of the model but make whatever changes in vocabulary that are necessary for the passage to make sense. Use your imagination treely.[21]

This is our contribution to the women's liberation movement; the resulting compositions from this exercise are always very funny. The reader can concoct his own.

Transformation Conversions The usual transformation conversions are exercises on changing the imperative to various tenses, passive to active and active to passive, statements to questions and questions to answers, negative to positive and positive to negative, adjectives and adverbs to clauses and phrases and phrases to clauses, direct to indirect and indirect to direct speech. There are as well, in Dacanay's terminology, integration, reduction, and transposition exercises.[22]

Here is a typical transformation conversion from Baskoff:

Change the following sentences from passive to active voice.
Note: If there is no agent you must supply one as the subject in the active voice.

---

[21]Ibid, p. 57.

[22]Fe R. Decanay, *Techniques and Procedures in Second Language Teaching* (Dobbs Ferry, New York: Oceana Publications, 1963), pp. 107-151.

1. First I was directed to my seat by the stewardess.
2. We were told to fasten our seatbelts.
3. A few minutes after take-off, magazines and newspapers were distributed.
4. I was given some gum to chew because my ears hurt.
5. We were given instructions on what to do in case of an emergency.

The student's composition will be something like this:

First the stewardess directed me to my seat. Then she told us to fasten our seatbelts. A few minutes after takeoff, the stewardesses distributed magazines and newspapers. One of them gave me some gum to chew because my ears hurt. The captain gave us instructions on what to do in case of an emergency.[23]

The next exercise is a direct to indirect speech transformation conversion from Arapoff. This exercise is very complicated and is followed by two pages of analysis (in the form of questions) in order to enable the student to write such a conversation himself.

Conversation:

John: I've heard San Francisco is a beautiful city.
Bob went there on his vacation.

Don: I didn't know that. I've been thinking he'd gone to Los Angeles. I'd have liked to've heard about San Francisco. I am planning to go there on vacation.

John: He might've visited both cities. He'll be arriving in a few minutes. You can ask him then.

Indirect address:

John mentioned to Don that he had heard San Francisco was a beautiful city. Bob had gone there on his vacation.
Don replied that he hadn't known that. He had been thinking Bob had gone to Los Angeles. He would have liked to have heard about San Francisco. He was planning to go there on his vacation.
John said that Bob might have visited both cities. He would be arriving in a few minutes. Don could ask him then.[24]

Integration exercises—joining sentences by conjunctions and

---

[23]Florence Baskoff, *Guided Composition* (Philadelphia: Center for Curriculum Development, 1971), p. 156.
[24]Nancy Arapoff, *Writing through Understanding* (New York: Holt, Rinehart and Winston, 1970), p. 25.

relative pronouns—appear in most texts. These examples are on the sentence level:

> Cue: The suitcase is lost, and the handle of the suitcase is red.
> Response: The suitcase, whose handle is red, is lost.[25]
> Cue: Steve never watches commercials. Stan does not like them.
> Response: Steve never watches commercials, nor does Stan like them.[26]

They are pure pattern drill, and very effective. They should be taken to the paragraph level:

> Model: from Ernest Hemingway, *A Farewell to Arms*
>
> I did not believe the Germans did it. I did not believe they had to. There was no need to confuse our retreat. The size of the army and the fewness of the roads did that. Nobody gave any orders, let alone Germans. Still, they would shoot us for Germans. They shot Aymo. The hay smelled good and lying in the barn in the hay took away all the years in between . . . . I listened to the firing to the north toward Udine. I could hear machine gun firing. There was no shelling. That was something. They must have gotten some troops along the road. I looked down in the half-light of the hay barn and saw Piani standing on the hauling floor. He had a long sausage, a jar of something and two bottles of wine under his arm.
> "Come up," I said. "There is the ladder."
>
> Assignment:
>
> Hemingway is describing the retreat in Italy during World War I. One of his stylistic characteristics is his short sentences. Rewrite the entire passage, combining with subordinate conjunctions as many sentences as you can with ease. See Appendix V (which contains a list of conjunctions).[27]

A less controlled integration exercise presents a model with the directions to add a relative clause, a reason clause, a purpose clause, etc. to certain specified sentences:

> Model: from Irving Howe, "T.E. Lawrence: The Problem of Heroism"
>
> (1) To an age that usually takes its prose plain, Lawrence's style is likely to

---

[25]Earl Rand, *Constructing Sentences* (New York: Holt, Rinehart and Winston, 1969), p. 75.

[26]Jacqueline P. Griffin and G. Howard Poteet, *Sentence Strategies* (New York: Harcourt, Brace, Jovanovich, 1971), p. 267.

[27]Paulston and Dykstra, p. 54.

seem mannered. (2) Unquestionably there are passages that fail through a surplus of effort; passages that contain more sensibility than Lawrence could handle or justify. (3) But it is dangerous to dismiss such writing simply because we have been trained to suspect the grand.

Assignment:

Rewrite the entire passage, adding comparison clauses to sentences 1 and 3. See Appendix V (which lists conjunctions to use for comparison clauses).

The student's composition may look like this:

To an age that usually takes its prose plain, Lawrence's style is likely to seem *more* mannered *than we are used to.* Unquestionably there are passages that fail through a surplus of effort; passages which contain more sensibility than Lawrence could handle or justify. But it is *as* dangerous to dismiss such writing simply because we have been trained to suspect the grand *as it is consistently to submit to bathos.* [28]

This adding of clauses type of controlled composition is a much more complicated kind of language manipulation than it seems at first, and requires very clear thinking on the part of the student.

Many writers have been concerned about reduction exercises, i.e., reducing sentences or clauses to verbal phrases (embedding) in order to pack information into a sentence. A high degree of predication within a sentence is typical of mature written English, and this type of exercise is a primary concern of many writing texts, especially those for native speakers.

Cue:	A boy was frightened by a dog. The boy quickly ran to the door.
Response:	Frightened by the dog, the boy quickly ran to the door. [29]
Cue:	Even if Phil is drafted, he will propose to Nadyne.
Response:	Even if drafted, Phil will propose to Nadyne. [30]

These exercises should also be taken to the paragraph level. Janet Ross suggests one way of doing so:

Directions:

Included clauses help indicate the precise relationship between ideas. In

---

[28]Ibid, p. 22.

[29]Rand, p. 83.

[30]Mary E. Whitten, *Creative Pattern Practice: A New Approach to Writing* (New York: Harcourt, Brace and World, 1966), p. 133.

order to make the following selection less wordy, express in one sentence the ideas between the bars. You will probably use included clauses to do this.

At the Airport

/At the airport I always like to conjecture about the people. I see many people at the airport./ That lady is a grandmother. She is standing beside a jewelry counter. She is meeting a plane. Her daughter and two small grandchildren are on the plane./

This is a composition which one of her students wrote:

I always like to conjecture about the many people I see at the airport. That lady standing by a jewelry counter is a grandmother meeting a plane on which are her daughter and two grandchildren.[31]

Reduction exercises may also be done as modifications, in which case the student is simply asked to add certain types of verbal phrases to indicated sentences. Earl Rand reports on an interesting procedure for teaching embedding, which he calls synthesis, following traditional British terminology. The model paragraph, which contains many embeddings, is rewritten in simple sentences.

The problem of how these atoms are arranged in a protein molecule is one of the most interesting and challenging now being attacked by workers in the physical and biological sciences.

The students rewrite this sentence, which is the last of a paragraph, as they have done all the others, in simple, active sentences:

The problem is one of the most interesting and challenging problems.
The problem is that these atoms are arranged somehow in a protein molecule.
Workers are now attacking the problem.
The workers are in the physical and biological sciences.

A week later the student is asked to combine the paraphrased, simple sentences into one sentence. "He is urged (1) to place the new or main information in the independent clause and the secondary,

[31]Janet Ross, "Controlled Writing: A Transformational Approach." *Tesol Quarterly* II, no. 4 (December 1968): 260-261.

supporting material in the subordinate clauses or phrases, (2) to pronominalize, (3) to make a sentence with an unimportant actor-subject into a passive and to delete the *by*-phrase, and (4) to use transition words."[32]

Modification Conversions. Modification exercises are primarily compositions to which the student has added or completed some patterns of the model. They are similar to expansion drills in pattern practice. They lend themselves primarily to the adding of adjectives and adverbs, articles and noun modifiers, phrases and clauses, and transition words. Completing a sentence which has been partially begun can also be considered a modification exercise.

The following are some typical exercises on the sentence level:

Complete the following sentences using adjective clauses.
 a. This is the house where _____.
 b. The lawyer whom _____ lives in San Diego.
 c. The class which _____ starts at 9:00 A.M.[33]

Complete the following sentences using noun clauses.
 a. I believe _____.
 b. I asked the policeman _____.
 c. I don't know_____.[34]

They can be done equally well on the paragraph level:

A Familiar Procedure

Directions:

Complete the four following paragraphs of partial statements with time clauses in the simple present tense, underlining the time clauses.

Hing will go to the college cafeteria in a few minutes for another meal. He will take off his cap as soon as . . . He will not take off his coat until after . . . He will continue to carry his briefcase while . . .[35]

[32]Earl Rand, "Analysis and Synthesis: Two Steps Toward Proficiency in Composition," *Workpapers in English as a Second Language: Matter, Methods, Materials.* Department of English, University of California at Los Angeles, (Los Angeles: April 1967), pp. 87-91.

[33]Baskoff, p. 156.

[34]Ibid, p. 157.

[35]Lois Robinson, *Guided Writing and Free Writing: A Text in Composition for English as a Second Language* (New York: Harper and Row, 1967), p. 28.

The degree of control in these exercises depends on the degree to which possible answers have been discussed in class. There may be oral preparation or the exercises may be based on a previous reading. The student may also simply be presented with a passage and asked to add certain patterns to indicated sentences. Passages taken from fiction lend themselves best to this kind of writing activity; it is not as easy as it may seem to find appropriate passages. Here is one which lends itself particularly well to modification conversions:

> (1)I was on the patio, pulling faces, when I noticed Tom Wells standing in the shadow of the fountain. (2)I do not know how long he had been standing there watching me.
>
> (3)The object of my facial contortions was to attempt to discover what it felt like to be Jimmie and Tom Wells respectively. (4)My method was not infallible, but it sometimes served as an aid to perception. (5)I had practiced it since childhood. (6)You simply twist your face into the expression of the person whose state of mind and heart you wish to know, and then wait and see what sort of emotions you feel. (7)I had begun with Jimmie. (8)First I considered myself to be standing high and lean, very fair, with a straight wide mouth; and I pulled my mouth straight and wide, I made my eyes close down at the far corners, widening at the inner corners; I raised my eyebrows and furrowed my brows; I put my tongue inside my lower lip, pulling my chin long; my nose, so concentratedly did I imagine it, curving up slightly at the bridge. (9)Then I was self-consciously Jimmie.[36]

With this passage the student can be asked to add verbal phrases to sentences 5, 7, and 9; relative clauses at his own discretion; reason clauses to sentences 2, 4, and 7; purpose or result clauses to 2, 5, and 7; or concessive clauses to 2, 5, and 7. It must be emphasized that directions for rewriting passages must be very clear, and that examples of reason clauses, etc. should always be given. Because there is a considerable degree of copying involved in writing these types of controlled compositions, the student should not be asked to do the same passage twice just because several language manipulations are possible with one passage.

Here is a last example of a modification conversion in sentence connectives:

Factual Account:

American higher education has a rural tradition. America began as a

---

[36]Paulston and Dykstra, page 53.

civilized but rural nation. Its first colleges and universities quite naturally began in the country. Land was cheap in rural areas. It was less expensive to build schools there. Country people thought city life would have a bad influence on their children. They wanted them to go to rural schools.

Unified Report:

American higher education has a rural tradition for three reasons. First, America began as a civilized but rural nation. Therefore, its first colleges and universities quite naturally began in the country. Also, land was cheap in rural areas, so it was less expensive to build schools there. In addition, country people thought city life would have a bad influence on their children; thus they wanted them to go to rural schools.[37]

Techniques of Semicontrolled Composition

As Maryruth Bracy has pointed out, there "exists a broad gap between the least-controlled writing and entirely free compositions."[38] Left to his own devices the student will still make a great number of errors, but his proficiency is such that he needs to move beyond carefully controlled manipulation of structures and vocabulary. Bracy comments on an experiment where her students wrote fewer errors when the content was controlled:

The problem is not to structure the content so that specific sentence structures will result; otherwise, the students are back to controlled writing. The suggestion is to explore ways of re-structuring topics so as to graduate the control .... The result would be a range of "freeness" in composition similar to the already well-defined range of control in writing.[39]

In the absence of such an established range, we can merely list some established techniques of semicontrol. The one principle that they all share is that the model supplies the content or the ideas for the composition, while there is little structural control. A common

---

[37]Arapoff, *Writing through Understanding*, p. 87.

[38]Maryruth Bracy, "The Move from Controlled Writing to Free Composition, or, "Write 300 Words on "Being a Foreign Student at UCLA" *Workpapers in English as a Second Language,* Vol. IV. Department of English, University of California at Los Angeles, (Los Angeles: June 1970), p. 22.

[39]Ibid, p. 22.

procedure is to present the student with a model passage and ask him to paraphrase it, to write a summary of it, to add a beginning, middle or end to it, or to outline it. Or he may be given an outline and asked to write a composition from it. Another technique uses topic sentences to control the student's composition:

Directions:

Add three more sentences that develop the topic sentence:
1. Once I visited a village which was located . . . .

_____

_____

_____

2. The people of the village had their own distinct customs.

_____

_____

_____ 40

Karl C. Sandberg suggests drills for what he calls "writing laboratories" and we quote examples from his NAFSA paper at length, since his suggestions are excellent.

Instructions: Write a biographical sketch of the imaginary Russian novelist Ivan Ivanovich. You may describe him as you like, but the following questions and information may help you. Most of the action will, of course, be in the past tense.

Parentage

> Born 1812. Father dies when Ivan is three—How? from tuberculosis? by political assassination? of grief over his wife's infidelity? from being thrown from a horse? Mother—rich or poor? beautiful or homely? aristocratic or commoner? strong (domineering, self-willed) or weak? selfish or generous? like or unlike her husband?

Ivan's Education

> Was it solid or sketchy? Did he study classical or modern subjects? How many languages did he learn to read? to speak? French? German? Spanish? Chinese? Latin? How widely did he read in economics and political theory?

---

[40] Slager, p. 82.

Early Manifestations of Revolutionary Tendencies

Why? Because of social abuse of his mother? Revolt against maternal authority? Being influenced by a group of young intellectuals who were anarchists in disguise?

His Siberian Experience

Arrested in 1842 for plotting on the Czar's life. Was he guilty or not guilty? How was he treated in Siberia? harshly or kindly? How did he stand the weather? Did he lose his mind or remain sane? Released in 1847.

Declining Years in Paris

Writes his masterpiece *Confessions of a Siberian Exile*–acclaimed or rejected by Parisian society? Died rich or poor? from starvation, gout, or tuberculosis?

If the student possesses a large vocabulary he branches out from the possibilities suggested. If he does not, he still finds enough alternatives in the drill for him to do something imaginative and original (no two biographies of Ivan Ivanovich resembled each other).

The next drill is less controlled and is intended for a more advanced group. It presupposes previous drill on the patterns of conjecture. After these patterns are reviewed in class, the following announcement is made: You have probably heard of the revolution yesterday in Costra Incognita. The information which has come to us by radio and TV is unfortunately quite incomplete. We have only the facts listed below. Tell what you think must have happened.

7:10 A.M. The national radio goes off the air. What did people think had happened? Power failure in the electrical system? Strike by the broadcasters' union?

7:30 A.M. The national radio comes back on the air. A different announcer plays the national anthem. Why?

7:50 A.M. Numerous shots are heard in the vicinity of the presidential palace. What did people think was happening? Fireworks in celebration of the president's wife's birthday? A fire in a nearby ammunition factory? A bank was being robbed? What do you think was happening?

9:50 A.M. The national radio announces that the air force has gone over to the rebels.

10:00 A.M. Airplanes bomb rebel positions. Who was flying the planes? Did the air force remain loyal to the president? Did rebel air pilots mistakenly bomb their own positions?

11:00 A.M. The radio has gone off the air. No further word has been received. What do you think has happened? What do you think will happen?[41]

Another technique which has proved helpful is to ask the students to write on a topic similar to that of the model passage. Here is a writing assignment from Ross and Doty:

Model passage:

Language and Culture

To know a person's language is to understand his culture, for language grows out of and reflects culture. The Tzeltal tribe in Mexico, for instance, has twenty-five different words for expressing the idea *to carry*. Tzeltal speakers can indicate by one word each of these concepts: carrying on the shoulder, carrying on the head, carrying in a bundle, carrying in the palm of the hand, or carrying in a container.

Writing assignment:

Following the model in the preceding exercise, write a composition in which you show how knowing your own native language helps a person understand your culture. Underline the verbal constructions in your paragraph, using as many as are appropriate to express your ideas but varying their function in the sentence. Also underline the subject sentence of your paragraph.[42]

J. A. Bright has some good exercises for letter writing:

SUDAN LIGHT AND POWER COMPANY, LTD.
(Incorporated in England)

Khartoum   BRANCHES:
P. O. Box 86   Omdurman. Tel. No. 5623
Tel. No. 2217 (Accounts)   Khartoum N. Tel. No. 2723
Tel. No. 2479 (Repairs)

KHARTOUM ELECTRICITY AND WATER SUPPLY

---

[41]Sandberg, pp. 56-57.

[42]Janet Ross and Gladys Doty, *Writing English: A Composition Text in English as a Foreign Language* (New York: Harper and Row, 1965), p. 144

(a) Write to the above company saying that you have been sent the bill for somebody else's house.

(b) Write to the above company asking whether it is not possible for them to run later buses between Omdurman and Khartoum, and whether the bus service could not be extended to cover Khartoum North.

(c) Reply to (b), agreeing to the first suggestion, but rejecting the second. Give reasons.

(d) Write to the above company asking about the terms upon which special buses may be hired. Answer your own letter.[43]

And finally here is a semicontrolled composition exercise on parallelism. This differs from the others in that there is still an attempt at guiding the structures.

Model: from Gerald Dykstra, "A New Dimension in Writing Laboratories"

Such supporting materials should also contribute toward meeting one of the major shortcomings inherent in most classroom teaching—oversize classes. Yet, if having thirty to eighty students under one teacher is not conducive to normal interpersonal linguistic communication, neither is the ideal to be found in the opposite extreme of having each student hermetically sealed off from his fellows in a laboratory booth.

Neither classroom situation nor laboratory nor textbook nor trained teacher nor any other element by itself will provide us with a panacea for all our ills, but through use of varying combinations of these some people seem to be learning some English. There is every reason to believe, and little reason to doubt, that English teaching can be further improved by new and better supporting materials which may take the best from current materials or classroom situations while meeting some of the shortcomings.

Assignment:

Rewrite the entire passage, changing *such supporting materials* to *such a political system*. Make up your own shortcomings or change *oversize classes* to *overcrowded housing in slum apartments*. Follow the general structure of the model, especially in the parallel structures, but make whatever changes in vocabulary that are necessary for the passage to make sense. Use your imagination freely.[44]

---

[43]J. A. Bright, *English Composition Course for Overseas Students* (London: Longmans, 1962), p. 121

[44]Paulston and Dykstra, p. 60.

PROCEDURES

Specific procedures in teaching with controlled composition will vary from text to text. Some will allow the students to work at their own pace on individual assignments while others require that the entire class do the same assignment at the same time. The following steps constitute the basic procedures.

1. The teacher gives the assignment. He must make certain that the students understand the model. Even more important, he must make certain that the students understand and know the particular linguistic rule which will generate the specific language manipulation of the controlled composition. In practice, this does lead to teacher talk about language, and it cannot be avoided. Such linguistic explanations should be carefully planned and timed prior to their presentation in class or they will become rambling and time consuming. On the beginning levels, when the students' writing is no more complex than the patterns they are taught for oral use in grammar, very little explanation is necessary and our students work at their own pace with primarily individual explanations. But on the intermediate and advanced levels many of the patterns they are taught are typical of written usage only and are quite complicated, and we have found it more efficient to keep the entire class working on the same exercises preceded by a brief linguistic explanation. Following the presentation of the model and the explanation, the teacher makes sure the students understand the directions of what they are supposed to do. Even if the composition is to be written outside of class, it is a good idea to have them all get started on it in class so the teacher can make sure they have understood the assignment.

2. The students write. Our students have been known to hand in compositions on three by five inch note paper. Now we tell them on the first day that compositions are to be written only on eight and a half by eleven inch standard size lined paper and on every other line in order to facilitate corrections. With controlled compositions, the students are instructed to underline that part of the composition which differs from the model so that the teacher can primarily check the underlined parts. With free compositions, the students are told to write on only one side of each page so that they can later cut and paste to improve on organizational weaknesses. Writing is one area of language learning where fastidious insistence on neatness (penmanship, paper) and carefulness (correct language) does

pay off. It may seem old-fashioned to the reader, but when we know how susceptible we are ourselves to the face value of the examinations we correct, it would simply not be fair to our students to insist on anything less than neat, legible, and correct compositions.

It is also necessary to decide whether the students are to write in class or at home. Our beginning students always write in class so that they can have the teacher's help whenever they need it, the emphasis of controlled composition being to help the students write *correct* compositions.

The attitudes of students toward their composition in a course of controlled composition differ markedly from students who only write free compositions. Students become accustomed to writing correct compositions, and they will carefully ask questions if they are not certain of the correct response. Because of the nature of the control, they know exactly what questions to ask before they make a mistake, and this is a habit that we want to reinforce from the very beginning. On more advanced levels, when students can work with reference grammars, controlled composition lends itself very well to homework.

3. Compositions are corrected. It is important that the students receive feedback as soon as possible on their writing. Some exercises lend themselves to oral checking in the same way as the reading comprehension questions were checked. The teacher needs to make sure that the students do check their papers, so after the oral checking the compositions should be collected and briefly checked through. Mistakes should be indicated by underlining and corrected by the students themselves. In order for the student to be able to do that, the teacher will either have to explain the mistake to him, or indicate the page in the reference grammar where the rule is explained, or mark the mistake with a proofreader's symbol. It saves a lot of time if the students are given a list of symbols for common mistakes in the beginning of the term, like this one:

sp	spelling
s-v	subject-verb agreement
prep	wrong preposition
tns	wrong tense
¶	new paragraph
ww	wrong word
neg	wrong negation form
	etc.

Errors on patterns for which no rules can be found (like in this sentence: "Certainly operations research was develop (*sic,* but there is a rule) in many ways, *as fields where can be apply it,*" will have to be proofed by the teacher, i.e., he will have to write in the correct version above the erroneous pattern—if he wants the student to learn that pattern. Otherwise he can just ignore it. Incorrect vocabulary choice is also best proofed by the teacher, certainly on beginning and intermediate levels, and for vocabulary all mistakes should be indicated. Advanced level students should become familiar with a thesaurus although it is doubtful that it will help them correct a wrong word choice. With all indicated mistakes, the student should then copy over the entire sentence in his corrections. It makes no sense at all to have the teacher spend time in correcting a composition which the student then barely glances at. To have the student copy the same sentence more than once seems like fruitless drudgery; written pattern practice of the type discussed in the chapter on grammar is much more efficient.

No students like to do corrections, and it is easy for the teacher to forget to check up on them. If the teacher explains to the class that he will not record the grade or credit for the composition until after he has okayed the corrections, the students will soon chase the teacher with their corrections, rather than the other way around.

There are times when half the class makes the same mistake. Whatever the reason, that particular pattern was apparently not well taught, and it usually makes sense to go back and reteach it to the entire class, maybe with some written exercises on the sentence level as reinforcement.

Free Composition

In addition to the controlled compositions, students on the beginning levels need to write occasional free compositions. Students need to give vent to their feelings, put across their own ideas and get a feeling of independent achievement in the new language. The major guideline, then, to procedures dealing with free compositions on this level should be to preserve this sense of achievement by minimizing the possibility for and emphasis on errors. Students on the intermediate and advanced levels need much practice in writing free compositions. Our students write a composition a week, but a more useful guideline is probably to have the students write as many free compositions as the teacher can reasonably correct.

Topics should be selected with care. On the higher levels, topics will depend on the particular point of rhetorical organization the students are studying, but on the beginning levels, students are usually assigned topics which require only description or straight narrative, such as *My Best Friend* or *My First Day in School. A Hero of My Country, Folktales and Legends of My Country, National Holidays,* and the like seem ideal topics of this type, but in fact they often lead directly to trouble. The vocabulary and mode of expressions of such topics are permeated by the students' culture and mother tongue. They very likely have written about them before in their own language, and the resultant compositions are often a great mish-mash of translation and interference errors. A simple guideline for the selection of topics is to pick subjects which: (1) the students are interested in and (2) they know something about. Hence topics for free composition lend themselves ideally to be correlated with the reading selections.

The students should be trained to work with a checklist for sentence level errors. It can very well be the same as the list of symbols for common errors. Prior to handing in the composition, they read through it only for the purpose of looking for these errors. Such a checklist can also be used for controlled composition. On the more advanced levels, they might also be trained to work with a checklist like Knapp's:

Rough Outline

A clear thesis statement that can be supported or proved
Three or more useful supporting points

Rough Draft

Show examples of thoughtful editing

Final Draft

Mechanics give a clean, orderly impression
The title—is correctly capitalized,
shows imagination in phrasing,
indicates the subject clearly
Adequate margins—sides, top, bottom
Clear indentation for paragraphs
Clear, easy-to-read handwriting or typing
Logical development of one idea in a paragraph
A topic sentence that gives the idea of the paragraph

A clear controlling idea in the topic sentence
Supporting statements that focus on the controlling idea
Clear relationship or transition between sentences

Imaginative, precise use of language

Connectives used with precision to show relationship (1)
Careful, correct use of expanded vocabulary (2)
Examples of artful phrasing (3)
Correct spelling and hyphenating (4)
Correct punctuation to develop the meaning of sentences (5)
Good use of parallel structure in series (6)
Good use of phrases or clauses to modify or to tighten the expression of an idea (7)
Good selection of detail to suggest larger meaning (8)
A good conclusion that draws the paragraph together (9)

Good idea content

A clearly expressed idea, easy for the reader to understand
An interesting idea, worthy of adult communication
Challenging, original thinking

Corrections—with adequate practice to insure mastery

Corrections under all "Red Marks"
Spelling: 5 times + used in five sentences. Listed.
Focus items used in at least 10 true sentences. Listed.[45]

Knapp uses his checklist for correction purposes as well. An item on the checklist receives a plus if that item appears in the composition; the absence of a plus indicates that the students have not mastered this particular point or at least that it has not appeared in their composition. The hope is that the students in future compositions will endeavor to remedy particular shortcomings in past compositions.

The procedures for correcting free compositions are similar to those for controlled compositions. The composition teacher is not a proofreader and should most certainly not rewrite the students' compositions or even necessarily correct all mistakes. Free composi-

---

[45]Donald Knapp, "A Focused, Efficient Method to Relate Composition Correction to Teaching Aims," *Teaching English as a Second Language*, H. Allen and R. Campbell, eds. New York: McGraw-Hill 1972), pp. 213-221.

tions have very many more mistakes than controlled compositions, and it is very disheartening for both teacher and student to have the composition end up covered with red marks. This is especially true on the beginning level.

There are some alternatives. The teacher can mark as incorrect only those patterns that the students have covered in the grammar class. He can announce at the time he assigns the composition that he will only correct certain patterns, and then list them. He can select the "worst" three or four errors in each composition and check those. He can correct errors on the patterns the students are expected to know with red ink and others with green. Knapp suggests that the teacher simply underline performance errors so that the students can see the extent of their sloppiness, and then no further issue is made of them. Instead, Knapp recommends, the emphasis should be on competence errors in patterns the students are expected to learn during the course. Each student keeps an individualized list of "patterns to be learned" on which list are entered the patterns selected by the teacher from the student's own set of errors. The student then writes from ten to forty true (meaningful and verifiable) sentences until the pattern to be learned has been mastered.

Each teacher will have his own idiosyncracies when it comes to correcting compositions. Certainly we don't know that one system is better than another. We do believe that competence errors on patterns the teacher wants the student to learn should be corrected, that is, used by the student in a sentence or preferably more than one (although forty sounds a bit extreme). We tend to have students correct performance errors as well—those errors for which the students know the rule once the error is pointed out to them—for the reason that it is very difficult to tell competence errors from true performance errors with foreign students. Negative reinforcement—students do dislike correcting errors for which they think they know the rule—is quite efficient in promoting carefulness in writing.

Some of our instructors feel that giving grades on the compositions also serves to encourage carefulness in writing. We willingly concede that such practice may not conform with the highest principles of testing and grading; after all, it is encouragement of the "an offer he couldn't refuse" type, and the grading serves a punitive purpose as much as an evaluative one. But, alas, our students do not always conform with the highest principles of studenthood either, and it is a fact, however deplorable, that with some classes their compositions improve when they are graded. We leave the matter of grading free compositions to the individual strategies of teacher personality. Also, one should remember that many students like to be graded. But surely there is no need to grade free compositions given in a beginner's program of controlled composition, nor is there any need to grade controlled compositions. If compositions are graded, they should be given two grades, one for language and style, and another for organization, content, and general thoughtfulness.

MECHANICS OF PUNCTUATION

Punctuation may seem exceedingly trivial in a program of composition but nevertheless it is necessary. Principles of punctuation differ from language to language, and our students do not know how to punctuate in English. They need this knowledge for two reasons: one, to be able to write comprehensibly and two, for their reading.

> we are much more dependent on punctuation for clues for efficient reading than we are likely to think but even something so simple as lack of periods and commas is likely to confuse us more important dashes and semicolons also serve as transition words and syntactic markers of a semantic nature and our students need to recognize that punctuation serves a more serious purpose than decoration the at times only apparent purpose in their own production we hope this paragraph has convinced the reader of the point we are making

No specific rules need to be discussed here. Any high school or college text in freshman English will include a chapter on punctuation. The important thing to remember is not to teach more than one thing at a time and to give the students sentences for exercises. In the Institute we teach punctuation in the language laboratory, a practice which has turned out to be remarkably successful for reasons we can only speculate at. The punctuation exercise takes on aspects of a game. The student reads the rules for, say, ellipsis. He does the exercise but he can only do it by listening to the tape. When he has finished he checks his answer with the correct one in the back of the book, adds up his score and figures it into percentages, and finally enters it into his own progress chart. It is very much like the word quizzes and tests on sundry matters that keep appearing in the newspapers, presumably because of their popularity with the readers.

We ourselves can never pass up a word quiz. Here is a sample lesson from Jaramillo's *Conventions in the Mechanics of Writing:*

An Ellipsis (. . .) consists of three spaced periods.

An Ellipsis (. . .) indicates that one or more words have been omitted from a quotation.

> example: "All governments depend on the honesty and good will of the people."
>
> becomes
>
> "All governments depend on . . . the good will of the people."

Note that "honesty and" from the original quotation has been omitted. These words have been replaced by an ellipsis (. . .).

Punctuate the following quotations. If something has been omitted from the quotation, a space for an ellipsis (. . .) has been provided.

I will read each quotation in its ORIGINAL FORM, followed by the author's name. If I read something that is *not* included in your quotation, place an ellipsis (. . .) there.

Be sure that all punctuation is correct for the following quotations.

Listen carefully, NOT all quotations will need an ellipsis.

POINTS

1. things that we have to learn to do,
   we learn   them

   aristotle _____

2. knowing how to do a thing is easier
   than doing it

   Anonymous _____

3. everything   tells a different story to
   all eyes that see and ears that hear

   ingersoll _____

4. comparison   makes men happy or
   wretched

   thomas fuller _____

5. a man travels   in search of what he
   needs and returns home to find it

   george more _____

   _____

TOTAL _____

POSSIBLE NUMBER RIGHT ___30___   NUMBER RIGHT _____
                                  −UNNECESSARY MARKS _____
                                  TOTAL   _____
                                  PERCENTAGE   _____ [46]

ORGANIZATION OF CONTENT

Objectives

It is frequently said that writing is a thinking process. At this level of writing compositions, of organizing thought and argument into a coherent and logical whole, writing is undeniably based on thought. The difficulty is, as Kaplan[47] has pointed out, that logic as an organizing principle of phenomena is not an extension of intelligence but culturally conditioned. Our students do think, but they organize and express those thoughts in ways which differ from what we are accustomed to in analytical writing. Frequently, therefore, their compositions strike us as illogical, long-winded, unfocused and bad. This is a complaint that instructors in writing for foreign students share with instructors in writing for native students. Principles of good writing as we know it come naturally to very few people and must be carefully spelled out. Our students not only have not been taught principles of American English rhetoric, they have frequently been taught systems which conflict with our rhetoric. Consequently, a large part of the curriculum in writing on the intermediate and advanced levels deals with an explicit analysis of principles of writing in English and does not differ markedly in content from a class in freshman composition. Indeed, it is not uncommon for the instructors to comment that teaching such a course has improved their own writing.

There are three basic teaching points: paragraph development, development of paragraphs in a series, and the organization and development of a composition. These three share the basic problem of making the sentences and paragraphs stick together, of relating

---

[46]Barbara Jaramillo, *Conventions in the Mechanics of Writing: A Language Manual for Foreign Students* (Pittsburgh: English Language Institute, 1973), p. 31.

[47]Robert Kaplan, "Cultural Thought Patterns in Inter-Cultural Education," in K. Croft, ed., *Readings in English as a Second Language* (Cambridge, Massachusetts: Winthrop Publishers, Inc., 1972).

thought to argument in an orderly and logical manner. We achieve coherence in writing by rhetorical devices and by logic of thought, and these we must teach.

The following discussion deals primarily with writing on the intermediate and advanced levels. Our beginning students do work on simple outlining, but most of their writing is spent on controlled and semicontrolled composition in order to perfect their written language skills. Their English is still so awful that little is gained by having them work primarily on free compositions, nor would they be able to follow the explanations in English. If students can't understand, in the target language, the reading of analytical prose or the explanations of their rhetorical principles, there is no sense in having them attempt such writing.

The main objective of our writing courses after the beginning course is to write a full-fledged research paper. For nonacademic situations, a research paper can easily be modified to a report, an essay and the like, but the important point is that there be one important overriding objective. From this objective follows the selection of all items in the curriculum, and all activities serve to support the successful writing of, in our case, a research paper, a major accomplishment for the students.

At the beginning of the term the students are handed what amounts to a list of deadlines:

Week 2:	Selection of topic
Week 3:	Bibliography cards (at least 2)
Week 4:	Thesis statement
Week 4:	Rough outline
Week 7:	Sample note cards
Week 8:	Second polished outline
	(if needed a revised thesis statement)
Week 10:	Rough draft
Week 12:	Footnotes and bibliography
Week 14:	The finished research paper[48]

Again, these items can easily enough be adapted to fit individual classes' needs. Such a list serves to break down the major objectives

---

[48]Lois I. Wilson, *Curriculum Notes*; mimeographed (Pittsburgh: English Language Institute, 1974).

into subgoals and gives the students purpose and direction in their work, and a sense of continued achievement. It also keeps everyone on schedule.

Procedures

Procedures in the classroom break down into five types of activities: (1) exercises and discussion of rhetorical organization, (2) exercises and discussion of rhetorical devices for coherency, (3) the preparation of bibliographies and footnotes and note-taking, (4) discussion of weekly minor compositions, either individually or with the whole class, and (5) writing grammar pattern exercises and controlled composition.

Rhetorical organization

The exact procedures in teaching rhetorical organization will of course be based on the particular text which the class uses, but the basic steps are these:

(1) Presentation of model and rule, i.e., a linguistic explanation
(2) Study of rhetorical devices
(3) One or more exercises, based on a model
(4) The writing of original outlines, paragraphs or compositions

This exercise will serve as an example of this principle:

A well-written paragraph usually consists of (1) a topic sentence (TS) which expresses the central idea of the paragraph, (2) one or more supporting sentences (SS) which relate directly to the central idea of the paragraph, and (3) a concluding sentence (CS).

Look at Paragraph 4. If you outline the paragraph it will look like this:

1. Topic Sentence:	Ford developed the assembly line.
2. Supporting Sentence:	Before, each car built by hand
3. Supporting Sentence:	Work slow
4. Supporting Sentence:	Therefore cars expensive
5. Supporting Sentence:	In Ford's system, each worker has special job
6. Supporting Sentence:	E.g., one man made part of wheels
7. Supporting Sentence:	Another man placed wheels on car
8. Supporting Sentence:	Third man inserted bolts
9. Concluding Sentence:	Each man needed to learn only one act.

Now outline Paragraph 5 yourself:

1. TS: Ford brought _____
2. SS: An automobile frame_____
3. SS: Each man_____
4. SS: At the end of the line_____
5. SS: Fuel and water_____
6. CS: The assembly line _____

Now outline paragraph 9. The wording in the outline is not important, but the outline should reflect the central idea and the added comments which progressively support the central idea.

Is there a concluding sentence?

1. TS: _____
2. SS: _____

etc.

7. SS: _____
8. CS: _____

Outline a paragraph of your own on the disadvantages of automobiles.[49]

The students either read the model at home or in class.

The importance of always working with models cannot be overemphasized. Abstract linguistic rules are meaningless to students if they cannot see how they function. The same principle that we discussed about modeling drills rather than giving directions as how to do them also applies here. Furthermore, and this should be kept in mind throughout this discussion, at this level reading and writing reinforce each other so that using models for writing is also practice in reading.

The teacher will discuss the reading passage with the students, asking many questions to make sure that they understand the rhetorical principles. One exercise may very well be done orally in class so that all students understand what they are expected to do before they turn to individual work.

First, students need to learn general principles of paragraph development and composition outlining. It may be true that native writers do not always begin a paragraph with a topic sentence, but it

---

[49]Christina Bratt Paulston, Composition Exercises to appear in *English For Today, Book IV* with William Slager and William Norris (New York: McGraw-Hill, forthcoming).

is also true that foreign students' writing improves remarkably if they are held strictly to this requirement. After students have learned the general principles of paragraph development and outlining, they need to work on specific principles of organization which go with different types of writing. Lafene's outline serves as well for writing as for reading and we repeat it here:

I. Major Types of Writing

  1. Explanation and analysis

    (a) a process
    (b) an opinion or point of view
    (c) event(s) and phenomena
    (d) instructions and directions

  2. Argument

    (a) persuasion
    (b) refutation
    (c) examining both sides of a point

  3. Description and summary

    (a) a thing
    (b) a person
    (c) a place
    (d) an event
    (e) concepts

  4. Narration

    (a) a series of events; a report
    (b) biography or autobiography
    (c) historical events
    (d) fiction or nonfiction

II. Methods of development for major types of writing

  1. Illustration and/or exemplification
  2. Comparisons and contrasts
  3. Partition—dividing something into parts and explaining or describing each
  4. Classification—putting things into categories
  5. Definition—formal, descriptive or operational

6. Cause and effect
7. Reasoning—if. . .therefore. . .[50]

Students need practice with all of these different types of writing, with special emphasis on the organizational principles particular to each type. In his chapter on "Analytical Development (by comparison)," Bander points out that we *compare* by pointing out similarities and *contrast* by pointing out differences.[51] We can compare two topics by first discussing one and then going on to the other topic in the next paragraph, or we can compare them in pairs, turning alternately to one and then the other. He recommends the development of pairs or a combination of the two methods. He goes on to discuss models with comparison only, with comparison and contrast, and finally with comparison, contrast, and analogy. This type of clarification of rhetorical principles is crucial before students can undertake to write analysis by comparison themselves.

The next step is a study of the rhetorical syntactic devices which are typical of this type of writing. This step will be discussed below. Depending on the level and ability of the class, they next spend some time on controlled or semicontrolled exercises on comparison or go on directly to write original paragraphs of their own.

When the students write original paragraphs, they need access to lists of transition words, prepositions and conjunctions. General phrases and sentences of the type that Flowers lists are also very helpful:

PRACTICE IN LOGICAL SEQUENCE

1. Point of view: X may be discussed from several points of view.
The viewpoint of the freshmen regarding X must be noted.
Let us investigate the financial aspects of X.

2. Enumeration: There are five Xs to be considered.
We saw a number of interesting Xs.
Statistical analysis of X is revealing.

---

[50]Julia Lafene, "Prospectus for Suggested Project for Materials Development," (Pittsburgh: Department of General Linguistics, University of Pittsburgh, 1974).

[51]Robert G. Bander, *American English Rhetoric* (New York: Holt, Rinehart and Winston, 1971; pp. 212-217.

9. Definition: There are several definitions of X.
Before we begin our analysis of X, let us determine exactly what we mean by the term.
Language is "a system of arbitrary vocal symbols by which thought is conveyed from one human being to another."
(Here, since the term *language* is defined formally, the extensional possibility is that the writer will define in order the technical terms that make up the topical lead.)[52]

Rhetorical devices

There are three major rhetorical devices for achieving coherence within and between paragraphs: transition words, parallelism and punctuation marks. Transition words may be either (1) the same word or a synonym repeated in the following sentence, (2) substitute words, such as some pronouns or summary words for ideas or concepts, like *problem, approach, point,* or (3) sentence connectives, like *furthermore, however.* As we said, students need to have access to lists of these when they write their exercises and compositions.

The particular type of writing the students are currently working on will decide which set of transition words they need to study for that particular passage. Here is an exercise on transition words which follows the exercise on paragraph organization on page 238 above:

There are different techniques for achieving coherency within a paragraph, i.e., for making the sentences stick together. One such technique is used in Paragraph 4:

5. SS: Ford suggested a system in which *each worker* would have a special job to do.
6. SS: *One man,* for example, would make only a portion of the wheels.
7. SS: *Another* would place the wheels on the car.
8. SS: And *still another* would insert the bolts that held the wheels to the car.
9. CS: *Each* needed to learn only one or two simple acts.

Each sentence has a pronoun which connects that sentence to the others. These pronouns are called indefinite pronouns, and they are very useful in writing. Some of the most important are:

---

[52]Frank C. Flowers, *Practical Linguistics for Composition* (New York: The Odyssey Press, 1968), pp. 83-89.

all	everybody	no one
another	everyone	one
any	few	other(s)
anybody	many	several
anyone	most	some
both	neither	somebody
each	nobody	someone
either	none	such

See how many of these you can find in Paragraph 3.

Now rewrite sentences 5 through 9 from Paragraph 4 listed above with your own words but keep the indefinite pronouns, so that your composition looks something like this:

> The teacher suggested a system in which *each student* would have a special job to do. *One student,* e.g., would clean the blackboard. *Another* would place all the books on the shelves. And *still another . . .*

Add some extra sentences of your own in which you use some of the other indefinite pronouns listed above. You may choose either of these topics:

> A. The teacher suggested . . .
> B. The principal suggested . . .
> C. The students suggested . . .
> D. The President suggested . . . [53]

The procedures are the same as those discussed earlier: model and rules, a controlled exercise and finally the student's original composition.

In the chapter on comparison, Bander discusses the use of the semicolon in sentences with paired comparisons. He lists the following transition words as useful in writing comparisons:

also	another	furthermore	moreover
both	equally important	too	at the same time
in the same way	besides	then	accordingly
just as . . . so	in fact	in addition to	like[54]
similarly			

In addition to those we would add the conjunctions *as . . . as, so . . . as* (only negative); *-er . . . than, more . . . than* and the correlative pronouns *the former . . . the latter, the one . . . the other.*

---

[53]Paulston, *English For Today.*
[54]Bander, p. 218.

Multiple substitution conversions of a model lend themselves well to controlled exercises. Either the students can be asked to keep the transition words and change the topic, or they can be asked to keep the topic and change the sentence connectives. The passage "A New Dimension in the Laboratory," which was discussed in the section on controlled composition, also lends itself for practice on transition words. The assignment now reads: "Rewrite the entire passage, changing the two sentence connectives to two other suitable connectives. Draw a double line under all the other transition words. (See Appendix II)" Here is an example of an exercise on paragraphs in a series where the topic is changed and the transition words remain the same:

> In lesson 5, you learned that sometimes paragraphs are written in a series where all the paragraphs deal with the same central idea. This reading contains a good example of this type of writing. You will see this if you outline the discussion of problems in space travel, which is the central idea of paragraphs 3-8. Now copy the sentences verbatim, which are indicated below.

Paragraph 3:
    Sentence 1 TS (introducing the series). . . . .
    Sentence 2 TS (introducing the first problem). . . . .
Paragraph 4
    Sentence 1 TS . . . .
Paragraph 5
    Sentence 1 TS . . . .
Paragraph 6
    Sentence 1 TS . . . .
Paragraph 7
    Sentence 1 TS . . . .
Paragraph 8
    Sentence 1 TS . . . .

Now go back and underline the transition words that keep the paragraphs together, i.e., which indicate that all of these paragraphs occur in a series. Then rewrite these paragraphs, using another topic but keeping the transition words the same. Pick a problem of your own or choose one of the topics suggested below.

A. There are are many problems connected with passing school examinations.
B. There are many problems connected with travel in my country.
C. There are many problems connected with fixing faulty electrical appliances at home.

When you are finished your composition should be similar in format to this one:

There are many problems connected with fixing faulty electrical appliances at home. *The first and greatest of them* is identifying the broken part. You can rarely tell just by looking at the outside so one has to take the appliance apart in order to find the difficulty.

Another problem is being able to find the extra part which is needed. Often electrical appliances are imported and spare parts are difficult to find.

Once the appliance is in a million parts, *still another problem* becomes very obvious. How are all the pieces going to fit together again? There always seem to be extra pieces left over at the end.

Workmen are *also* affected by spectators. It seems impossible to mend an appliance without attracting an audience that is full of well-meaning advice of the most contradictory nature. Workmen must train themselves to ignore all such comments.

The lack of proper tools is another problem. *Someone* has disappeared with the screwdriver, the scissors are gone, etc. The hammer is of little use, and a knife doesn't work very well. The electric shock which one can get from an improperly mended appliance is *also a serious problem* in this sort of work. Of course, if the shock is serious enough, you will have no more problems.[55]

The students may also work simply on the sentence level. Here is an exercise with isolated sentences:

Write five sets of sentences. In the first sentence of a set make a statement or comment; in the second, contrast or limit that statement.

Example:

I prefer classical music. On the other hand, folk songs are very nice too. Fleming discovered penicillin in 1928. Nevertheless, it did not come into general use until 1941.

1. _____
2. _____
3. _____
4. _____
5. _____ [56]

---

[55]Paulston, *English For Today.*
[56]Ibid.

Such sentences are easily based on a reading passage, which eliminates the disjointed quality of writing isolated sentences. Students may also be asked to underline all the transition words in a paragraph or two from their reading assignment, and then the class discusses the function or use of these transition words in class. The teacher can easily figure out additional types of exercises. The fact that they are easy should not detract from their importance, especially in classes which may use a text in rhetoric intended for native speakers.

Parallelism is very easy to teach students, and occasionally they need to be cautioned of its overuse. A very effective way to teach parallelism is to give the students a passage with many parallel constructions and then have them rewrite the passage with all parallel constructions in the same slot. The first two or three sentences are best worked out on the blackboard. Here is an example:

> "We observe today not a victory of party but a celebration of freedom, symbolizing an end as well as a beginning, signifying renewal as well as change."

This is rewritten as

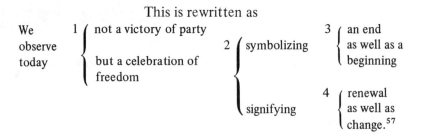

After students have caught on to this procedure, which they do very quickly, the teacher may inductively discuss (How do you know this is a parallel construction?) the various techniques of parallelism: (1) using conjunctions (1 above), (2) by the repetition of identical words or phrases (*as well as* occurs in both 3 and 4 above and serves to join two parallelisms into a parallel construction), and (3) by the repetition of similar structures in a series (2 above).

Next the students write their own exercises:

> In the last lesson you learned about parallelism. Paragraph 3 in this reading has a sentence which exemplifies this type of writing:

---

[57]Paulston and Dykstra, p. 80.

International calls *have been made* clearer, charges *have been* greatly *reduced,* and transmission and dependability *have been* greatly *upgraded.* Here parallelism has been achieved by using similar structures in a series. Write five such sentences, taking great care that all the structures within the same sentence are parallel. For example:

Microwaves are used to transmit television calls, television programs, and data messages.

Television provides jobs for many, it brings cultural events to the home, and it offers teaching in various subjects.

(If it is hard for you to think of ideas of your own, you might look at past readings for some suggestions.)[58]

Students enjoy working on parallelism, and they very quickly learn to make very sophisticated mistakes indeed. It is just as important to teach students when it is appropriate to write in parallel constructions and to avoid their overuse as it is to teach the parallelisms.

Bibliographies, Footnotes, and Note-Taking

Not much needs to be said about footnotes, bibliographies and note-taking. Any standard manual will have such information. For our intermediate students, we use with great success a highly simplified manual called *10 Steps in Writing the Research Paper.*[59] The most important teaching point is to convince the students of the absolute necessity of documentation; plagiarism is a new concept to many students. More important, scholarly work without references is frustrating to those readers who wish to pursue the subject. Many a time we have been driven to apoplexy in reading European and Latin American monographs with their disregard for references, and we are determined our students will learn better.

Our students learn to be familiar with two systems of documentation (internal and external to the text). They use only the one which is appropriate to their field, but they need familiarity with both for their reading. Paulston has written elsewhere about techniques for teaching footnotes and bibliographical entries, and we

---

[58]Paulston, *English For Today.*

[59]Roberta Markman & Marie L. Waddell, *10 Steps in Writing the Research Paper* (New York: Barrons, 1971).

won't discuss that here.[60] One point only needs to be made; students need to practice writing in class initially under the teacher's supervision so that the students can be helped before they go too far astray. Proper documentation is difficult for students, and it is a topic which should be taught slowly, i.e., over a long period of time with a minimum of new information for each lesson.

Discussion of Students' Compositions

Discussion of individual compositions is an important aspect of an efficient composition program. It can of course be done outside of class, but it is also efficient use of teacher time to spend five to ten minutes with individual students while the rest of the students are writing in class. The focus of the discussion should center on rhetorical organization and on sorting out performance errors from competence errors (the teacher simply asks the student what this or that sentence ought to be, and if the student can't answer, it is presumably a competence error), so that students can do exercises on the latter type of patterns.

Grammar Pattern Exercises

Intermediate and even advanced students still need to work on correct language forms. Our students spend about a fifth of their class time on grammar patterns typical of written English and on the perennial trouble spots, like articles and tenses. The teacher gives a grammatical explanation which is as brief as possible but still sufficient. At times this might mean a ten to fifteen minute lecture-discussion on a grammatical point but we don't see how, for example, the definite article can be dealt with in any less time if the explanation is to make any sense. And the students do need sensible grammatical explanations at this level. The audio-lingual purist can always look at such an activity as an exercise in listening comprehension. Which, incidentally, it is.

Next the students write. Mostly they write controlled and semicontrolled compositions, but on very difficult teaching points (like the definite article) they may do sentence level exercises first.

---

[60]C. B. Paulston, "Teaching Footnotes and Bibliographical Entries to Foreign Students: A Tagmemic Approach," *English Language Teaching* XXX:1 (1970).

Some of the patterns on which they made mistakes in their free compositions are also practiced during this time. It is also a good idea to have the students do their corrections at this time; it assures that the corrections get done and the teacher is also there to help if the student gets lost in his reference grammar.

Teaching writing is a time-consuming job because, in spite of all that has been said to the contrary, there is no way out of correcting compositions if the students are to learn to write well. But it is a satisfying job in that the students' progress can be so very marked, and judicious use of controlled composition will take a lot of the frustration and drudgery out of teaching writing.

Index

A

Accent, 82
Adams, J., 172
Alexander, L., 142
Allen, H., 232
Allen, R., 102-3, 138
Allen, V., 103, 107-8, 111-13, 138, 154, 176, 177-78
Analogy, 8
Analysis, 8, 37
Anderson, J., 159, 161
Anthony, E., 195
Arapoff, N., 209, 212, 217, 223
Articulation (*see* Phonology)
Asimov, I., 160
Auditory ability, 204

B

Bander, R., 241, 243

Barnard, H., 134
Baskoff, F., 217, 221
Bilingual-bicultural, 58
Bracy, M., 223
Briere, E., 96
Bright, J., 227
Britton, D., 55, 71, 74, 78
Bruder, M., 10, 13, 47, 145
Brunetti, B., 55, 65
Bumpass, F., 158
Burgess, A., 196

C

Campbell, R., 95, 232
Carroll, J., 10, 204
Cazden, C., 57
Chall, D., 160
Chall, J., 160
Chastain, K., 82, 128

Classification of structural pattern
  drills (*see* Drills, classification)
Cloze test (*see* Reading formula)
Communicative competence (Chapter
  Two):
  goals in teaching, 58
  procedures, 59
Communicative interaction activities,
  59
  community oriented tasks, 63
  problem-solving activities, 67
  roleplay, 70
  social formulas and dialogues, 60
Communicative performance, 59, 102
Comprehension questions:
  grammar lesson, 8, 35
  reading lesson, 165, 181
Composition (Chapter Six):
  controlled, 205-23
    types of exercises, 208
  correction of, 228
  free, 205, 230
  motives and objectives, 203
  semi-controlled, 223
  techniques and procedures, 205, 223,
    228
Consonants (*see* Phonology)
Content words, 168, 183
Correcting errors (*see* Errors)
Costinett, S., 209
Cowan, G., 181
Croft, K., 98, 118, 169, 236
Crowell, T., 165

D

Dance, F., 57
Davison, W., 101-2
Decanay, F., 23, 99, 101, 158, 216
Decoding, 100, 134, 158, 183
Dialogues, 34, 62, 74, 108, 144
Dictation, 135
Dictionary usage, 164, 90
Documentation:
  bibliographies and footnotes, 247
Doty, G., 226
Drills, structural pattern:
  classification, 3
  meaningful, 6
  mechanical, 4
  communicative, 8
  procedures, 39-44
  typology, 10-33
Dykstra, G., 208, 215-16, 218, 222,
  227, 246

E

Errors:
  competence, 233, 248
  correction:
    communicative activities, 59, 69
    composition, 228-29, 232, 249
    grammar drills, 44
    listening, 130
    pronunciation, 115
    performance, 45, 233, 248
Ervin-Tripp, S., 56
Esarey, G., 110, 151
Explanation, linguistic:
  grammar, 8, 37-38, 40
  pronunciation, 83
  reading, 170, 172, 175

F

Finocchiaro, M., 158
Flowers, F., 241-42
Fluency:
  speaking, 9, 82
  listening, 138, 155
Francis, G., 142-43
Freebairn-Smith, I., 56
Fries, C. C., 84, 92, 159, 169, 195
Fry, E., 185
Function words, 168, 183
Furey, P., 151, 171

G

Goodman, K., 158
Grammar lesson:
  design, 33
  procedures, 34-46

Grammar patterns:
 exercises for composition, 248
 identification, 36
 list, 2, 47-54
 presentation in context, 34
 recognition in reading, 175, 178
Grammatical rules, place of, 8
Greenbaum, S., 165
Griffen, J., 218
Grimshaw, A., 56
Gumperz, J., 56
Gunderson, D., 158

H

Hannerz, U., 56-57
Harris, D., 194
Haskell, J., 160
Higa, M., 169
Higgins, J., 108-9
Hockett, C., 82
Homework, 34
Holmes, J., 57
Hoover, J., 55, 65, 71, 151
Hymes, D., 56-57

I

Interaction activities, 10, 59 (*see also*
 Communicative interaction
 activities)
Intonation (*see* Phonology;
 Pronunciation)

J

Jaramillo, B., 236
John, V., 57
Johnson, F., 11-12, 56, 158
Joiner, E., 3
Jones, D., 55, 76
Juncture (*see* Phonology)

K

Kaplan, R., 213, 236

Katona, G., 3
Kelly, L., 162, 165
Kettering, J., 55, 60-61, 63-64, 66-68,
 151
Kinetic memory, 12
Knapp, D., 231-33
Knight, M., 55
Kreidler, C., 105
Krohn, R., 14

L

Lado, R., 31, 162, 169
Lafene, J., 181, 241
Lagoze, H., 55, 71, 77
Lawrence, M., 130
Learning, styles of, 204
Leon, P., 96, 100
Levenson, C., 118, 173
Lewis, J., 108-9
Linguistic competence, 58
Listening comprehension (Chapter
 Four):
 and other skills, 74, 82, 97, 106, 114
 objectives, 131
 procedures, 131
 techniques, 132
Lorge, I., 169

M

McPherson, E., 181
Malmberg, B., 91
Markman, R., 247
Marty, F., 162
Meaning (*see* Vocabulary, Reading):
 guessing from context, 194
Michigan test, 2, 174
Moody, K., 207, 209
Morley, J., 129, 130, 133, 135-36,
 139-41, 154
Morrey, R., 3

N

Nida, E., 189
Nonverbal behavior, 57

Norris, W., 166, 185, 187
Note-taking, 145, 247

O

Oller, J., 160
Oral reports, 114

P

Palmer, H. E., 162
Paulston, C., 3-4, 10, 55-56, 59, 203,
    208, 213-16, 218, 222, 227, 239,
    243, 245-48
Perkins, K., 178
Phatic language, 29
Phonology (*see also* Pronunciation):
  articulation, 87
  phonemes:
    segmental, 82-83
      consonants, 84
        chart for English, 85-86
        minor features, 87
      vowels, 88
        chart for English, 88-89
        minor features, 89
    suprasegmental, 91
      intonation, 81-82, 93
      juncture, 93
      stress and rhythm, 81, 83, 91
Pierce, M., 178
Pike, K., 84, 117-18
Pimsleur, P., 204
Pincas, A., 212
Politzer, R., 8
Poteet, G., 218
Prator, C., Jr., 93, 103, 106
Pride, J., 57
Proficiency:
  levels, 2, 12
  measures, 2
Pronunciation:
  correction 115 ff.
  drills, 100
  goals and objectives, 81
  lesson design, 94

modeling, 100
problems, 90
procedures and techniques:
  segmental phonemes, 95
  suprasegmental phonemes, 106
  intonation, 107
  stress and rhythm, 109
Punctuation, mechanics of, 234-36

Q

Quirk, R., 165

R

Rand, E., 218-19, 221
Read and look up, 189
Reading (Chapter Five):
  comprehension questions, types,
    165, 173
  extensive, 162, 199-201
  formula:
    Cloze technique, 160
  intensive, 162-199
    lesson organization, 163
    procedures, 163-65
    techniques, 165 ff.
  levels of difficulty, 160-61, 199
  objectives, 159
  speed, 193
  text selection, 159
Recoding, 136, 164
Reed, C., 128
Register, 63, 71, 108, 130
Restructuring range, 11
Rhetorical organization:
  devices, 205, 242
  procedures, 238
  teaching points, 236
Rivers, W., 3, 30, 56, 58-59, 127, 204
Robinett, B., 93, 118, 213
Robinson, F., 201
Robinson, L., 221
Roleplay, 9, 63, 65, 70, 114
  procedures, 73

Ross, J., 213, 220, 226
Rutherford, W., 7, 10, 16, 24-30, 32

S

Sandberg, K., 208, 226
Savignon, S., 3, 59
Schumann, F., 69
Schumann, J., 69
Selekman, H., 151
Shute, M., 103
Slager, W., 213, 224
Smith, F., 159, 164
Sound-symbol correspondence:
  homographs, 105
  homophones, 105
  in reading, 158
  name sound/base sound, 104
  sight words, 104
Spelling (*see* Sound-symbol
  correspondence)
Spencer, D., 206, 212
SQ3R, 201
Stageberg, N., 93
Stevick, E., 63
Stieglitz, F., 22
Strain, J., 98, 102
Stress (*see* Phonology; Pronunciation)
Style variation (*see* Register)

T

Thomason, S., 56
Thorndike, E., 169
TOEFL test, 2, 174
Translation, 35, 37, 95, 171

Traver, A., 169
Trow-Madigan, M., 147-48
Typology of structural pattern drills
  (*see* Drills, typology)

V

Valdman, A., 204
Vernick, J., 103, 105-6
Vocabulary (*see also* Word study;
  Content words; Function words),
  18, 34, 134, 168
  productive, 168
  receptive, 168
  selection, 168
Vodden, M., 110
Vowels (*see* Phonology; Pronunciation)

W

Waddell, M., 247
Wang, W., 128
Wardhaugh, R., 21, 92
West, M., 159, 169, 189
Whitten, M., 219
Wilson, L., 157, 175, 189, 192, 237
Word study, 183-89
Writing (*see* Composition):
  types of, 180, 240

Y

Yorio, C., 178
Yorkey, R., 201